Recognizing Satan

A Case for Exorcism in Modern Times

by Audrey Kenner

PublishAmerica
Baltimore

© 2007 by Audrey Kenner.

All rights reserved. No part of this book may be reproduced, stored in a retrieval system or transmitted in any form or by any means without the prior written permission of the publishers, except by a reviewer who may quote brief passages in a review to be printed in a newspaper, magazine or journal.

First printing

ISBN: 1-4241-9599-3
PUBLISHED BY PUBLISHAMERICA, LLLP
www.publishamerica.com
Baltimore

Printed in the United States of America

CHAPTER 1

In the movie *The Exorcist*, Regan, a twelve-year-old girl, is possessed so completely by the devil that at one point during the exorcism she literally transforms into a demon. Through powers manifested by the demons, she is able to manipulate objects in her environment though her hands and feet are securely tied to bedposts. Her body, no longer under her control, is destroyed and defiled by the demons that possessed her soul. Foul language, deep and raspy, spews from the mouth of the young girl as she spits and regurgitates gobs of disgusting matter onto everyone who manages to get into her line of fire. Through her, these demons kill a man and defile religious symbols with malicious abandon. Her bedroom, where the exorcism takes place, is cold, frigid and permeated by a wretched smell that one could only imagine to be putrid, to say the least.

As the demonic activity within this young girl progresses, she spirals deeper and deeper into Satan's pit, and the real Regan, the part of the human soul that belongs to God, is buried deep within the confines of a prison that the devil created within and around her. Her will, though weak and contaminated, manages to come through via a message of "help" written with the raised skin of her abdomen as a desperate cry from deep within. It is the human spirit that yearns for life. It refuses to let go of hope and relinquish her soul forever to the devil.

In this movie, it wasn't the girl's faith in God that saved her. The emphasis was more on the exorcism ritual, the method, than the name of Jesus. The audience is led to focus on the horror of the mayhem of the devil physically devouring the girl from inside out and the uncertainty of whether the ritual of the exorcism will succeed against such a ghastly foe. What finally expels the demons and severs the young girl's ties to the devil: the ritual of the exorcism or the power of the name of Jesus Christ?

Well, you can't throw the name of Jesus around too much on the big screen. You can allude to it, hint at it, but you just cannot ascribe too much power to the Son of God without some kind of buffer that would make the movie more palatable to the general audience. You cannot offend people unless, of course, you are cursing a blue streak, showing sexual situations that are not appropriate for children, exposing naked body parts, or brutally killing someone and making a bloody mess. But you cannot offend someone by using the name of Jesus with reverence but that's just how movies go. In movie world, had it been faith in God and the name of Jesus that saved her, the movie probably would have been labeled too "religious," and never would have seen the light of the big screen because nobody would fund such an undertaking. Movie moguls don't back movies because they are good Samaritans; they back movies because they want to make money! They have formulas that they use in order to calculate and project just how much money a movie will bring in. If the formula is not favorable, they don't want to put their money behind it.

If you want to make a movie about Jesus, you'd better be willing to spend your own money to do it. That's what Mel Gibson did in order to make *The Passion of the Christ.* Nobody wanted to back such a risky undertaking, and if he had not put his own money behind it, that movie would not have seen the light of day. The movie turned out to be a huge success despite what the formula might have predicted. Jesus was the hero, and his deity was not compromised in any way.

In times past, movie makers have been wary of attributing any positive outcome of a movie to God or Jesus. However, they have no problem whatsoever in attributing negative behavior that is evil to the devil or some demonic force from hell. Why? Because the devil makes more money at the box office than Jesus.

Aside from the fact that *The Exorcist* was made for the purpose of entertainment, what was the purpose of this violent possession? On the most obvious level, the demon wanted to take over her body, to possess her soul, to own her, to live in her. On another level, however, the purpose of the demon was also to kill or possess the soul of anyone else it could manage to get a hold of. The younger priest, for example, who assisted in the exorcism, was portrayed as being a primary target because of his inexperience and emotional problems. He was a psychiatrist who admittedly had lost faith and wanted out. The older, more experienced priest actually died during the exorcism, but we don't know exactly how. We know that his heart was weak so we speculate that perhaps he was unable to endure the sheer magnitude of the exorcism itself. Yet, in the very scene of his death, Regan, unencumbered by restraints, is sitting at the opposite corner of the bed with a look of devilish glee as the older priest, now dead, lays motionless, eyes open, opposite her. Did he really have a heart attack, or did the demons kill him? The audience shudders with gleeful horror as our imagination speculates the worse.

The movie implies that the older priest understood that it was his destiny or fate and it was to be just a matter of time before he met up with the evil that he had seen earlier in the desert. The younger and less assured priest's death it seems came about because of frustration, anger and lack of knowledge. He let his guard down when dealing with the devil—if his guard had ever been up; caving in emotionally because of his unresolved issues of guilt, lack of faith, and ultimately a type of ego gratification. He yields to the flesh. The devil has placed the straw that has broken the camel's back. In an angry rage, he decides that it is up to him, not God, to get rid of the demons once and for all. He'll take on the devil and kill him with his bare hands! In his emotional rage in he invites the devil to take him, BIG MISTAKE! Inviting the devil into your body is never a good idea, and in this priest's case, it results in his death.

It was just a matter of time before the younger priest did such a thing anyhow. He was constantly tortured by demons in one way or another and his wavering commitment to his priestly vocation did not help his situation. He knew Christ and the rituals that his religion required, but he was not totally committed to living his life for God. The issues of guilt surrounding his mother's death were conveniently used by the demons to arouse his emotions and affect his performance as part of the exorcism team. He had issues about his strength of character and his ability to serve God; his anger was ignited and his ego challenged rendering him ill-prepared to fight the good fight at such an inauspicious time in his life. Unfortunately such an inopportune time in a person's life is a most opportune time for the antics of the evil one, Satan.

The Exorcist, a movie based on a book about the true story of a twelve-year-old boy possessed by the devil, uses creative license to entertain the audience and I'm pretty sure that the story didn't go exactly as was portrayed on film. The good thing about this movie, aside from the fact that it can scare the daylights out of you, is that it causes one to seriously think about the nature of the devil and what he can and cannot do. What *is* the devil really capable of? If he can possess the soul of a child, who is most likely more innocent than most adults, how deeply and completely can Satan infiltrate a sinful human adult body and what impact can such people have on the world in which we live? How difficult *is* it to rid our bodies of these demonic forces? Just how much of this movie can be considered truth and how much is purely fictional entertainment contrived by the movie industry with the thought of getting a sizeable return on their investment?

Movies can be inspired or based on fact. Generally when a movie is based on fact, we must always remember that there is an element of money-making creative license that is heavily weighed into the final cut. In this movie of demonic infiltration and possession, despite what may have been added or deleted for theatrical purposes, the knowledge and understanding that we are expected to walk away with is fear of the devil and what he can do to us. The knowledge and understanding that we *need* to walk away with is that demons can inhabit the human body, demons do inhabit the human body, and the demons *can* be expelled. We need to understand that sometimes the task is not easy; in fact it can be dangerous. It is a "fact" that this movie is based on the demonic possession of a twelve-year-old boy. It is a fact that an exorcism took place. The gory details, however, can always be embellished. How much embellishment took place, I don't know. What I do know is that this movie is frightening, but even more, it's disturbing. However, rather than fear, we should come away from this movie with a clear understanding that Satan's demons cannot be allowed to languish and take up residence in the human body. He should not be given full rein do with our flesh as he very well pleases on any level.

When dealing with Satan one must be aware of his tactics and just how far he can go, because there is an inherent danger when we lack knowledge of such spiritual things. This is why I cannot stress enough, how important it is for us to be educated on the spiritual. *The Exorcist* doesn't deal with the how's and why's of the possession as much as the drama of the demonic possession. The two priests in the movie were focused on getting the devil out of the young girl by performing an exorcism, not necessarily acquainting the girl and her mother with Christ for their souls' salvation.

They never even talked to the girl's mother about the love of Christ, Christ dying for our sins, or their salvation. While an exorcism is important and ignorance can permit the devil to constantly take advantage of us, our connection to Christ is the most important thing of all. Without knowledge, we may unwittingly allow Satan to enter our lives in many different forms, on many different levels, and in many different ways. If, however, we are able to recognized his schemes, we would be better able to avoid many of the pitfalls that he constantly throws onto our path hoping that one will make us stumble, another will make us lose faith, and another will totally swallow us whole so that we, our personality/soul, will forever remain unaware of the love of God and the victory of the cross.

While I am on the subject of movies, there is another movie based on the exorcism of this same twelve-year-old boy called *Possessed*. In this version, the movie explains why the boy is possessed and what led to him being possessed. The devil gains entrance into the boy because he is being taught by an older adult to dabble in the occult. *This* makes sense! The boy has been left spiritually vulnerable because of his occult activities. Also, it is evident that the devil has not entered this boy to take his soul to hell; it is depicted in the movie that the devil has it in for a particular priest whom he wants to defeat. So, the reason that the devil has entered this particular twelve-year-old is not necessarily for the boy, but to affect the people around him, especially the priest who is to perform the exorcism.

This version does not have the theatrics of *The Exorcist*, but it holds to a truer standard than *The Exorcist*. The devil is after the priest, who is a theology teacher at a college. The devil has an appointment with the priest and uses the boy as a vehicle to get to him. The boy, because of his occult activities, is ripe for the taking. If you think about it, this just makes more sense. If the devil can affect the priest, who is a college professor, the priest can in turn affect hundreds of young lives that will pass through his classes over the years. This would have more of an impact than inhabiting a twelve-year-old kid just to ruin his good looks because ruining one child isn't going to cut it. The devil is not all-powerful like God; he is not omnipresent.

Now, it's time to get down to basics so that we are more aware of the devil and his antics. Let's start with exorcism. While most people have a working idea about exorcism, I think that it's a good idea that we take a moment to embed in our minds more clearly what an exorcism is and what an exorcism does. Exorcism is not about monsters, nightmares, and horror. It is a spiritual process or procedure that can leave us cleansed and refreshed, better capable of following the voice of God and able to live a more satisfying and fulfilled life. It's about forcing to the surface weights that so easily beset us in order to expel these negative forces. Exorcism, or getting the demons out, allows us to enjoy a better quality of life, a more positive outlook on situations that appear hopeless, and the ability to have a closer relationship with our Lord and Savior, Jesus Christ. In many cases of demonic possession, without an exorcism, many fall victim to Satan and end up committing suicide or living a life without joy and peace. They are in a constant state of emptiness and confusion. I don't have statistics on this, but there have been many a suicide note bearing the words, "I just can't go on living this way!" or some such similar phrase. Demonic forces can be so powerful that they will **make** you want to leave the earth just to have relief. Life feels like a prison sentence in solitary confinement.

Am I making myself clear? The devil is nothing to play around with. He is a thief who will steal your joy, your health, your strength, your mind, and your money. He does not want you to have a relationship with Christ because he does not want you to know the truth. You may read statements such as this several times throughout this book, but this is only because it is so important for your mind to grasp this. Satan does not want you to realize the magnitude of the cross and the redemptive power of the blood of Christ. Living in misery is not how God would have us live. Christ suffered because he chose the cross for our salvation in obedience to God. Christ did not walk the earth misery, neither should we. If you are living a life of misery, this is not of God. This indicates that you need either Jesus, an exorcism, or both.

RECOGNITION TIP # 1

We must recognize and acknowledge our weaknesses. These are the areas Satan uses to tempt us.

CHAPTER 2

When the even was come, they brought unto him many that were possessed with devils and he cast out the spirits with his word, and healed all that were sick—Matthew 8:16

The following definitions are provided solely as a means of focus and clarity as we examine spiritual warfare, exorcism, and most importantly, recognition of Satan. These definitions are detailed and refined, not to insult your intelligence, but to prepare you for what you are about to learn about the devil. I pray that you read them thoroughly and completely.

Definition:
EXORCISM
To free (a person, place, etc.), of **evil spirits** or **malignant** influences.

Definition:
EVIL (evil spirits)
—Morally wrong or bad, immoral, wicked, harmful, injurious.
—Characterized or accompanied by misfortune or suffering.
—It is the force in nature that governs and gives rise to sin and wickedness.

Definition:
SPIRIT (evil spirits)
—Can be an angel or demon.
—The incorporeal part of humans.
—Conscious incorporeal being as opposed to matter.
—A supernatural incorporeal being as opposed to matter
—A supernatural incorporeal being especially one inhabiting a person, place, or object.
—Synonymous with: life, mind, consciousness, essence.

Definition:
CORPOREAL
Of the physical.

Definition:
INCORPOREAL
Not of the physical body.

Definition:
MALIGNANT (influences)
Disposed to cause harm, suffering or distress deliberately; feeling or showing ill-will or hatred.

The preceding definitions are indispensable when it comes to understanding the nature of exorcisms and why this process is so critical to the health and well-being of not only those who profess faith, but to those who claim to be agnostic or even atheist. Your familiarity with such terms is important. You may even find it helpful to refer back to these definitions on occasion while reading this book; for that matter it is important that many terms that will be used are clearly understood. Do not hesitate to stop reading and contemplate an issue or look up a term in the dictionary. We are dealing with a very serious issue that needs to be understood thoroughly and completely. Satan can be both cunning and baffling, mixing truth with lies and facts with fiction. I do not profess to know absolutely everything about this subject. I'm not sure that there is a person alive who does, but what I offer to you in this book is only a corner of the insight that God has allowed me to understand through the Holy Spirit. My story and discoveries will be illustrated and explained in various parts of this book as we go along. I have no problem checking with my spiritual leader, seeking wise counsel, and looking for and expecting confirmation of information and neither should you. Check with your spiritual leader for further understanding and clarity. If you do not have one, I suggest that you get into a church of God-fearing, bible-believing souls who strive to live as the Word has told us that we should. Do not be averse to consulting with wise counsel on this spiritual issue or any other issue such as this. God the Father has nothing to hide, nothing to be ashamed of, nothing to withhold from those who seek His way.

With that, let's talk about the nature of demonic activity. The nature of demonization can occur on many levels, demonic "possession" being the most serious. There is also demonic control (virtual puppetry), harassment (overshadowing), and infiltration (accessing and using the human body). Possession, the highest form, requires a reprobate mind, or the inability to perceive the unction of the Holy Spirit and various stages and levels within these conditions. Demons have no regard to person when it comes to carrying out a mission. Their vehicle of choice is the human body. First and foremost is the psyche or mind, the true battlefield of the demonic realm. Through the mind, they can control the heart and the body. Illnesses can be born, health problems can be increased, marriages can be broken, abuse can occur, and so on. They will, however, occupy a place through an incorporeal entity, or even an animal. The occupation can be intended as long-term, short-term, temporary, or permanent. Their only consideration is that the vehicle allow them to dwell unchallenged by anyone representing God, through his son Jesus, who defeated Satan on the cross at Calvary. This is why the name of Jesus is the devil's most dangerous and serious weapon of warfare.

The name of Jesus is powerful! We must not underestimate its power by getting too wrapped up in ritual. There is a place for ritual, but the ritual itself should not overshadow the name of Jesus and the purpose of his death on the cross. This is another very important thing to keep in mind as you read this book: Jesus died for our sins and therefore sin does not have the ability to control us. This is important to remember because the devil is a liar and will attempt to convince us through circumstances, trials and tribulations, that we are powerless against his attacks.

Demons cannot, however, abide and survive where the subtle vibrations of life are too positive **and** the Christ nature dwells. Positive vibrations such as love, faith, hope, righteous living and right intentions are a constant challenge to demonic activity, but unfortunately these ingredients alone are not enough. While they may offer a challenge to the devil, in no way are they a steadfast and concrete solution to the problem of demonic inhabitation. Positive qualities, by their very nature, do cover a multitude of sins, and it is very difficult for demons to survive in such an environment because of their nature. But, do not be deceived: a positive attitude is not the antidote. Demons do not care about your positive attitude; all they know is that they must be fed in order to survive. In the absence of Christ, demons will feed off of anything, including your good nature. Any person, regardless of their nature or efforts, is still vulnerable to be enslaved to the devil if Christ is denied access by them. This includes specific areas of your life that you may have denied Christ access to.

Let's look at the teen, who accepts Christ as her Lord and Savior, and yet when it comes to humility, she denies Christ access because she feels the need to protect herself. To be humble, in her opinion, is to let her guard down. Let's look at the housewife who goes to church every Sunday and yet is partaking of her husband's sin in order not to lose him. She is denying Christ access to her marriage. How about the gruff businessman with a heart of gold, very giving and concerned, except he refuses to allow Christ full access into his mind by using profanity. Each time he uses profanity, he separates himself and denies association with Christ as Peter did, denying that he was a follower and punctuating this lie with a slew of profanities. What about the preacher who fasts and prays and studies and prays and preaches and prays, but is deeply involved in secret sinful activities that if found out would make a congregation of believers gasp in horror. This preacher has to deny Christ access to the flesh in order to continue in such activities.

Christ died that we might be redeemed, and it is through him that we are free from bondage and Satan's grip is broken. No matter how "nice" we are as individuals, we do not have the power to save ourselves and break free from demonic strongholds. Unlike Jesus, who walked the earth as God wrapped in flesh, we are flesh and we are prone to sin. We humans, though the spirit of Christ dwells within us all, need to rely on the redeeming power of Jesus' death on the cross and Calvary to save us from these evil forces.

Now, if you will, consider the following translated version of exorcism.

EXORCISM
(Expanded, detailed version):
To release a person bound by wicked, immoral, and injurious behavior that immediately or eventually leads them to sin, misfortune, suffering, or death (body or spiritual). The influencing factors are not of a physical body or mental illness, but of a presence; the purpose of this presence is to cause harm, suffering or even death. Its major purpose is to compromise the spiritual integrity of a person by binding or at least relegating them to a state of confusion, concerning God, God's will in their life, or their holy position in God's divine plan. The ultimate purpose of the evil presence is to use an instrument,

preferably the body, to accept and embody evil and all that this evil perpetuates whether against oneself and/or others.

The word "exorcism" comes from the Greek word meaning to ask or pray deeply.

When we are up against evil that has infiltrated our home or our flesh, this is not time for ordinary prayer. This is the time for deep prayer, a time to dig deep and go deep because if the spiritual situation has progressed to the point of needing an exorcism, the devil's power is now an evil physical energy or presence. In short, it's time for war!

RECOGNITION TIP # 2

Recognize and acknowledge when you're most vulnerable and go into a state of radical high praise and worship until this season passes.

CHAPTER 3

...upon this rock I will build my church; and the gates of hell shall not prevail against it—Matthew 16:18

It seems that the modern-day church would prefer to call such tasks deliverance ministry or spiritual warfare which is quite accurate to a point. However, if we take into consideration that as long as we are on this earth, studying God's word, going to church, under the guidance of our spiritual leaders, praying, fasting, meditating on God's word, we're in *constant* spiritual warfare. If you take into account that a deliverance ministry can be done on mass scale and does not necessarily have to include a one-on-one encounter, it is not direct enough. Jesus never had deliverance meetings. He cast devils out of individuals. Jesus was not general when he cast out demons; he was very specific. It is quite natural for the flesh to contend with the spirit and the spirit with the flesh—that's why God gave us the church as part of His awesome genius. The church is established to handle much of the general. His disciples or the individuals who make up the church, are supposed to handle the details or specifics of taking care of each other.

The problem with delegating such tasks or ridding the body of demons to spiritual warfare or deliverance ministries can be attributed to the fact that these ministries may better be suited for maintenance than an actual pointed address of the demons that we may harbor. This is especially so when infestation has moved beyond a certain point and the demonic activity has escalated to a point where the individual can find no place of contentment in his life, including church. An exorcism to cast out these demons is what is needed to achieve the relief that people are longing for. Demons, by nature, attempt to fill up places within our soul where God belongs, so that portions of us are so full of evil and malcontent that God will not dwell there; the biggest reason is our condition won't allow Him to.

How much longer will we neglect the benefit of exorcism when it should be such a vital area of spiritual warfare? By the time an individual is plagued by such demonic darkness, their ability to achieve a true sense of peace, joy and happiness with such routine religious practices is almost nonexistent. There are demons that need to be forced to the surface so that they may be cast out. We must face the fact that this demonic activity is keeping them bound to an ineffective spiritual experience. When demonic activity is rampant, we are at the least relegated to the routine, but it does not allow us the freedom to grow and excel in Christ. We are caught up in an ineffective loop of sorts that goes nowhere. We do not grow while we are in this state, and while we may not be "dead," we certainly are not living. We are ineffective when we are caught up in routine spirituality. Satan does not care if we remain in such a state, saying our feeble prayers by rote without even seeking God's presence. Satan doesn't care that we go to church. We can go to church whenever we want to—the devil does not want us to go to church to worship Christ! If we do not love God and worship Him in spirit and in truth, what does the devil care about us going to church? He loves it! He wants us to go and perhaps we can gain a few souls for him in the process.

We serve a living God and by definition, anything that lives cannot be stagnant; it must grow or die. The devil would have us be stagnant and never grow to discover the power of the Christ that dwells within each and every one of us. He would have us die and walk the earth as zombies as a testament on his behalf as to how miserable life can be. God's word is given to us that we might absorb its truth and be drawn to Him. God wants to fill us with His love so that we grow and drop seeds of love and mercy on others that they may be touched and be drawn to Him through us because of it. Those who are touched touch others and they too are drawn to the one and only living Christ.

The devil does not want this type of relationship with us. He wants to take over where God belongs in our life. He does not want us to have life in Christ; he wants us to have *him* in us. This is one way to recognize his works. When our ability to set or accomplish positive and meaningful goals in our life is constantly derailed, not so much by outside forces but by forces that are within us, this is a concrete problem that needs concrete attention. When forces snatch our thoughts, taunt and discourage us, trap and imprison us in negativity, these are demonic forces and must be treated as such. It's no fun house, it's a chamber of horrors and it's very real.

These forces seem to overpower our best intentions, desires and abilities, and can be very costly, especially in our personal lives. This is demonic activity at work, trapping us, discouraging us, confusing us, stealing our peace, and making our joy oh-so-elusive. The most costly result of this demonic activity is that many a soul will be lost to the works of the devil. This does not have to continue to happen in our time. The number of souls drawn to Christ can increase exponentially if we kick the devil out of these poor ailing Christians instead of allowing them to suffer as so many are doing right this minute. Our spiritual walk is important and we must be free to comprehend spiritual things. Our life "vein," which is the Holy Spirit, is the force of God within our spirit and must be open and receptive, with little or no blockage.

If the Holy Spirit is not allowed to flow, there is trouble. There are areas in our spiritual walk where strongholds must be discerned and addressed specifically so that we are not blind and deaf to the gospel of Christ. How can we learn of Him, lest we hear of Him? How can we see Him if we have been rendered temporarily spiritually blind not only because of sin, which can be readily detected, but by invading malevolent forces? There are people who are already in this unfortunate position and don't even realize it. They won't hear the word because they *can't* hear it and therefore the preacher is in essence preaching to a brick wall. These people don't even know that they are not hearing the word of God. These people are not receiving the word because they are compromised and not spiritually attuned. Evil forces oppress or depress the spirit and need to be expelled so that the line of communication is opened. When the line is opened, this gives us our "ears" to hear the Word of God.

There are many who shun the word "exorcism;" why they do is a mystery. Maybe they feel that it is too harsh a word, regardless of how people should treat the malady of demonization. Many people that I know take offense to this word because it is a practice that is associated predominantly with the Catholic Church. Because the Catholic Church created the ritual of exorcism, many denominations don't subscribe to it. Exorcism *is* a strong word, giving us a sense of violence and force but, as you can see from the definition of exorcism given earlier, the essence of spiritual warfare is clearly defined in the word. However, exorcism hints at something more specific and wrenching than spiritual warfare, a more potent form of warfare.

We need something more direct than general, something which speaks of a specific hard-hitting act that focuses on driving the demons out from us and destroying their effect. We need the word "exorcism" to define more specifically the casting out of devils, especially the ones that won't go nicely and won't go easily because they need to be addressed strongly and specifically, and at times even violently. These demonic forces will not respond to the everyday generalities because they can be hidden and manage to remain hidden because of their chameleon-like nature. These demons need to be ferreted out and sometimes a direct face-to-face confrontation must occur. Jesus was quite confrontational and direct with demons when he walked the earth. When he spoke to the demons, he spoke authoritatively. When Satan spoke through Peter, saying that Jesus should be protected from death, Jesus immediately knew who was speaking. He knew that it was not Peter who spoke these words, but Satan. Jesus loved Peter, but his love for Peter did not dull his senses to the works of the devil. Jesus didn't play around with the devil, and neither should we.

This scripture goes to show that the spirit of a man can be invaded at any time, but especially during emotional situations. In the Gospels, Satan uses Peter's love of Christ, one of Christ's very own disciples, as an opportunity to try to thwart God's plan of salvation for mankind, and Jesus immediately recognizes it. How many times have we allowed Satan to use our emotions as a vehicle to thwart God's plan for us or someone we love? We must be able, as Jesus did, to discern the spirit of the devil regardless of whom he may operate through. We must learn to recognize Satan as Jesus did with his companions, his very own disciples, and do as he did and order Satan to get behind us, regardless of the form he might choose show up in. We cannot allow our affections for a person, place, or thing override the instructions of Holy Ghost. That kind of affection is not of God and we should resist the temptation to give in to the devil because we are fond of the vehicle that he is using.

The evangelist Billy Graham tells the story of being called to the ministry as a young man. At the time that he was called he was going out with a girl whom he thought himself to be in love with. According to him, the Holy Spirit told him that he was to terminate the relationship with the girl. She wasn't a bad person or someone to be ashamed of, but he knew beyond a doubt that God didn't want him to see her anymore. He dreaded that he had to terminate the relationship but in obedience to God he did. This was a very difficult thing for him to do. She cried, he cried, but he did it because he knew that it was what God wanted him to do. He knew that the Lord was calling him to be used for His service and the girl that he was seeing was not a believer.

RECOGNIZING SATAN

While Billy Graham was fond of the girl, he was not willing to have something that God had clearly forbidden him to have. If he'd chosen to disobey God, Satan could have very well worked through the girl to disrupt, delay, or cause him not to enter into a ministry that has draw millions of people to Christ. Our relationship with God is more important than the most important relationship in our life. I don't care how much we may desire something, if God tells us no and we go ahead and do it anyway, Satan can and most likely will use our disobedience for his purposes.

Situations like Billy Graham's, believe it or not, are why a person who is demonized can acquire an unhealthy affection for these alien forces within them and around them. They refuse to let go when it is time to let go and become used to living in disobedience. Had he stayed with the girl, who didn't seem to be so bad by the standards of the world, the whole course of his life would have been affected. This is why God told him to end the relationship. Billy Graham refused to put his personal feelings before God. He was willing to release the familiar and grab onto faith, the spiritual. Had he put the girl before God, this would have been a sin and we all know, to do such a thing opens the door for the devil.

In the cases of sin, familiarity does not breed contempt but acceptance and even a sense of false security. Once sin has opened the door for evil, demonic occupancy can occur. Sin, left unchallenged, permits demons to creep in, plant themselves, and initiates the process of taking over our souls. Once this begins, the occupied souls are compelled to protect these demons in every way that they can. Why? Because sin feels good to the flesh. Sin feels good to the ego. We can all recall the sense of euphoria that we feel when we get away with something forbidden that feels good to our flesh. For the average person who follows Christ, conviction may kick in immediately following the act, but that does not mean that our flesh immediately forgets. This does not mean that the flesh will not long for the experience again. It is this part of our nature that Satan uses to convince us to continue in sin. God, on the other hand, uses this part of our nature as a part of His divine design to permit us to exercise choice and draw us into a closer relationship with him. The more that we consciously choose to follow Christ, the stronger we become. The more we are conscious about making choices, the better chance we have in avoiding the snares of the devil, and the more likely it is that we will find that Christ dwells within us.

Remember, Satan does not want us to believe that we have freedom of choice. He wants us to live as mindless as possible so that he can control us.

He wants our mind to operate in constant error, accepting the first thing that flits through it without examination or introspection. God wants us to take every thought into subjection. He *wants* us to think! He wants us to know that we have choice because He designed us to be free. The devil wants us in bondage to him. It is the only way that he can succeed in his process of preventing us from discovering Truth.

RECOGNITION TIP # 3

Recognize and acknowledge the power of God. It is impossible to defeat the devil if we do not understand God's power and His plan of salvation for us.

CHAPTER 4

...I have set before you life and death, blessing and cursing: therefore choose life, that both thou and thy seed may live—Deuteronomy 30:19

In order for demons to successfully occupy a soul, the first order of business is to make us think that we cannot help it, or that we have no choice in various matters. I tell my kids all the time, you don't *have* to do anything but die. This is my way of letting them know that whatever decision that they make, be it right or wrong, it is their choice—not somebody else's choice, but theirs. We must not get comfortable with thinking that someone else has made a decision that we have managed to get caught up in; this puts our soul in danger. Even if we go along with another person's decision, it has to be our decision to go along with that person. Do not hand over your power of decision to someone else thinking that it will make life a lot simpler. If you do this, you can be assured that the devil is lurking about in such an atmosphere and it's just a matter of time before he infiltrates your soul with bad or wrong decisions that lead you away from the path of becoming whole through Christ.

One example of this is when a mother allows the man in her life to abuse her child or children. Many times what has happened is that the woman has shut down her thought process in deference to the man and is allowing him to take on the role of being the "thinker" in the relationship. She has chosen to shut down, for whatever reason, abdicating her role as a mother and as a thinking human being. Before she knows it, she *can't* think clearly because she has chosen not to think at all. Meanwhile, Satan is having his way through this man because the conditions are favorable to do so. While his demons have her mind bound and preoccupied with his shenanigans, Satan is operating through him to destroy her children.

Another situation that comes to mind is people who are involved in gang activities. I don't just mean teenagers either. I'm also talking about members of the mob, corporate America, cults, and churches. People in situations such as these can easily find themselves in a position where to think for themselves is to alienate themselves from a group that they have become familiar with and are in many ways dependent upon. It's easy for them to slip into a state of mindless adherence to a principle or ideology. You can see where I'm going with this, right? When we allow others to do the thinking for us and make choices for us, this is not good and a trick of the devil. It feels good because to be a part of something that is supposed to benefit us, protect us, put food on our table or prevent loneliness is a feeling we all enjoy—but to give up our freedom of choice and our natural instinct to think is to have these things undermine a gift that God has given us, as well as a disrespect of His position in our lives. Love, protection, food, and so on are the things that God is to provide, and for us to look to man to be responsible for providing them is to allow man to play a dangerous role in our lives. Yes, God works through people, but people are not God.

When we shut down our thought process, Satan has freedom to do his work uninhibited without challenge. When we command ourselves to shut down our thought process, we automatically open ourselves up to oppression. How do we shut ourselves down? We shut ourselves down by our words and by our attitude. If you notice when you want to do something that is not particularly moral or right, certain things have to occur. First of all, we have to make a decision to stop thinking and to let the lowest part of our psyche be in control of the matter—like having an angel on one shoulder and the devil on the other. In order to do wrong, we have to shut up that angel! The devil wouldn't win if we didn't. As long as the angel is present, we cannot comply with the devil. We may be momentarily caught between doing what's right and what's wrong, a state of stagnation, but in order for us to do wrong we have got to voluntarily shut up that angel on our shoulder.

Some of the words and phrases we use to do so are:

WHATEVER!
I REALLY DON'T HAVE (MUCH OF) A CHOICE!
FORGET IT!
WHAT'S THE USE!

Words and phrases such as these give the devil a clue that our guard is down and he can ride in on the fear and negativity of our spoken words. Our words are very powerful and words such as these can literally stop the thought process, the very avenue that wisdom and the Holy Spirit operate through. Words and phrases such as these close the blinds of our mind and we proceed mindlessly into the world of sin, and sin for all of its negative connotations, has some very pleasant effects on the mind and the flesh.

This is the problem with sin. Many times sin does not feel bad, especially in the beginning. Sin can make us feel in control, sexy, powerful, giddy, fearless, and even god-like. Sin is the devil's playground. When we sin we are at variance with God and we give Satan permission to peddle his wares and position his demons in our lives *and* in our bodies. Usually the devil makes us feel good before he makes us feel rotten. If he made us feel rotten from the beginning, he wouldn't have very much to offer us.

This is why many people live with demons and don't want them evacuated. Without these forces operating within them, *they* feel incomplete, vulnerable and naked. For years, and for some people, as long as they can remember, they have used the demons for protection against forces on the outside of them, forces in their environment that they needed to feel power over. They *allow* these demons to "protect" them. This happens when the person is either unfamiliar with the protection of Jesus or has been spiritually molested in such a way that he is angry with God and feels that he cannot trust Him. Some allow the demons to dwell in them because they feel that their sins are so bad and horrendous that there is no way that they could ever hope for God's love and forgiveness to be bestowed upon them—and this way of thinking is just fine with the devil! But, we know that the devil loves lies. He loves lies and doesn't care who's doing the lying, whether it is us lying to ourselves or others lying to us for him. He doesn't care; he just wants to use the lies to destroy us so that God won't have another soul in His kingdom.

Sin offers immediate gratification and therefore sin is easy to embrace. The flesh, that part of us that strives with the spirit, exists to be gratified. Satan caters to the flesh on a regular basis. The nature of sin makes it easy for us not to think of consequences because for the moment everything feels fine. If the essence of exorcism is to renounce the devil and his works, it is no simple matter to get a person to renounce what is familiar and comfortable to the flesh—and to convince a person that the "safety" that they feel in sin and evil is a lie. It is serious warfare!

This is precisely why we should refuse to water down such a serious matter. Why should we call it spiritual warfare when what we really want to do is wrench these demons' claws from our very soul? We want to exorcise them! We want to purge our physical being of them! We want them to exit! Who cares who invented the word, where it came from, and which religious sect uses it more? Satan exercises spiritual warfare on us every day. He attempts to turn our spirit against God and his principles even when he cannot physically invade us. It is Satan who seeks to take over our "land," as in a war. God owns the land; Satan wants to take it over even though he knows that can never own it. But, if he can at least harass the tenants and convince some to willingly hand over the mortgage, that'll do for him. Exorcism is the process of expulsion. We seek to physically eradicate malignant spiritual forces from our "land" that eventually, after the party is over, causes suffering and harm and even death. We strive to maintain God's original purpose for the human design, to love and worship Him and only Him. Sure it *is* spiritual warfare on one level because battles are constantly raging and we must fight the good fight and put on the whole armor of God. Armor protects against penetration, but if the armor was not on or the armor was on improperly and penetration occurred, it's time to move to the next level of warfare: exorcism. Intentions at this level are spiritual expulsion which is why exorcism seems a more appropriate term.

RECOGNITION TIP # 4

Recognize and acknowledge that the devil is already defeated. Jesus' death and resurrection accomplished this.

CHAPTER 5

But now are they many members, yet but one body. And the eye cannot say unto the hand, I have no need of thee: nor again the head to the feet, I have no need of you. Nay, much more those members of the body, which seem to be more feeble, are necessary:
And those members of the body, which we think to be less honourable, upon these we bestow more abundant honour; and our uncomely parts have more abundant comeliness.—1 Corinthians 12:20-24

Whether someone needs to go to an exorcist or not is relative. A godly church that has a diligent, well-trained, healthy, and viable deliverance ministry is just as capable of freeing us from demons as it is capable of instructing us on how to remain free of demons. However, there are people who are gifted in the discerning of spirits and detecting their presence. These are people who have a gift from God for such things that are above and beyond the ordinary. Their ability to discern demons, along with the gift that an exorcist has, can prove invaluable. While the bible states that all who believe in Jesus should be able to heal the sick and cast out demons, there are some who seem to be more gifted in these areas than others. If there are people who have a gift for healing, why wouldn't there be people who have a gift of casting out demons? Jesus said that we could do these things and even greater things than this.

Unfortunately, there are still a number of churches that refuse to even allow such talk, other than on a perfunctory level. They feel as though this is a negative topic. These churches figure that if there are people in their church who think they have demons, they are either crazy or they should learn to ignore them and lean on Christ. Meanwhile demonic forces are constantly gaining ground in their lives, running rampant in Christians because they do not have the knowledge or strength to resist the devil. Demons have closed their ears to the word and therefore they are, quite frankly, simply ignorant of a very large portion of God's word. Their ears have been blocked by the devil so they have not heard about the armor. They live their lives cuffed and bound, never experiencing peace in Christ because Sunday after Sunday they are missing the Word and nobody realizes it. *They* don't even realize it! Because of this, demons have now had an opportunity to enter, fester, and multiply and anyone who reaches the point of demonic multiplication is a candidate for the services of an exorcist or at least person who can serve as an exorcist.

Some say that there is really no need for an exorcist or that there is no particular calling for one to become an exorcist, but God calls his people to do a variety of things in life and graces them with the gifts and talents that they need to carry them out. He can anoint us with a special ability to do what he has called us to do or to perform a particular job in an *extra ordinary* way at a specific time in our lives or even for the duration of our earthly journey. He can anoint us for service at His desired time according to His will and purpose. He can give us abilities above and beyond our natural or ordinary capabilities. Just as He opened Sarah's womb for a season for a specific purpose, so He is able to do for us. He is able to birth in us what He will, even if we think that our season has passed and anoint us for service at His desired time. Eyes have not seen nor have ears heard *ALL* that our heavenly Father can do! We, on the other hand, are so limited by our humanity that we cannot begin to imagine awesome gravity of God's power.

We all have a place in God's church. We all have gifts and abilities that God has blessed us with that are special for us according to His will. We cannot operate outside of these gifts according to our own desires and purpose without asking for trouble. For example, we are capable of spreading the gospel of Christ, and Christians *should* spread the gospel of Christ. However, that does not mean that all believers are called to preach the word of God in front of a congregation as a pastor of a church or that everyone who is familiar with the bible should be Sunday school teachers. We should all sing praises unto the Lord, but that does not mean that we all have a talent *to* sing or are meant to be soloists or professional singers of the gospel. We should cherish and respect the gifts that God gives us, just as we should respect and cherish the gifts that God has given to others, and if you do not feel that the Lord has called you to be an exorcist, I would definitely discourage you from trying to be one!

However, if someone is called to be an exorcist, why should we find it odd or unacceptable? If someone has an extraordinary talent to rid people of demons, by all means, shouldn't we respect that and allow them to exercise their gift to help people to get rid of these ungodly varmints? Actually, why should we care what they're called—exorcists, deliverance ministers, prayer warriors, or whatever—there are definitely people within God's church who have this talent, and whatever name we choose to call them, they are needed just like any other ministry. They should be able to exercise their gift as part of the whole body of Christ just like anybody else. It may be necessary that these people be trained to deal with the nature of exorcisms as opposed to spiritual warfare, but how can we go wrong? To *not* do this is preposterous. To leave a hole in this very necessary part of the Body of Christ is an awful mistake because as we will see, Satan loves "holes."

Satan, no doubt, loves the fact that many people underestimate his mission on earth. As matter of fact, I would even venture to say that he is probably responsible for perpetuating such erroneous thinking in the first place; keeping us either over-occupied with the devil so that we ignore the significance of Christ in our lives, or under-occupied and ignorant so that we are not aware of his devious schemes and remain locked in spiritual err. God would have us be diligent in all our ways. He would have us watch and not close our eyes to his love, grace, and mercy, as well as have us be aware of the wiles of the devil. God would have us resist the devil but how can we resist that which we are not familiar with, especially if it comes as a wolf in sheep's clothing? If we expect no harm from the "sheep," why would we take precaution? We may think the wolf really is a sheep because we don't recognize the masquerade and invite him into our homes. If we learn to recognize Satan and his deplorable schemes and masquerades, we are better able to protect ourselves. Consequently, we are more capable of understanding the full significance of needing the full armor of God. We are more attuned to the importance of the Word in our lives being the significant part of the ammunition that we need to resist the devil and understand that he is already a defeated foe.

RECOGNITION TIP # 5

Recognize and acknowledge that there must be a constant and continuous cleansing of our mind and heart of evil. We do this by studying the word to gain knowledge of the nature of Jesus. We do this through prayer, confessing our sins, asking for forgiveness, and forgiving others. These things make our soul tender to the will of God.

CHAPTER 6

Put on the whole armour of God, that ye may be able to stand against the wiles of the devil. For we wrestle not against flesh and blood, but against principalities, against powers, against the rulers of the darkness of this world, against spiritual wickedness in high places. Wherefore take unto you the whole armour of God, that ye may be able to withstand in the evil day, and having done all, to stand.—Ephesians 6:11-13

The Old Testament with all its wars, victories and defeats, foreshadows our battles with Satan. During those times the people made armor that would protect primarily their head, chest and groin area during battle. However, the victory or defeat did not lie in the constitution of their armor. The victory was in what God said would be the victory. The victory was in the words that He spoke concerning His will and purpose. When God's will was obeyed, and it was His will that there be victory, victory was the outcome. When the people turned their backs on God and disregarded His words as He related them to His prophets, defeat was inevitable. Victory was not possible without God. In order to achieve victory over the enemy during Old Testament times, not only did they have to know that they had an enemy, they also had to understand that the victory was not in the power of their sword or in the efficiency of their armor but the victory was in the power of God. The sword and armor were tools that served a significant purpose in protecting the body from harm. The warriors for or against God's purpose, as a matter of practice, never went to battle without their armor, and neither should we.

God spoke the word that determined the victor, during those times, however daunting the opponent may have been. Even opposing armies, who believed in other gods, trembled when they found out that their opponents had God's favor, and they worshiped idols! One of Satan's biggest weapons that he uses against us is our ignorance of the Word of God, and our failure to realize that we have

God's favor for victory over the enemy. The devil used it back then and he still uses it today.

During Old Testament times, the enemy always came to steal, kill and destroy. Such battles had the same satanic overtones that we face today, only now the battlefield is the mind and spirit, though not excluding physical battles that involve flesh and blood. The mission, however, is the same—to take over and destroy God's people, take their land, and plunder possessions that are rightly given by God. God's mission is the same today as it was back then—to protect His people, enlighten His people, and deliver them from the enemy. God has a plan of salvation that must go forth. He sent His son Jesus to help us to accomplish this task because we are His people, it is He who has made us, and therefore He knows us to the very number of hairs on our head. In our obedience, and sometimes despite our disobedience, God's chosen people are always victorious over evil whether directly or indirectly.

In Old Testament times, it did not matter who had the weakest army or who had the strongest army. It did not matter who had the largest army or who had the smallest army. What mattered during that time was who had the one and only true living God on their side. All victories and defeats during that time were at the discretion of God. If any faction initiating a war against God's people expected to achieve victory by might and power, they were sadly mistaken. No, He did not always allow the "good guy" to win every battle because regardless of what we think, God's actions are always purposeful. He sometimes uses the battles within the war to bring His people closer to him and under His subjection so that they can realize that they are to depend on Him. God needs us to understand that to turn our backs on Him is to defy Him and to deify ourselves. When these people defied God, they put themselves in harm's way and gave the enemy, an ever-present threat during those times, the opportunity to destroy them and seize their land.

For those who repented after realizing what they'd done, He never fails to come to their rescue no matter how far they had strayed. God is always merciful and quick to forgive, saving us from our enemies when we call on His name. Sure, those people had to deal with the consequences of their action, for there is always a price to pay, but it was nothing compared to the price at the hands of their enemies. People were pretty barbaric during biblical times. Think about it, they beat the Savior of the world beyond recognition; you can imagine what they cared about those who were rumored to be even less. That is why proclaiming Jesus as the Christ and the one and only true and living God was so dangerously radical back then. That's why poor Peter, who said that he would never deny Christ, did. Those people were crazier than Peter was, and Peter knew it! Peter, who was one of Jesus' companions, cut off a soldier's ear! Imagine what someone during such barbaric times who was *not* a companion of the Christ would do. Jesus understood Peter because he understands all things; he also understood the barbaric nature of his captors and he did not hold a grudge against Peter's humanity because of this. The situation of Peter's denial is merely an illustration of how difficult it is to adhere to Christ when we feel threatened no matter how well-meaning our intentions are.

This is why those who turn to God are never disappointed in the end; God knows what we're up against. Those not in the will of God were defeated. Sometimes they had what appeared to be a victory, but it wasn't. God used their disobedience in accomplishing His will. The same holds true today. God will at times allow evil to accomplish what it needs to accomplish. This is a hard thing for some of us to hear, that God uses bad people, bad situations, and bad circumstances or evil to accomplish His will, but He does. Since God is the very antithesis of Satan, God is incapable of evil so He needs to use people who are capable of evil to accomplish things that go against his nature. "Bad guys," however, only remain "victorious" at God's discretion and even then to the degree that His divine plan should prevail.

The wars and battles that are represented in the Old Testament are all indications of what Satan desires to do in our lives. The kings wanted the people of God to fear them because of their military power. They wanted to plunder their possessions and kill and enslave the people of God. They wanted them to worship *their* gods and live life according to how they saw fit that they should live. In the Old Testament, Satan was not mentioned much although his presence is prevalent. While there is mention of evil spirits, there is no mention of devils being cast out. God sent evil spirits to plague people on occasion during Old Testament times and He had His reasons for this and if He sent them back then, He can send them today. Whatever God did during Old Testament times He is quite capable of doing today; as to *whether* he chooses to send an evil spirit or even needs to send one is another matter. It seems that during those times, Satan's biggest role was in the gods that the people kept turning to worship. When the people turned away from God, Satan was there in the form of other gods, commonly called idols. It isn't apparent that these gods did anything except give the people the illusion that they could live sinful lives and ignore God in relative comfort. This is exactly what Satan wants us to do. At this time the Holy Spirit had not yet come to convict man so they figured that they needed a god or gods who would allow them permission to do what the true and living God would not allow them to do in comfort—cater to all their fleshly desires. Jesus' role as savior had not yet come to be, so there was no one to cast the devil out "in the name of," as our savior. They were under the law, and if God gave the laws which they had to live by and they didn't like these laws, then what they figured they needed were other gods to give more laws or "better" laws that were more amicable to their sinful nature. They needed gods who had a better understanding of their fleshly urges and desires; they needed gods who would do what *they* wanted them to do.

RECOGNITION TIP # 6

Recognize and acknowledge that we cannot develop a relationship without communication. Communicate with God on a daily basis.

CHAPTER 7

For when ye were the servants of sin, ye were free from righteousness. What fruit had ye then in those things whereof ye are now ashamed? For the end of those things is death. But now being made free from sin, and become servants to God, ye have your fruit unto holiness, and the end everlasting life. For the wages of sin is death; but the gift of God is eternal life through Jesus Christ our Lord.—Romans 6:20-23

I once had a conversation with a young lady who insisted that the reason people have such negative reactions to sin is because society makes us think that a behavior is bad or sinful. In other words, it is not so much the action that makes a sin a sin, but what society thinks of the action that determines whether a sin is a sin. If the behavior was not considered "bad" by society, then people who are sinning would not have such negative reactions such as emotional disturbances, negative outcomes, or general feelings of guilt to be plagued by. One example she used, was promiscuity and teen sex. In other cultures, this young lady insisted, people have sex at a young age and no one thinks much of it.

While I did not get to complete this conversation with this very idealistic young lady, I wondered what society she was talking about. To be honest with you, the first thing that came to my mind was the culture of the sixties when drugs were experimental and love was "free." It took that generation to grow up to realize that nothing is free and that they indeed had to pay for their "freedom." If they wanted to experience making a living in the work force, the "experimental" aspect of drugs did not fit into the picture; they had to pull themselves together and clean up their act if they wanted a certain quality of life. Most of these young people, when they became adults, taught their children the dangers of drugs, promiscuity, and lack of self-control. They taught them to be mindful of the choices that they made in life. Many of the offspring of the sixties who were not taught these life lessons intuitively felt eerily uncomfortable with the freedom that these parents had allowed them.

As far as what this young lady spoke of, I could not address it intelligently because I knew of no such civilization. This is not to say that such a civilization does not exist; there may very well be such a place. And physically what was their health like? What was the emotional maturity level of these young people as compared to our society? To what extent were they exposed to people other than people who think almost identically to how they and their family think? Is there any way to do a psychological evaluation of this promiscuous society to validate the mental state of these people? Is everybody happy, well-adjusted and in a healthy state of mind? Is the Word of God being taught to these people and if it is, how can it be taught accurately? According to the bible, similar societies were worthy, according to God, of destruction. Most of the people didn't mind in that society either, but God did.

I wondered if those people believe in God, if they believe in Jesus as their Savior and *still* act in such a fashion, or if they worship idols crafted of wood or stone. If such a society or culture exists, wouldn't the scientists of today have a field day with this one? At the same time, I know that such ingredients can ignite stories that make for tall tales, myths, and legend; all these genres' typical venues for encouraging good behavior or excusing bad behavior.

I don't profess to know what the case may be regarding these people if they exist. What I do know is that history leads me to believe that bad and sinful behavior once thought to be good, just, and warranted, has a way of being the teacher of future generations. History teaches what those who have had an experience learned and what those who contemplate having the experience should to expect. Through history, we can understand how negative and sinful behavior affects individuals as well as groups of peoples, illustrating the destructive effects of evil. Throughout the ages, ever since Eve ate of the fruit and gave some to Adam to eat, the wages of sin have been death and the devil has been a liar.

It is a lie to believe that sin is relative to a culture or society's beliefs. If it is part of a culture to worship idols, according to the Word of God, it is sin. Just because that's what you grew up seeing your mother, father and neighbors doing, does not mean that God accepts it. There are certain types of behaviors that are sinful according to God's word and not necessarily according to society's standards, whatever or wherever that society may be. These sinful behaviors, according to the word of God, lead to death—spiritual, physical, or emotional. Sin is acting contrary to the will of God and if we were to search the scriptures, we would see that sinful behavior was not based on what society said was sinful, but what God said was sinful. Some behaviors are specified, some implied and with some we are given a portrait in the form of parables. Jesus came that he might show society the foolishness of their ways and the wisdom of the Father, not to forfeit the laws of the land. Society's beliefs may change during certain eras for whatever reason, but this does not mean that God will find sinful behavior acceptable at any time.

When Jesus walked the earth, that particular society believed in stoning people to death because of sin, but Jesus came to tell us that we are all sinners and it's not our job to kill off sinners. Had Jesus condoned such a thing, the entire society would have had to be stoned to death—why, the last man standing would have had to stone himself to death if he were truly bent on following the laws of the day. Jesus came to show that the efforts of man to rid the world of sin and evil are futile, and that this domain belongs exclusively to God the Father. There is no man righteous enough to sacrifice his son or his own life to save a wicked person and bring down redemption for the entire world. God did this through Jesus because there is no man that is worthy enough do His job. We are sinful by nature and God understands this. He made us! There is nothing we can *do* to justify our worthiness because we are not saved by works.

While we may not build gods made of wood and stone or set up Asherah poles as in biblical times, Satan still caters to our sinful nature. Our attempts to justify sinful behavior are rebellion and idolatry. Each time we are rebellious we build a god of stone: hard, dense and opaque. Each time we lose faith and look to ourselves or our worldly comforts to save and protect us, we're worshiping idols of gold, silver, and wood. Just as during biblical times when people built physical idols of gold, silver, wood, or stone with their hands, we do the same thing without picking up a single tool. Satan uses our idols and our attitude and reliance on certain physical comforts in order to gain access into our minds and hearts.

If we *knew* our Lord and Savior, we would not consider what society says as our barometer and moral compass as to what is acceptable. We could not call that which is bad, good and that which is good, bad. If we study God's word and invite him into our hearts, our level of confusion would be minimal at best. Giving our attention to living for Christ, we would know God's word and as His sheep, we would know His voice. This is why it is so important for us to get to know our Lord and Savior and have a personal relationship with Him. If we know Him, we will not desire to rebel against Him. When we truly know Him, it troubles our spirit when we are disobedient and in the midst of sin. When we commit ourselves to have a more personal relationship with God, we are drawn to Him and our ability to recognize Satan's devious schemes in our lives are more apparent than ever.

We must never lose sight of the fact that Satan has a certain nature that equips him to do a certain job. His job, along with various other goals that are an integral part of his character, is to perpetuate evil and go against God in any way that he can. That's what he does and no one will ever be able to convince him to do otherwise. Nowhere in scripture will you find Jesus trying to convince the devil not to be evil. You won't find Jesus coddling or loving on the devil to bring about change in his nature. He does not address the devil at anytime as a friend; he only addresses him as an enemy and a foe. Jesus understands the nature of the devil and how spiritual law dictates that his evil nature is unchanging. He will tempt us. Satan tempts us to worship other gods that have their "laws." He would have us abide by laws that are "better" suited to our sinful nature. Satan would have us live in chaos rather than harmony, another indication of the work of the devil. Jesus, on the other hand, implores us to take the high road. Rather than going to a place and bowing low before an animal or pole to pay homage, Satan would have us hold fast to a lifestyle and set of rules that keep us in mental, physical and emotional bondage. Once ensnared, he knows that we will be reluctant to break the rules of that lifestyle because we do not want to risk being excommunicated or alienated from the people, places, and things that have become familiar to us along with the byproducts of that lifestyle. By nature, most human beings have a tendency to resist change. Even good changes affect the levels of stress-related hormones that our body releases. Once something becomes an accepted part of our lives, be it good or bad, it's difficult to change and this is something that Satan understands. Satan's way is to offer us the world, if we would just bow down and worship him. The more we give in to the devil, the harder it is for us to change. If we accept his offers in any way, we've got ourselves a problem. There is only one God, one Christ. When we do not honor and worship Him, we honor and worship the god of this world, Satan, and just let me take a minute to state here that Satan's world can appear to be very attractive. His world can be very tempting and delectable *at first glance*!

RECOGNITION TIP # 7

Recognize and acknowledge that disobedience to God can nullify blessings that God has for us; blessings that we cannot comprehend with our humanity. Obedience to God extinguishes the work of the devil so that we remain free in Christ.

CHAPTER 8

Little children, keep yourselves from idols. Amen.—1 John 5:21

 The likelihood that we would build a god made of wood or stone in this day and age is highly unlikely. Yet we do worship people, objects, ideals and MONEY. None of these things can take the place of God, yet we hold them in such high esteem and we put them in such positions of prominence in our lives that to live without them would seem a horrendous punishment that we would find essentially unbearable. We would kill, steal, and maim rather than lose a loved one were it up to us and it is not an unlikely thing for us to surrender our morals and ideals in order to keep our paycheck. This is a noble and acceptable concept to us. Protecting our families is viewed as an act of love.

 When there is an immediate threat to our families and loved ones, our emotional compass kicks into high gear. When there is a present threat to their survival, our instinct for survival takes a back seat and we will risk all. The thing is, we naturally have a desire to protect those that we love and this is not a bad thing. This is what makes us human; to protect those that we love and to expect those that we love to protect us. There is a desire to please those that we love and an expectation that those that we love will contribute to our sense of happiness. Of course, Satan uses these same emotions as he is prone to do, to cause us to do unscrupulous things without fully thinking them through or weighing the consequences. This, once again, is an example of how Satan exploits our propensity for nurturing to accomplish his tasks by using twisted reasoning that caters to our fears and insecurities. Once again, because of his work, the thought process is aborted and we go with what feels good at the time. We never get past emotional blocks to a level of Christ love that centers and balances us, allowing us to make wise choices and decisions. We ultimately end up making poor choices all in the name of "love" that transport us deeper into the lair of the devil.

Satan uses our instinct for survival pretty much the same way. Our instinct for survival is one of our most base instincts and because of that it should be monitored by us very carefully. While it is a valuable tool that God has furnished us with to continue to perpetuate the species, it is also one of the tools that Satan uses for his work because it *is* so base. This "baseness" in our nature is what we must rise above in order to have a strong relationship with God; this is a part of not yielding to the flesh. If we do not consciously rise above this base instinct, it allows the devil to take us to places we don't want to go and to do things that we should never do. This base instinct is very animalistic in nature and is being played out amongst animals in the wild at this very moment, a factor that helps to keep the world ecologically balanced but does nothing to perpetuate mankind. God created us in His image, higher than animals; He made us with dominion over them, not to live according to the "laws of the jungle" as they do. This is living according to flesh and an invitation to demonic activity in our lives.

When we live according to the flesh, we live in a very animalistic way. Many criminals in society live in such a way, which is why Satan has such access to their souls. They worship their flesh, attending to the needs of it and the baseness that it requires. We are to worship God, not our flesh, so to worship the flesh is like worshiping a type of god, an idol. I cannot express enough that idol worship is something that we should be very careful of because it can be very subtle. Worshiping, or tending to what makes the flesh content, as a way of life can be a form of idol worship.

The idea of worshiping other "gods" does not play out the same in today's society as in biblical times. The most common type of idol worship back then was to worship something that was physical and made by hand. Today many of our idols are not made by hand with few exceptions, money being one. Our idol worship is mostly conceptual—how we look at people, places, things, or activities that we are involved in. For example, activity that we engage in on a continuous basis that falls into the category of anti-God, anti-Christ, and disobedience are behaviors that appeal to Satan and the very thing that he relishes. He would have us at least dilute our Christianity if he cannot persuade us to reject it altogether. As long as the devil can keep our mind and conscious on certain people, certain things, and certain activities that we are involved with, and as long as it's not God, its okay. The devil knows that unhealthy attention to such things is a form of idolatry. He knows that the whole purpose of idols, back then and today, is to have us focus on *them* and *their* power, and not **God** and the power of the **Holy Trinity**. Satan knows how limited his power is; it is we who must struggle to remember that Satan is a defeated foe, regardless of what has happened or what will happen in our lives.

Nowadays, many Christians do not sit before carved objects praying that the object itself would answer their prayers; this we consider primitive and uncivilized heathenism. If we do sit before carved objects these days, what we *may* call it, to soften the idea of it being idolatry, is having an object of focus. People who meditate or pray in this fashion say that they are not expecting to receive a blessing because of the object or that they are putting trust in the object to solve their problems. They tell me that the object is simply an article of focus. It reminds them, they say, to stay focused on their prayers or the purpose of their meditation. It is not, they insist, that they are putting trust in an inanimate thing.

We will put more trust in our finances than God, and we won't hesitate to soften the blow by saying the money is just an object of focus. We'll put more trust in a successful company than we will in God, without even giving thought to it. We offer the sacrifice of our health, our families, children, or the sacrifice of a weekly "Sabbath" that is needed to recharge our engines and contemplate spiritual matters. I heard a woman admit that she gave up her children to her husband and moved out of the house so that she could go back to school without distraction in order to follow her dreams of being a success. This woman had faith in her success. She believed in the blessings that the success would yield. She believed that her children being out of the way would allow success to flow to her. This woman sacrificed her children to the god of success. This is idolatry, and this is spiritually error. Did this work out for her? Yes. Did this work out for her children? No. They have issues of abandonment and rejection that Satan is conveniently using to try to ruin their lives. Do you recognize Satan in this scenario of "virtual" idolatry?

This virtual idolatry is commonplace in lieu of people fashioning physical idols with their hands. Many idol worshipers back in biblical times had no problems with virtual idolatry. They made a god for pretty much anything they saw fit to make a god for—the harvest, the moon, the sun, fertility, love, etc. Pagan religions covered large areas of concern with gods to fit any occasion; this pretty much took away the desire to look to the unseen and intangible for results. They looked to the god of that thing for results. If they wanted to win a war, they did not get wrapped up in the war itself expecting victory; they bowed down and worshiped a god of war and expected the god of war to give them the victory.

People becoming Christians during that time must have had a difficult time coming out of idolatry and worshiping one God. It must have been difficult to go from looking to manmade idols to address many issues, to having faith in one God to deal with all of their issues. With idol worship, they did not have to take responsibility for their actions; they could blame their trouble on the wrath of an unappeased god. I can imagine that this would have led to fear of having a close relationship with an omniscient and omnipresent God because in their minds, He would have had to be pleased all the time for everything, just like the idols. They had come to expect either punishment or results from their idol gods and it would have been foreign to them to accept the radical message that this God loved them with a holy love even when they were at their worst.

In the New Testament, as well as now, the blood of Jesus is the everlasting protection for those who accept Jesus Christ as their Lord and Savior. The name Jesus differentiates between us just serving any god, any idol, saying "Lord, Lord," and serving the one and only true and living God. Satan cannot deceive God's people into believing that they are worshiping God and doing His will, because of the distinction of His Son. When we say God, there is no distinction in the pronunciation. Jesus and the name of Jesus are like the anti-venom serum to snakebites (no pun intended). Satan cannot abide where the presence of Christ is because darkness cannot comprehend light. Also, as an added bonus of our protection against the devil's deception, in the New Testament we are given access to the Holy Spirit which is our internal protector, compass and guide to assist us on our earthly journey. The Holy Spirit acts as our protector against invading forces by warning us when the enemy is at hand. It also opens us up for messages from God that help us to resist the devil so that we are not tempted beyond what we can endure. It activates us so that we are capable of doing God's will, despite the fact that we might not think that we're clever enough, articulate enough, or strong enough to do so.

The Holy Spirit is like the director in a play. He tells us what is good, what is bad, where we should stand, what we should stand for, and in what direction we should go. He helps us to give our best and to put our best foot forward. The Holy Spirit is what activates us to do the work of Christ, think Christ-like thoughts, and say the things that God would have us say. He helps us rise above the imperfection of our mere humanity. With the Holy Spirit our humanity cannot impede us because what is impossible in our humanity, God can work through the Holy Spirit to accomplish.

So you see, through the Holy Spirit, God has provided other spiritual avenues. We have God the Father, God the Son, and God the Holy Spirit available to us and because they are all a very present help, we don't *have* to eat what Satan sets before us. There is always a choice when it comes to the devil! We must know how Satan works, but even more importantly, we must understand the provisions that have been provided to us by God our Father. We are not bumps on a log, powerless fodder for Satan's amusement. We have been given Christ as an example of how to live as a human on this earth, the Holy Spirit to give us warning and clarify incoming information to the spirit, and of course we are fiercely and wonderfully made in the image of God.

RECOGNITION TIP # 8

Recognize and acknowledge that we always have more than one choice, and one of those choices is what God would have us do. We make our choices in life; God did not make us to be robots.

CHAPTER 9

Stand fast therefore in the liberty wherewith Christ hath made us free, and be not entangled again with the yoke of bondage.—Galatians 5:1

People perish for lack of knowledge. Many a person's spirit has been invaded because of ignorance. Many people have thought that they *had* to deal with Satan's work. They have been caught up in a particular sin or particular sins for so long that they think that they have done all that is humanly possible, and therefore are doomed to accept a life that is demon-infested. Here's the good news; we don't have to do that, people! God is powerful, and it is imperative that we gain knowledge on this subject of just how powerful He really is. He is so much more than a meal, a house, money in our pocket. In our seeking of Christ, we discover keys that allow us direct access to all the weapons of warfare that the Lord has given us. We discover keys to unlocking blessings and keys that unlock chains that have us in bondage. In addition to the blood of Jesus, God has an army of angels and an infinite supply of workers that help us and act as a bridge to guide us, in our weaker moments, back to Christ our Savior. Through Him we get clean, and we can stay clean. He LOVES us and *WANTS* us to have the victory. He no more wants to see us ignorant and hurt as any loving parent would want to see their child unprotected, ignorant of evil, hurt by consequences, and bound in iniquity.

As you proceed, try to keep in mind that the whole purpose of this book is to expose Satan for what he is, what he does, and how he does it. When Satan is exposed, he can be defeated and the Christ within can reveal himself to you and those around you with minor opposition. Satan can no longer deceive you with his lies about how inadequate, unlovable, imperfect, unworthy, etc., you are. His adversarial antics are exposed and rendered powerless because we now know that we have power through Christ Jesus and we KNOW how to use it. The quality of our life has to change because we will know the truth, and as a consequence the truth MAKES us, or CAUSES us, to be FREE to live a life that is pleasing to God.

Just as physical ills affect the physical body, spiritual ills affect the spirit of a man. The spiritual and the physical exist parallel to each other and yet they are intricately dependent upon each other. There are laws that apply to how the spirit world operates just as there are laws of physics. The laws that apply to the spirit world are called immutable laws. The laws of the physical world are changeable to an extent. For instance, nothing exists that is not constantly changing on some level: getting older, collecting dust, evaporating, reacting to chemicals, or being acted upon by some force or another. In the spiritual realm, everything that exists has existed in some shape fashion or form forever. There is no oxidation in the spirit realm; nothing has gotten older or better or worse. In the spiritual realm, it would be safe to say that everything falls into a category of black and white and there are no gray areas. They may seem gray to us but in reality they are either God's permissive will or His sovereign will. In other words, an immutable law cannot be changed; nobody and nothing can change those laws except an override by God himself. When this does happens, this is called either divine intervention or a miracle.

Spiritual ills are subject to spiritual laws. One cannot cure a spiritual ill with a physical substance. Symptoms may be temporarily managed, but the cure has to be spiritual. This spiritual law is one of the major reasons for unhappiness in the world. People refuse to understand this and try and try again to remedy or cure situations in their lives that are of a spiritual nature with non-spiritual things. One reason for this is that we have been conditioned by society to look for tangible solutions to our problems. The media, our friends, our family, all tell us that we need to *do* something, *stop* doing something, *buy* something, *change* something, *take* medications, *get* more money, and *have* more things. Don't get me wrong, the advice can be good and valid, IF we are talking about a problem that is physical problem. If we want a job whether we need it or not, it's not going to happen unless we actually *do* something to bring this to pass. Jobs don't just let themselves in your door, pick you up off of the couch, and put you to work while you are asleep. If we want to save money for a rainy day we must *stop* spending every dime that we get our hands on and save. You cannot save what is spent. Sometimes we must *buy* things that we need, *change* our clothes, *take* medication, or *get* more money. These are all physical solutions to concrete problems. However, if a problem is spiritual, the solution has to be spiritual and must originate from a spiritual source.

Even so, this is not to say that because a problem is spiritual, the answer is going to magically appear written on a wall, or that it will come from a priest, rabbi, or preacher—or even while you worship in your church, although it certainly can. What I am saying is that just as Jesus knew that the spirit had revealed to Peter that he was the Christ, if anyone answers a spiritual question accurately, or attends to another's spiritual need on any level, the source of these things *are*, because they must be, spiritual in nature. Answers to spiritual problems are spiritual and a solution cannot be found otherwise.

Hence, while the spiritual can be connected to the emotional, the emotions and spirit are separate. We can be emotional about a thing that has nothing to do with the spiritual. We can also be so spiritually moved that it evokes emotion in us. That emotion is not the spirit, but the emotion may be a physical byproduct of the impact that the spirit is having on us. It's easy to get the two confused if we don't know any better. When we come to understand what is spirit and what is emotion, this makes it more difficult for Satan to deceive us and easier for us to differentiate between the need to heal spiritually and the need to heal emotionally.

For instance, a person may be diagnosed with an emotional ailment that responds successfully to medication and/or therapy. That person will continue to heal and get better by adhering to and following the doctor's orders because the problem is not of a spiritual nature. On a spiritual level, a person may be diagnosed as having demons and will not respond to therapy and medication. If there is any reaction to therapy and medication at all, it would be a temporary symptomatic relief at best. The demons may hide for a season, but they will not go away. In some cases, medication may actually break down the natural barriers within that person that are resisting the demon's efforts to take over. It is vital, for this reason, that a person be examined and observed closely because such a mistreatment of symptoms can make the difference between life and death as far as the spirit is concerned. There has to be proper diagnosis otherwise the wrong cure can be applied. In other cases, sometimes therapy and medication can be used and may offer a much-needed moment of clarity in the thought process in order for the Word to penetrate and be received into spirit. In essence, the demonic activity is curtailed long enough in order for the word to reach the *person* without such severe hindrances. This gives a spiritually compromised individual a much-needed window of opportunity to make the crucial decision of renouncing Satan and his works. The use of medication, however, is no guarantees that a window of opportunity will ever present itself. Ultimately, the problem of demons is progressive; the more we allow demons to dwell within us the more room there is for their evil companions.

In the physical world such maladies may mistakenly be called mental illness if not diagnosed from the proper perspective and we fail to examine spiritual laws. By the same token, an illness that is purely physical or emotional may be misdiagnosed as spiritual if a proper diagnosis is not given. This is why it is so important for us to be able to distinguish and discern between what is spiritual and what is purely a physical or emotional ailment. Some people are gifted with the gift of discernment, and some are not. Since most people do not have medical training and have very limited knowledge on even the most common of medical terminology, it is recommended that a professional be consulted, first and foremost when at all possible, for a proper diagnosis. This is important! We do not want to put ourselves in the position of "crying wolf" every time we **think** we've encountered a demon in ourselves or in others. We don't want to belittle the importance of recognizing when people are truly in bondage to Satan, and a medical condition; the stakes are too high.

We must understand the law that spirit communicates with spirit. One has to be open spiritually in order to have access to the spiritual on any level. Once we are opened to things of the spirit; access into that world is now possible for better or worse. A minister has to be open to the Holy Spirit in order to give a spirit-filled sermon, other than that, it is just information gleaned from the bible. The spirit world does not consist solely of angelic creatures from heaven filled with good intentions from the Almighty Himself. The clergy, if not diligent about keeping in right relationship with God, are very vulnerable, more vulnerable than the average person. While everything that is spiritual was created by God, everything that is spiritual is not necessarily holy unto God. After all, when Lucifer rebelled and was ejected from heaven he took a third of the angels with him and since then, there is and has been opposing forces in the natural as well as the spiritual. Just as there are positive and negatively charged ions, there are positive and negative forces that exist in the spiritual realm. The positive and negative both have their place and their purpose; both are useful and serve a purpose as we will see.

I can relate this to you with much confidence. My oldest sister died after having fought a miraculous battle overcoming obstacles during her illness that the doctors never thought she would overcome. She crashed through barriers that left them scratching their heads, surviving victory after victory and crisis after crisis that made my family believe in miracles like we'd never believed in them before. During her long illness she had opportunity to visit in this spiritual realm, and I was fortunate enough to be blessed to be a there with her to hear about it.

She would tell me about the people she would see. She called them ghosts, or dead people. Some of these "people" would come to her to comfort her and others would come to torment her. The bad people would try to confuse her and trick her into thinking that they were the good people only to gain her trust and then proceed to hurt her. She never explained to me in detail about the nature of this hurt, but the pain was real. These people would try to get her to trust them so that she would relate things to them that they would later use to hurt her.

She came to know these entities by name and she would describe them to me, what they were wearing and how they looked. Some of them would be dressed like doctors and nurses to confuse her enough so that she was suspicious of any new doctor or nurse that came to attend to her. Some of them would not. She told me their names and just to be sure that these "people" were not real, I would take the name to the nurses' station to ask if they had any nurses employed in that unit that went by the names that she'd given me. I would describe the people like she described them to me but nobody had seen a doctor or nurse fitting that description and there was no one on that unit with the names that she'd given me.

My sister was a very gentle person. Not given to loud talk, boisterous ways, never one for negative or hurtful words. By our worldly standards, she would have been considered a good person, a nice person, and a likeable person. Even so, she had to battle through these beings and discover what was true and holy and what was evil and deceptive. This went on for a while until she overcame them and was able to see the beauty and truth of the love that God held for her and how he had operated all along in her life, keeping her, preserving her, and loving her. Once she was able to maneuver through this spiritual field of horrors and discover truth, these entities could no longer deceive her. She became more peaceful in her spirit and more anxious to leave her sick and ravaged body to go "home." That's what she told me in the end, that God said that it was time to come home. She had seen the glory of the Lord in the spiritual realm and she was ready because God had not only told her, but revealed to her what the devil had tried to hide from her in order to frighten her enough to keep her from the glory that God had planned for her. After she'd reached this level, she died peacefully; no fighting death, no hesitation, only acceptance. There is no doubt in my mind that she went home to be with the Father in the place that He had revealed to her, because not only did *I* witness her stubbornness and tenacity to refuse to die when the odds said that she should have, many others did too. My sister held on long enough to prove that the devil is a liar and that God is good and merciful and forgiving and that He loves us with an everlasting love.

That is what we must do. We must get past the lies of the devil when he is tempting us and harassing us and hold on long enough, to get to the glory and the love of the Father. This is what Satan tries to do in our lives: deceive us into thinking that we will never be worthy of the love of our Father. Some of us give up when we shouldn't, and just succumb to whatever lie he tosses our way. We need to fight through our unpleasant battles, like my sister did, until the glory of God can be revealed to us in our life. During her time on her death bed, many people were praying for my sister, and I believe the prayers of others reached heaven on the wings of doves, and God does answer prayer. Our prayers were answered in the form of my sister having the strength not to die and give up at such a terrible time in her life of torment and pain and make it to a place of peace and sweet surrender into the arms of the Lord.

My sister's death confirmed in my spirit what the bible says in words. Not all "angels" are messengers from God. The third of the angels in heaven who severed their holy relationship with God to follow Lucifer are his "angels" and he is their leader. These too were angels who were created by God to do His bidding right along with Lucifer. These creatures dwelled in the very presence of the Lord Himself and somehow Lucifer was able to convince these holy creatures that they should go against God, their creator, and follow him. We aren't privileged as human beings to physically dwell in the heavens, saturated by the presence of the Lord; how vulnerable does this make us to do what Lucifer did? Just think, Lucifer, in the awesome physical presence of God, rejected Him! Not only did he reject God, he persuaded a third of the angels to leave the heavenly presence of the Holy Father! Is this not someone we need to know about?

Why should we have only the foggiest idea of how to recognize and defeat someone who convinced a third of God's angels to turn against Him? How dangerous is it for us not to be clear on the spiritual laws that are designed to protect us from this enemy? The gospels informs us on many levels and in many ways about the power of the devil. Knowledge is power, especially when it comes to matters such as demonic activity. Satan will use what we know and especially what we don't know, to get us to live for him and not God. Maybe he believes deep within his evil little heart that if he is clever enough, he ought to at least be clever enough or persistent enough bring at least a *third* of the souls on this earth under his power so that *they* worship *him*! Is the story of Lucifer an indication that it is possible for him to convince one out of every three people to follow him? I don't know, but it is something to think about.

RECOGNITION TIP # 9

Recognize and acknowledge that Satan is real. God created him and allows him to exist in order to strengthen us for Him.

CHAPTER 10

It is the spirit that quickeneth; the flesh profiteth nothing: the words that I speak unto you, they are spirit, and they are life.—John 6:63

We all are spirits wrapped in flesh regardless of whether we practice a religion or not. Since we all had to come from somewhere; we all had to have a source. God is the only existing entity that does not have a source. God is the creator of all things, and God created man, animal, Lucifer and the angels that he took with him.

When God breathed the spirit of life into man, he became a living soul. The spirit that God breathed into each and every one of us is that invisible connection to Him. It is what connects the earthly to the heavenly. His spirit is that part of us that strives toward what we do not understand but instinctively knows what is good and possible. It is that part of any one of us that longs for happiness and completeness. It's the part of us that yearns for "home," a base of acceptance, understanding and love. We yearn because we instinctively know that there is such a "home." His spirit compels us to seek this connection; therefore we innately desire to feel "connected" to something greater than ourselves. This spirit is that part of us that compels us to cry out for help when none seems apparent. This spirit of God within us makes us believe that the impossible is possible and that miracles do abound. It is that thing in each of us that rises like a phoenix from its ashes because we feel that somehow if we persevere, a way will be made out of no way and a new day holds invisible promises just for us.

Though our spirituality is directly linked to the emotional, the emotional is not the spiritual and the spiritual is not the emotional. Our desire for this connection is not an emotional one although this desire is not void of emotion. It is natural and necessary part of our life force. It cannot be restrained without negative consequences; it can only be attended to or ignored, strong or weak. How we attend to this desire and the measure of its force to connect can make the difference between a soul redeemed and a soul forfeited.

Every human being is spiritual because every human being was created by God, be they good, evil, or somewhere in between, this is indisputable because only God has the power to create life. By the way, this is why evolution makes no sense. Exactly how long is it going to take the dog to evolve into a highly intelligent being according to this theory? How long before the monkey creates his own society and begins to worship a god? What's taking the cockroach, which's been here forever, so long to at least be able to develop and manufacture a body armor that can protect it from being crushed under the foot of man? Again, the real question is not whether we are spiritual, but how we choose to acknowledge or not acknowledge our spirituality.

Another question that we must address as undisputable spiritual beings is what do we as individuals consider the source of our spiritual essence, who are we spiritually? What motivates us to do the things we do because there has to be a spiritual source because we are spiritual beings? Which spiritual source is the motivating force that drives us? Who is it, or what is it that we have decided to connect ourselves to as our source? What well do we go to and fill up when we are low and what spiritual force is motivating us to go to this well? Remember there are only two forces within the spirit realm; a force of darkness and a force of light. Anything in between is invalid and will eventually be drawn into one of these two forces. No human being extracts their intentions and motivations from the light at all times, and very few human beings draw their motivation from the dark side at all times. Therefore it boils down to a simple math equation:

a = motivation $\quad\quad\quad$ l = light
$\quad\quad\quad\quad\quad\quad\quad\quad\quad\quad$ (love, wisdom, understanding, charity, faith)
b = intentions $\quad\quad\quad$ d = darkness
$\quad\quad\quad\quad\quad\quad\quad\quad\quad\quad$ (negativity, confusion, carnal satisfaction)

therefore:
$\quad$ If: $\quad a + b < l = d$ (moving toward spiritual darkness)
$\quad\quad\quad\quad a + b > d = l$ (moving toward spiritual enlightenment)

If we are capable of being honest with ourselves we will know which direction we're headed in and what well we have more of a propensity to draw from. If we discard our blinders we will understand whether we need to change or not. However, many of us are as blind men when it comes to such things but we can always ask God to show us and we will no longer be blind, we shall see.

What have we chosen as our source, our well? The intellect, the emotions, religion, people, places, and things outside of ourselves? How important is this source for our daily bread? Who or what is it that we have come to put our trust in? Where do we go to drink when we thirst? If by chance we dare to think that we have not chosen to put our trust in nothing or no one, we need to think again and take a look over our lives because more than likely if we think that we have not chosen, it is probably because we have chosen to idolize ourselves and our abilities. It's human nature to rely on something to get us through this life and this, my friend, cannot be avoided no matter who we are!

The first commandment that the children of Israel received was that they should have no god before Him. There must be some necessary importance in this being the first commandment. "Thou shall have no other go before me" is important because God understands the ramification of doing such a thing. To have other people or things to hold more importance in our lives makes us vulnerable. The breaking of this commandment seems to be the biggest prelude to demonic infiltration. Who or what we choose to serve or depend on for relief, to sustain our way of life, is what Satan uses as a portal or inlet. What we worship may not necessarily be evil, but because Satan sees how we depend on this, and because Satan knows that this thing is not God, the door is opened for infiltration.

Money, for example is not evil in and of itself, but the *love* of money is where the problem lies. The *love* of money opens the doors for Satan to use money as a tool to get us to do evil in God's sight, for the devil has discerned that *love* of money is the motivating factor in many of our ungodly decisions. When we come to think of money as a key to unlock joy, peace, and happiness, we'll do anything to get it, keep it, and protect it. Money should not be looked at as a key, but a tool. While money can save us from many situations that are difficult, money cannot save our soul. This statement may seem a bit trite, but truthfully we must constantly remind ourselves that who we are, what we believe about ourselves, how we feel about life, our ability to authentically embrace love, peace, and acceptance of God, are things that cannot be purchased. Money is so alluring that it us easy to forget ourselves while in pursuit of it. This makes it easy for the devil to convince us to obtain this tool with total disregard for the plight of our souls.

Another example of how we corrupt the first commandment and give place to Satan in our lives is with the people that we love. To love a person is not a bad thing. To love a person is a good thing. God wants us to love, just like he wants us to have money. The problem is, however, when the love of another person seems to be the key to our peace, joy and happiness. There that word is again, *key*. Recognize that when something seems to be *key* to the essence of our existence on any level, other than God, we are treading on unholy ground and if we are treading on unholy ground, we dance with the devil. A key opens doors; it is the solution to what is locked by revealing or releasing it. Our essence should belong to God; it should depend on nothing and no one else. We are not designed by the Almighty that another thing or human being should be able to fulfill our lives completely. No other human being can deliver our soul, and save us from the enemy. Jesus gave his life for us because He knew that there was power waiting to be released upon his death and resurrection. Jesus and his death on the cross, was the key that unlocked God's plan of salvation for the whole world. No other human being can do that, no other human being is God! When we substitute things and people in such a place in our lives, Satan has clearance to work through the very person or thing that we love so uncompromisingly, and turn us away from God. Why? Because we've become more interested in what satisfies that person, than what satisfies God. We have put that person before God and how dangerous is that?

It's a matter of survival, what we consciously or subconsciously choose as our source, the place that we go, mentally or physically to feel whole again. It's a matter of survival because we all need something to feel complete; we're just built that way! Sure, there are motivating factors which may influence who or what we choose as our source, but ultimately, it really doesn't matter why we make our choice. The motivating reason could be one among millions, some may seem legitimate, some not so legitimate. The point is that we *do* choose and this is what motivates our actions and colors our intentions. Consequently *why* we have chosen bears little relevance to the fact *that* we have chosen and whatever we have chosen has a strong influence on how we live our lives.

It is not unusual for our source to fluctuate from time to time depending on what's motivating our choice, but basically as time goes on, we do have a tendency to lean toward one source, more than another. This favorite source usually dominates our behavior. It is the major well that we have a tendency to draw from. It's usually something that we have found very possible for us to be successful at, or something that fits our personality like a glove. Our source, whatever it may be, provides a sense of reward and/or comfort. This thing makes us feel, however temporary the effects, more in control, more balanced. It enables us to feel like we can face whatever life has to offer and caters to our ego. This source is not God because God does not cater to our egos. Take away this source, and we flounder like a fish out of water desperate for our sustenance, and many times, we will do anything to hold on to it. This is why the bible warns us to be desperate for nothing because no *thing* in this world is so important that it can take the place of God. Desperation, such as it is, makes not only for foolish choices and unwise actions; it also makes us more likely to accept the temptations of the devil just to appease it.

This source of ours may not be common for the masses to readily attain or accomplish, but since we are capable of accessing this source; we feel that we can make things happen for us by using it. Whatever our source is, whether temporary or permanent, it is what we have chosen to depend upon! This is the person or thing in our lives that we have chosen as a substitute to deliver for us, in place of God in our lives. I understand that this is something that is hard to hear because many times a truth, any truth, is hard to accept. If it were easy for us to accept what is true, many people, especially in the psychiatric and social service industries would be out of work. Fortunately, however, once we accept truth, our journey to freedom and healing begins.

So what is it? Who or what is it that replaces God in your life. What have you put before God? Whom or what do you desire when your spirits are low? More money, a new job, a new boyfriend, girlfriend, parent or spouse? Is it drugs, alcohol, success, your children, food, or exercise that you feel will get you back on track? Do you feel that it is your church, your friends, your social standing, your work for charity, your reputation, your temper, your intellect that will make the difference when your back is up against the wall? Exactly what is it that you need to *do* in order for you to feel alive? What makes you feel that you matter and life is worth living?

God is not on the preceding list, and he is deliberately omitted. The reason is to bring to the attention those of us who consider ourselves to be goody two shoes, who would shout from the rooftops professing our religiosity and our spiritual integrity. This was done for those who go to church every Sunday and condemn those who don't; those who use Lord, God, Jesus in every other sentence and commit all sorts of grievous sins against him. This is for those who use the name of Jesus as a lucky amulet thinking to "trick" God into blessing them with things that are not meant for them to have no matter how much they choose ignore the word of God, and live how they choose to live. If you are one of those who climb into the pulpit Sunday after Sunday to impress man, have power, or pay bills with no regard as to whether you've allowed the word of God to go forth, a soul is led to Christ, *or* if you could care less if some poor soul who is suffering from spiritual starvation is fed, this list is for you to consider.

What about those of us who constantly examine the lives of others for errors and offences so much so that we fail to see how our preoccupation has stunted our own spiritual growth allowing Satan the opportunity to eat us alive as our own garden goes blindly unattended. Some of us have no love in our words of truth and because there is no love in our words, Satan uses these words of truth that come through our mouths to not comfort, teach, and elevate, but uses the words of truth to dredge up pain, insecurities, and hopelessness in others. These words of truth come from a negative space that the devil has come to occupy in your soul. The devil knows the truth and uses it and anything else that he can to destroy God's people.

A word to you truth speakers. If you feel no peace, no joy, and no contentment in your own life, the devil will use you to hurt people so if you're filled with pain and resentment, speak truth onto yourself before you go around picking on other people. In other words, you need to sit down and shut up until the Lord moves you to accept the truth about yourself first. You *may* be very intelligent and know the bible backwards and forward, scripture by scripture, line by line and *are* able to see the truth for someone's else's life. The devil, however, will use that knowledge in someone like you to turn people away from the word by having them to rebel against you and close their ears to the truth of the Lord because of you. When there is no love in your words, people know; even if they don't know what it is that they know. Young seekers who are on the fence many times are looking for reasons to continue a sinful lifestyle and you don't want to be the reason that they come up with. We should not use our knowledge of the Word to make ourselves look good in the eyes of others. The true experience of the Holy Spirit in our lives is very humbling and if you don't feel humbled, you need to think twice before uttering your truth all over everybody. Truth in the Holy Spirit has a way of humbling and strengthening us so that compassion and love are always present in abundance.

RECOGNIZING SATAN

This is your wake-up call to examine what the motivating factors are behind your deeds. Are they deeds of the flesh, or obedience to God? The two can look quite similar, until examined. Many of us will find that our motivations do not go beyond the ego and have nothing to do with God and everything to do with a desire to feel comfortable within our own flesh. Choice for us many times is based on the comfort of the flesh and has little to with whether a thing is right or wrong in the eyes of God.

I once heard a story about a young lady who would go to the park every day to feed the squirrels. The squirrels had come to expect this young lady and would gather at her feet, come up to her uninhibited, and basically behave like they were her personal pets. Soon people began to notice and admire this scene smiling and making complimentary remarks as they observed her. The young lady came to like the attention that feeding the squirrels brought to her, and soon her feedings took on a bizarre twist. She would go to the park to feed the squirrels everyday, but if there was no one around to watch her, she would withhold the food as the squirrels gathered at her feet, until there was an audience to watch and admire her!

I can just see in my mind's eye the little squirrels all gathering around her, up on their little hind legs, little paws at their chest, sniffing the air waiting and wondering when they would get their food. Unfortunately, some of us are like that, we will withhold what we have in our possession to offer until we are reasonably sure that our actions will result in some kind of notice or fanfare. When we're like "squirrel girl," what we do must be acknowledged or admired by others in order for us to feel a sense of satisfaction. While her original intentions may have been pure, she ended up feeding them for self-gratification. This, entertaining the ego, is indicative of a malfunction in the spirit. It is not proof that there is demonic activity going on, but it is proof that there is vulnerability within you that Satan can surely use for various temptations.

It does not stand to reason, for instance, that a person would want to help thousands of people and feel no compassion to help one suffering individual; thus the problem illustrated with of the feeding of the squirrels. It's a good thing to do, but if in your mind it's a better thing to do if you can garner compliments, admiration, and recognition from others while doing it, something is wrong. There's nothing wrong with compliments and accolades being given to those who help the less fortunate in our society, but it should never be the motivating factor for their actions. With all the things that go on in the world, both great and small, God's eye is on the sparrow. To get so caught up in the group that we fail to reach the individual is counter productive. This does not strengthen one's spirit to bring us into harmony with the almighty, this feeds the ego, and one of Satan's many favorite God given attributes that he uses relentlessly to destroy us. The devil understands that what is of the ego, feeds the ego, just as what is of the flesh, feeds the flesh, just as what is of the spirit feeds the spirit.

Knowledge of these principles alone can inhibit many of Satan's opportunities for attack. He knows of it and so should we. We too should become adept at knowing what moves us toward spiritual integrity and what moves us away from it. If we spend all day in prayer, and at the end of the day involve ourselves in activity that by its very nature negates much of what we have prayed for and believed for, our lives can be a series of two steps forward and two steps back. We remain stagnant, and this is where feelings of inadequacy can begin to arise, and of course we must recognize that Satan uses these feelings of inadequacy as an opportunity to introduce his nature of bitterness, sadness, hopelessness and anger into our psyches. The devil hopes that this introduction will then develop into a full fledged relationship between us and him and his demons. He hopes that we will wallow in this lake of negativity so that we can dwell with him and he can keep us in bondage.

RECOGNITION TIP # 10

Recognize and acknowledge that the most important thing to work for in life is a strong relationship with God the Father, which is an impossibility without his son Jesus. Jesus is our lifeline to God. Without him, there is no relationship with God.

CHAPTER 11

And he asked his father, How long is it ago since this came unto him? And he said, Of a child. And ofttimes it hath cast him into the fire, and into the waters, to destroy him: but if thou canst do any thing, have compassion on us, and help us. Jesus said unto him, If thou canst believe, all things are possible to him that believeth. And straightway the father of the child cried out, and said with tears, Lord, I believe: help thou mine unbelief. When Jesus saw that the people came running together, he rebuked the foul spirit, saying unto him, Thou dumb and deaf spirit, I charge thee, come out of him and enter no more into him.—Mark 9:21-25

Satan uses many things to keep us in bondage to him and as I have stated earlier, many of these means are natural God-given attributes that are meant to be used to aid us in ways that bring us closer to him and help us to learn of him. Fear is not bad in its proper place. Anger is not bad in its proper place. Sex is not bad in its proper place. Ambition is not bad in its proper place. Sadness is not bad in its proper place. Partying is not bad in its proper place. The devil, however, has a way of using these very things to tempt us to employ them negatively while taking us to levels that are ugly and destructive in nature.

I know of a man who does pretty well for himself. This individual never gives anything to anyone. He'll give only if he can prognosticate a return on his money, time, or actions. On birthdays and holidays, you might be able to expect him over but never should you expect a gift. NEVER! I've seem him put in a position where he is forced, for various reasons to hand over a few pennies. I wish that you could see the pained look on his face! It's like he's having a surgical procedure without anesthetics. Even after he's given the little that he's been forced to give, you can see the wheels turning to see what he can require of that person so that he truly would not have "given" anything at all. It's not that he's parsimonious, he enjoys his money. He has no problem spending money on himself and things that contribute to his personal comfort and well-being no matter how stupid and frivolous they may be, but when it comes to others and he can see no personal benefit, this is a very difficult thing for him to do. This is evidence that there is a demonic stronghold that needs to be broken. The demon that has inhabited his personality, just won't allow him to give freely in love and without expectation. In this instance, Satan has taken being a good steward with your blessings to this negative manifestation of stinginess and fear. This fear has opened the door within this person and has allowed the spirit of lack to enter. The spirit of lack will not allow him to feel comfortable with giving as long as it is resides within him. When there is a spirit of lack, I don't care how much a person may acquire in life, they can never achieve a sense of satisfaction.

Einstein said that for every action there is an equal and opposite reaction, and in the spiritual realm this absolutely holds true. For every one extreme, there is another, a twin if you will, that is on the opposite end of the spectrum that can cause just as much damage as the former may cause good. For every sincere Christian, there is a Christian whose actions may look the same on the surface, but who is just as insincere as the sincere Christian is sincere. For every good mother there is a mother whose actions look the same, but there is no sincerity in her efforts. The same goes for friend, father, boss, minister—you name it. There is a twin in the universe, whose ruler or master is the devil, this twin is an imposter that many times only the spirit of a man can recognize it.

There is also a polar opposite type of spirit that is equally as damaging. It is not the twin, but the direct opposite of what would be considered a negative. The man who suffers from a spirit of lack by being stingy and guarded is the opposite of someone who gives and gives with no sense of self-worth or boundaries. The demon that dwells in his opposite would be different than the one that gives without thought or limitation. This would not be a spirit of lack, but a spirit of people pleasing. A person plagued with this type of polar opposite demonic activity is the person who literally gives until it hurts. It doesn't matter if what they are giving should be given or not. These people do not give at the unction of the Holy Spirit. They have no boundaries and have no sense of discernment; a woman will give her body with little or no regard; a man will take or withhold needs from his family and gladly give them to others where he perceives that there is more satisfaction to be gained from the giving. Just as the man in the previous story feels pained when he's forced to give, these people feel pained when they cannot give and are plagued with feelings of guilt and remorse. It does not matter if the circumstance warrants it or not, whether they should or should not, this is not a pleasant feeling for these people.

No, is a very uncomfortable word for people plagued with this people-pleasing demon and they very often find themselves in very compromising, uncomfortable, and spiritually damaging situations because of this. They don't like to use the word no, and they don't want the word used when referring to them, which is why these people very rarely ask for anything for themselves. When this demon occupies a person, they want to be a hero or a "nice" person, more than they want to obey the will of God and this is the biggest problem of all. What we are looking at here is the same demon working from both ends of the spectrum, the desire to withhold out of fear of depletion and the desire to give, without regard to boundaries or discretion. The root of both of these demons is a demon of rejection. Those who live with a fear of lack and a fear of being depleted from giving, as well as people pleasers, are plagued with a demon of rejection.

I have seen the demon of rejection at work in many people caught up in lifestyles that they don't like and caught up and involved with people that they don't particularly care for. You see, the demon of rejection makes us think that we are so unacceptable, so unlovable, and unworthy, that we feel that we can do no better than we are doing at the moment. When we feel unlovable, we cannot love ourselves and we can't possibly expect that another will love us. When we feel unacceptable, we cannot feel comfortable in nonthreatening situations because we are constantly judging ourselves as so unacceptable that no one else could possibly accept us. When we feel unworthy, we cannot feel that we are worthy enough to have anything but misery and pain in life which is exactly what we come to expect out of life and exactly what we get. All of our actions and decisions are controlled by this subconscious belief system that this demon has put into our minds. We begin to play out this role, getting caught in a loop, planting bad seed after bad seed, and never expecting a harvest and we won't get one either because the devil has stolen our harvest!

This people-pleasing demon would have us give and give and give until we find that not only is our cupboard bare but we have stripped ourselves mentally, physically and spiritually leaving ourselves open, vulnerable, and naked. The aspect of the demon that constantly makes us feel lack is that he would have us hold on to what is meaningless, so that we won't have room for what is meaningful in our lives. The root of both of these demons is rejection, who's goal is the same as all demonic activity and that is to have us so preoccupied with satisfying the needs of our flesh that the call of our spirit nature goes unheeded. We are not acting out of the will of the Father by withholding and being guarded as in the former instance by being good stewards and being wise with what the good Lord has given us; what we *are* doing in fact is acting *out* of the will of the Father.

This is the problem with those who insist on problem solving situations that have nothing to do with them and are far too involved in the affairs of others. I believe the bible calls these types of people busybodies. If you help, when God has told you to keep your hands off of a situation so that His will goes forth, you are acting *outside* of the will of God and not out of the will of God. You are acting out of the flesh so that you can feel good and look good to yourself and others. Being a kind person because God wants you to be has taken a backseat to your ego. This same thing holds true for those who do not help when they should because they are having a bad day, they're broke, or things just aren't going how they would want them to go. God will not have us give what he has not provided for us to give, including our opinion. His wisdom is not based on our emotional state. For example it is not necessary for God to use one person's anger to get a point across to another person. In such an instance you are merely throwing your opinion around to relieve yourself, and it is not out of a sense of benevolence; you are angry. Emotions have a purpose in our lives, an issue to be discussed, but it is not their place to be in the driver's seat!

We may do many good things to hide the rotten way we feel inside from the outside world just as we may do many rotten things to hide our feelings of vulnerability. We habitually create tangible situations that we can make reference to, this makes us feel better, boosting our self-confidence and temporarily causing us to feel worthy in life. Of course, because the boost is only temporary it does not last. We find ourselves looking for things to *do*, in a cycle, depending on the state of our soul; doing rotten things to hide our vulnerability, or doing things that make us feel that we aren't so bad because a bad person wouldn't do such good things. The reality of what we are doing, however, is that we are caught up and are being held in a stronghold like an insect caught in a spider's web. When the spider returns and finds his prey, he will first suck it dry and then devour it piece by piece until the whole is consumed. Satan finds us caught in one of his webs and proceeds to suck us dry, before he proceeds to devour us bit by bit. In any case, doing either one of these things, holding on too tight or giving unrighteously without boundaries, leave us open to the devil because we bypass having to rely on the Holy Spirit for guidance and come to rely on what we do to make us feel secure. This is not something that is of God but one of the many deceptions that Satan uses to keep us in bondage.

By acting out in any way, we create situations in our lives that Satan uses to keep us in a state of bondage. Sometimes we create situations by deliberately pushing someone's buttons just so that we are able to act out in anger and rejection of the person, or set up situations to get hurt, knowing that we will be rejected, only to be reduced to tears to relieve ourselves of built up pressure and/or garner sympathy. Or we create situations so that we can feed off of the smiles, praises, and accolades of others. Demons can manipulate these situations we create to foster negativity and hurt in ourselves or others by using what *seems* good and but *is* bad.

When I was younger, there was this boy who was about fifteen or sixteen years old who would deliberately say things to anger his parents so that he would have a reason to storm out of the house to go drinking and partying with his buddies. When I got older I discovered that there are husbands and who deliberately create an atmosphere of tension in their own homes in order to justify having an affair. I realized that there are women who refuse to become upstanding, capable, and self-sufficient, because they're convinced that if they do, their man will abandon them. I've come to understand that there are people who are so convinced that they are unattractive and undesirable that every article of clothing that they buy is ill-fitted and unflattering. There are those who feel so unloved that they commit crimes that prove to themselves and the whole world just how unlovable they are. There are people who because of past mistakes, youthful indiscretions, and bad choices, hate themselves and shovel that hate like lose dirt on to whoever might be in their line of fire. These are not demons doing these awful things; these are people acting out, and the devil is using the situations that they have created as authorization to take up residence in them, *after* the fact.

For instance, a person seems generous but his generosity is not motivated by obedience and a love for the Father in Heaven. What is its purpose? If we give, we may prove to the world and ourselves that we are worthy but this means nothing to God if we do not give according to His will, with right intentions. We may think that we are being a goody two shoes and this will save us from the fiery pit or put us in right standing with God, but it can't. We're goody two shoes not by the unction of the Holy Spirit, but because being that way is what we do, and being that way makes *us* feel in **control**. This has nothing to do with the Holy Spirit. When we are in control, we must realize that a human being, who is fallible, is in control and therefore we can expect failure, disillusionment and/or disappointment. When we submit to God and allow Him to lead, guide, and direct us on our life path, we become as infallible as is humanly possible. Our heart is in the right place, our intentions are Christ like in nature and our actions are in alignment with the Word. The spirit of Christ dwells within us all and although Satan likes to operate like an eclipse to the "Son" and can seem to overshadow His presence in our lives, if we keep our eye focused on Jesus and the significance of His death and resurrection, we will see that there is not total darkness in our lives, but a only a shadow or a cloud passing by. We will discover that the light has not been consumed by the darkness, and if we wait on it, the light of Christ still resides within us. There is no other way to achieve a sense of peace without the light of Christ. When we are willing and prepared to submit to Him we can expect such peace to follow. Anything else that we do, we do on our own and what we end up doing is nothing more than works, busyness, avoidance and delay. The devil uses what we do to make ourselves feel good; the devil uses what makes our flesh feel good; the devil uses what is not of God—to gain entrance into our lives.

    This flies right in the face of those who want to blame the devil for all of our negative behavior when the truth is, we have choices. Unless we are experiencing a high level demonic infiltration, when we make choices, the devil didn't make them for us. When we make bad choices in life and continue to make bad choices in life, the devil uses this as authorization to become a part of our personality, our soul, and steer us away from Christ. He uses our choices to lead us away from the light and be drawn into the darkness. How do we know that it is us that is making the choice verses a "the devil made me do it" type situation? We know this because we will understand the right thing to do and yet consciously chose not to do it. When the devil is working his craft through us we do not see a more positive choice. There is no unction to do the right thing. This is not denial, for denial is when you kind of know something and refuse to abide in it, even if you know it only to the tiniest degree. Even if you can look back over the situation in your mind's eye, you will see that you knew you had another choice and did not take it. Some of our bad choices are more blatant that others and may carry far-reaching consequences that may be minor or severe. Some of the choices we make are an open invitation to the devil, an important fact to come to terms with in order for us to heal and become whole. The good news, however, is that our bad choices always have exit ramps that offer us opportunities to more positive roads despite bad choice previously made. In other words, we do not have to stay on a chosen path forever, be it good or bad; the choice is ours.

When we find that we have made bad choices, it's usually because we are trying to manipulate and control situations to satisfy the desires of the flesh. We have suppressed or dismissed what our instinct, our gut feeling, the Holy Spirit is trying to tell us in order to satisfy a deep longing in an inappropriate way or satisfy an inappropriate longing by whatever means necessary. When we do this, what we are doing is putting trust in our feelings which become an idol for many of us and therefore we are not putting our trust in God. We are not putting our trust in Christ's death and resurrection and choose to continue to operate in rebellion and disobedience, hence we cause delay and in some instances we may even derail God's plans for us. God has a purpose for each and every soul walking the earth, but…we also have free will. We do have the ability delay or derail our inheritance, but it *is* there for all to receive, a gift that is there for us whether we choose to open it not. Throughout all of or our trials and tribulations, the gift of salvation, forgiveness, and our God-given destiny is always there, it never goes away. We can choose to open this gift today, tomorrow, twenty years from now, or never. Satan desires to keep us from this very fundamental information and if we can ever come to realize this within the very depths of our soul, it is a profound realization! As long as the devil can keep us from this information by using diversions such as our emotions, idolatry, and other forms of sin to keep us off guard, he keeps us from not only realizing that such a gift exists he keeps us from opening this gift with irrelevant concerns.

We all sin; however, the nature of a multitude of sins is masquerade. Many times we sin in ways that we are not aware of. To sin is to operate in spiritual err and spiritual err is not always blatant negativity or ugliness. Sometimes it appears to be beautiful, right, prosperous, comforting and even good; after all, as my mom used to say, you can catch more flies with honey than with buttermilk, and you'd better believe Satan uses a considerable amount of honey to catch his prey. Many times, because of this masquerading nature of sin, we are in sin before we know that we are in it, which is why it is impossible for us not to sin. Sin does not always look like sin, and sin does not always feel like sin. In the word we are told to watch and pray lest we fall victim to sin. We'd better watch and pray because we *will* sin, but it's better to put a toe in and back away than to immerse the whole body in sin where demons await to take hold on us.

Our nature may be that we are prone to sin, but we do not have to sin to encounter the devil. Jesus, who was without sin, encountered him in the desert, a dry place. We too may encounter the devil during a spiritual drought. Satan tempted Jesus in three ways: hunger—desires of the flesh; spiritual deception—it doesn't matter what you do, since God loves you, He will take care of you; and finally the ego—the seat of pride, that part of us all that wants to be bigger and more than what is necessary for us to be, in order to have a fulfilling life.

TEMPTATIONS OF CHRIST
1. Command the stones be made bread—FLESH/GREED
2. Cast himself down from the holy temple, God's angels would take care that no harm came to him—SPIRITUAL DECEPTION
3. Bow down and worship Satan, and he would give Him all the kingdoms of the world—EGO

In the first temptation, Jesus' human body, his flesh, is weak and in need of sustenance. Satan tries to use this formidable condition to tempt him to use powers that were available to him in an untimely manner and for a frivolous cause. To turn the stones into bread, to satisfy what the flesh wanted at the time would have been Him depending on His power and not being in obedience to Father God. We all grow weak and weary in the flesh at times and many times Satan tries to get us to use our human skills, gifts, and talents, for immediate gratification, or for a piece of bread instead of depending on God to guide and provide. This is why it is so important to keep our spirit filled with the word for times such as these. Hunger pangs of the flesh, in whatever genre they may arise within us, should not be appeased by unholy means, regardless of whether we have the talent, money or means. We are to live by, and feed our flesh by attending to and embracing the word of God and all that it encompasses. We are not to partake in anything ungodly just to satisfy our appetite, or generate a sense of relief that would surely grieve the Holy Spirit.

In the second temptation, Satan attempts to coerce Jesus into a type of suicide by deception, mixing the truth with lies; this is spiritual temptation. With spiritual temptation, it is not uncommon for Satan to debase, confuse, and misrepresent the word of God; a method, by the way, that many cults use. Satan knows of angels and how they work because he was an angel. He knows of the spirit realm because it is where he dwells, in the spirit realm as well as on earth. Spiritual deception is one of the tactics he uses to confuse our natural knowledge of God, and undermine our studies of God no matter how minor or how extensive they may be. He can confuse us when we are not confident in what God reveals to us naturally through the Holy Spirit. If he can somehow make us unsure of His word, then his chances of having us commit a "suicide" or derail our godly destiny, increases. How many times have we been tempted to engage in behaviors that would end life as we know it and leave us mired in confusion, poverty, negativity? We may not have had a physical death, but because we succumbed to this particular temptation of the devil, a significant aspect of our lives may never be retrieved and our lives and our future can be altered forever. It is dead, gone, ended, or at least severely compromised because God did *not* intervene and he did *not* send his angels to prevent us from dashing our foot and we are left to deal with the consequences of yielding to temptation. Sure, God could have intervened and sent His angels, this is a fact according to scripture, but he didn't. Many people who have fallen into this type of temptation choose to be angry with God. They believe that God should have intervened rather than leave them to deal with the aftermath of what the temptation has wrought.

We are not to tempt the Lord our God into a frivolous display of power just to see if he will intervene. The devil tempts us to undertake suicidal measures and ignore the still small voice of the Holy Spirit. In the real world, when one attempts suicide, there's always a chance that one might succeed, and this is what the devil is counting on. He is hoping that we come to accept the deception that he has placed before us and live without hope, faith, and trust; not only in God but in ourselves; the very instrument that God uses to accomplish the things he needs to accomplish.

The final temptation that the devil uses is an appeal to the ego. The ego is rebellious by nature, a situation illustrated in the bible as the problem with Lucifer. The ego can be evil, as illustrated by Lucifer, because of his ego, being cast from heaven. Lucifer wanted to take over and run things, which is why this temptation is by far the most serious. Temptation of the ego can cause us to lose our place in the kingdom of heaven which is within us. The ego can desire position that is not ours and control of that which we are not meant to control. Just as Lucifer wanted to take over heaven and take the place of God, the ego can desire to take the place of God in our lives. Had Jesus succumbed to it, it would have been by far, the most detrimental to God's plan of salvation for the world. Jesus Christ's destiny was at stake and therefore the destiny of the world was at stake when Satan presented Him with the option of bowing down to him, that's why the devil offered it to Jesus. Whether he was able to actually give Jesus the world or not is not important, what is important is that symbolically by accepting the devil's offer; Christ would have denied his Father.

The devil would have us look to him as God who has the power to give us everything we want and everything we need. This is the big seduction that draws us into various situations that do not and will not bide well for us. The devil has a lot to offer that appeals to the ego. God's calls to us are deeper and more profitable that the fleeting gratification of the ego. This type of temptation is used to thwart the manifestation of our destiny; who we are, why we were created and the work that we were put down here to do. This type of temptation lulls us into a false sense of security that things are going well because through our ego we are temporarily satiated. Why work hard and persevere when someone is waving an easy out in our face? The devil is very superficial in his undertakings, which again is very appealing to our ego. On the surface it seems easier to let our ego run things and be done with the matter, allowing Satan to have his way with us and give us the desires of our flesh. Putting in the work and dealing with the temporary discomfort of the flesh, requires denying the ego and having the moral and conscientious integrity that it takes to realize the very thing that God wants us to experience, instead of opting for the thing at hand; the easy route.

We must deny ourselves such empty satisfaction. Many times we do not want to work at overcoming our desires; we want them not to be there in the first place. We want God to take away such evil desires while God wants us to *resist* temptation, *have* faith, *believe* that we can, *endure* the discomfort, and *learn* His word. The italicized words are words of action indicating that something is expected of us. There is something that *we* must *do* in order to make it through the temptations of life; all temptation is not meant to be prayed away. Sometimes we must be initiators of these action words in order that we can prove to ourselves, not to God, because he knows who we are and what we stand for, that we are ready and willing to move in or out of a situation in our lives. If God knows that we are capable, but we don't; what ends up happening is that we sabotage what God has for us because we don't believe we can handle the blessing. It is not necessary that we overcome all of our fears in order to receive what God has for us, but it is necessary that have enough courage to face our fears and move ahead despite them. Facing our fears help to build our faith muscles and faith is one of the weapons of spiritual warfare. Jesus did not ignore the devil and do nothing and the devil disappeared in a cloud of smoke. Jesus spoke the word. Not only did Jesus speak the Word, it is evident that he did not consider the physical conditions that were before him that begged to be taken care of.

Some of us speak the Word when we are face to face with the devil, but we do not do as Jesus did with his life which is to also resist. There are some of us who resist, but the temptation continues because we do not speak the word. There are many scenarios at play at this fateful time in the desert that we should note that Jesus had to resist:

Jesus is tired.
Jesus is thirsty.
Jesus is hungry.
Jesus is alone.
Jesus is in desert heat.

These are prime conditions for the devil to tempt. God did not put him in an easy situation because Jesus was his son. Had he put a mere human in such a situation for forty days and forty nights, he would have given in to the temptation or died. Jesus had to experience temptation in conditions that were perfect for the devil to achieve success, in order to show us how we are to deal with temptation in our weakest moments.

Many times conditions may appear to dictate that to resist the devil means death. We need our thirst quenched or we will die. We will die of starvation if we do not partake of the food of the devil. Our ego tells us that to reject the goodies that the devil has placed before us in such unfavorable conditions is to lose out. The ego hates to lose out on anything tangible. To lose the love, respect, or honor of the world is worse than death to the ego. The ego does not function in harmony with the spirit and does not care that despite all indications, the thing we desire is evil on many levels. The devil through the ego says; by any means necessary, feed me or you will surely die.

In order for Jesus to have given in to this final temptation, catering to the ego, Jesus would have had to be unsure of himself. In order for Satan to be successful in tempting us in this manner, we have to be unsure of who we are, what we stand for, our motivations, and who we belong to. We would have to ignore the tug of the Holy Spirit and allow the devil to be our guide because during this type of temptation, the ego is working with the flesh and Satan is at the wheel, and this is very powerful. We see status, power, acceptance, riches beyond our wildest dreams. We have fantasies of being in control of our own lives, our own destinies without a care in the world. If a care does come up, in our fantasy, it would be nothing that our power, money, or status couldn't handle; there is no pressing need for God.

God wants us to have faith in what he created us to be. Satan wants us to bypass Jesus and put our trust in what is worldly. Satan knows that if we look at the choices that lie before us and take time to examine them, what looks good is not necessarily what's best. Faith, on the other hand, moves us to choose, not what necessarily looks good for us, but the best thing in obedience to God, no matter how it looks. Faith does not consider the ego and the ego does not consider faith. Faith stands on it's own as a sincere belief that the outcome of any situation no matter how discouraging it looks, will work out to benefit us as we put our trust in the Lord and are obedient to Him.

Status is not a fleshly thing, power is not a fleshly thing, and being accepted is not a fleshly thing. All of these things are of the ego and all of these things feed the ego. Things of the flesh stimulate and feed the flesh. Things of the ego stimulate and feed the ego. This final temptation was geared toward the ego in to order convince Jesus to forfeit his birthright, just as the devil uses our ego to forfeit our birthright.

Esau sold his birthright because of laziness and lack of concern. He voluntarily and thoughtlessly gave it away for a full belly, soon to be empty again. The devil knows what he is doing when he offers us a full belly for something that is of such monumental importance. Esau could have told his brother to get lost with such a ridiculous offer, but he didn't. If someone can convince us that Jesus' death on the cross means little or nothing, and we forfeit all that Jesus died for us to have; the pity is on us not the one who saw the value in what we have rejected. Isaac, the father of the two boys could not see to whom he gave the blessing. He knew who he wanted to give the blessing to, this is human nature and human law, but spiritual law is blind in the sense that whoever is bold enough to step up to receive what is offered, will receive it. Spiritual law says that whoever will come; good, bad or indifferent for the blessing and does what it takes to receive the blessing, it is he who will receive the blessing. This principle holds true whether we are saint or sinner. I cannot tell you how important it is for the Christian to integrate this important information into his lifestyle. Non-Christians tend to understand this law better than Christians so they tend to reap the benefits of this spiritual law. It rains on the just and unjust, rain is rain! You can seek shelter out of the rain so that you won't get wet and feel a little uncomfortable, or you can let it drench you to the bone and use the rain to help you grow!

Satan would be satisfied with us ignoring such a law as this. He does not want us to become aware and fully conscious of this spiritual principle. He wants us to keep praying that it doesn't rain, or asking God to hide us from the rain. Rain helps things grow. There are crops in our lives that need to be watered and when we insist on praying the rain away, our crops die while others are out working their crops, getting drenched while their crops are soaking up every drop of moisture that they can. Deep roots need more rain. With some people whether they are believers or not, it doesn't matter what the crop is that they have planted; they are trying to understand the rain, learn from the rain. They are building trenches, and levees; maximizing its potential so that they can reap its benefits. They are not hiding in their prayer closets, complaining about the rain. They are working in the rain, they are working with the rain, and they are working despite the rain. They have a vision of their crops and the prosperity that they will reap from their crops. They are anxious and excited about this vision of the harvest that they expect to reap. This is why the unsaved appear to be more prosperous than the saved; they are applying a spiritual law that many Christians don't. This is shameful!

A drug dealer is willing to do what it takes to get his product out and get his money. He knows that it is illegal; he knows that he may be thrown in prison, he knows that there are many people that he cannot trust and few that he can. Does this stop him? No! And do you know why? It does not stop him because he knows that if he can come up with a plan that might work and he is successful at executing the plan, he WILL end up with more money in his pocket. His vision and his goal are wealth and opulence. He is not thinking about your strung out son, or your strung out daughter or husband or wife. He is not thinking about a long term prison sentence, all he sees is his vision of wealth and opulence. He is willing to take the risks, he is willing to have a plan, he is willing to know the obstacles and he is prepared to accept the reality of all of this in order to realize his vision. How many of God's people are willing to have a plan and execute that plan because we have a vision that must not be hindered? How many of us refuse to learn about the enemy and are allowing the enemy to keep us from having a plan, not to mention having a vision.

Need I say it here? Do you recognize how Satan hides the truth from the saints and reveals it to those who would do his work? Satan can keep us preoccupied with religion until we miss the point. God speaks of this principle when Jesus is confronted by the learned Sadducees and Pharisees. They are so busy in practicing their religion until the reason why they practice escapes them. If they do well, they do well to make themselves look good to others and to feel good about themselves, God is not in the picture. Many of God's people do not have a vision, and the ones that do, often don't have a plan. We want things to happen by osmosis, and this has got to stop!

Satan works through the flesh and the ego to corrupt our spiritual connection and derail our plans. We all long for something but it is important to realize where our longing is coming from because it could be one of three main sources: the ego, the flesh, or the spirit, which is God's domain. Satan works through the longings of the flesh and ego. This may seem a bit too simplistic, but think about the things that you long for and you will see that if they do not fall into the category of the spirit, they fall into the categories of flesh and/or ego. This is why it is important to determine where the longing is coming from.

Here are some things to search for within yourself in order to examine your motivations and whether your longings are of the spirit, the flesh, or ego.

FLESH: **Any and all physical sensations.** Choices motivated by the flesh means that the choice itself may not be good, but it will bring about sensation and stimulation of the body whether:

sexual
Any and all activities directed or used to achieve the result of sexual stimulation, pleasure and/or release

mouth
Eating for no reason, or not exercising prudence when talking because it just has to come out so that the flesh gets relief

eyes
Motivated to look at evil or ungodly events, situations and materials that cause stimulation, positive or negative

ears
Motivated in much the same way as the eyes. There is a desire to hear about or listen to ungodly or evil events, situations and materials that cause stimulation. This stimulation may "feel" positive or negative. Gossip or other people's business is a good example of this fleshly portal

nose
Certain smells stimulate memory and evoke certain emotions. The bible speaks of fragrances many times. They brought fragrances to the baby Jesus. Many times when there is a problem of demonic activity, there will be smells that are putrid to say the least.

If a choice is motivated by the EGO—
Physical, psychological, social, financial, gain or status is not only expected, but required. This also applies to emotional and spiritual situations, wanting to have more knowledge or power in these areas than others has nothing to do with serving God.

The ego is the source of pride and self-preservation, and many times, this is rooted in the spirit of fear. This fear is often rooted in, and/or connected to a spirit of rejection which is rooted in a lack of faith which has been compromised or molested somewhere along the line. This spirit of rejection, if it is followed back in time through the memory, more likely than not, was acquired, usually during childhood where faith in a parent or parents was shattered for some reason. If you have a feeling of rejection within you, and you cannot recall feeling rejection during your childhood by a major caregiver—it could be attributed to rejection from peers, teachers, relatives or strangers. It is also a possibility, however, that this spirit of rejection was acquired in the womb. You may want to investigate what happened during your mother's pregnancy, there may be clues there as to how the spirit of rejection may have entered you. What was happening in her life at that time, what kind of trials and tribulations was she going through during her pregnancy?

It is so important that a child have faith in his parents. This is where faith is honed because an infant knows nothing of God on a conscious level. A child has to depend on his parents until he learns to depend on God. The ego is very demanding, and like a child, the ego would have us make decisions based on this spirit of rejection and lack of faith that was developed long ago.

An indication that a decision was made according to something that was moved in our spirit—

These decisions are based on following what we have come to understand about God, what we have been taught about the nature of God, and what we know innately. Spiritual decisions will be based on life lessons that we have truly learned and **do not** contradict the bible. Our decisions will be quite sound if we are willing to listen to and obey the prompting of the Holy Spirit. The prompting of God is based on love and not necessarily rational thought, if the thought is irrational, it still will not contradict biblical principles. The decision may not based on love as we generally think of it either because our emotions have a tendency to cloud the pureness of love. If an action or decision is based on spiritual prompting from God, it will have God's name or nature written all over it. We are compelled to act out of godly principles even though our emotions may tell us otherwise. God is spirit, God is love. God's love is pure and unadulterated. God's nature is more wise than rational and always based in love. There is nothing negative in God's work, unlike the work of an evil spirit. Decisions based on evil spirit are filled with negative, hurtful, and unhealthy expectations for ourselves and others. Decisions based on godly principles are just the opposite; they are not made to perpetuate negativity. Godly decisions expand our consciousness and makes us better people. Ungodly decisions contract us making us smaller and pettier and ultimately unhappy.

But everything works out for those who love the Lord, right? I know you've heard this uttered in some respect at least once in your life. If we examine this statement and what it is saying, we will realize that an important part of this statement is that there must be a love for the Lord in us. If there is a love for the Lord in us, our actions and behaviors will be different preceding the event. If we cultivate our love for the Lord our choices will be more Godly, and we will consider our path more carefully. Our thoughts will be more focused on trying to understand the will of God in our situation because we actively, not passively love Him. Those who "love" the Lord, the word "love" being a verb, an action word, a word of action; is what counts. All things work for good for those who *love* the Lord in such an active sense of the word can expect that things will work out for good no matter how bad they may seem. Under these conditions, whether our decisions or behavior is right or wrong, the love of the Lord comes into play. No matter what Satan may have tricked us into, because our thought process took a spiritual route, and not the route of the ego or the flesh, we can be assured that we will come out of it a better person because we loved the Lord enough to act out of love for Him. We considered the spiritual. It does not matter that the decision wasn't perfect; as humans nobody will ever be 100% on target, 100% of the time; what matters is that we love the Lord enough to consider His way and made a conscious decision and effort to act on His word because we are actively loving him in the first place.

It is illogical both in the physical and the spiritual world, to expect that there will not be consequences for our actions. How much sense does it make that we can make haphazard choices, do anything to anybody, break any law and our lives will be happy, peaceful, successful, and fulfilled? We have a free will that free will moves us onto paths and may take us off certain paths; sometimes temporarily, sometimes permanently; sometimes for better, sometimes for worse. It does not behoove us to live our lives any kind of way and expect good results regardless of what we do. In the end things can work out, that's true, but it is a gamble, and things don't necessarily have to work out to our advantage. Our actions and choices may result in a consequence of an untimely death of something or someone along the way.

Consider the source and your motivations! If your source is anything or anyone aside from the Lord Jesus Christ, the likelihood that you are operating from the flesh or the ego, in spiritual err, missing the mark, or sin if you will, is 100%. Don't be afraid to be honest with yourself about what you've come to depend on as your source. Do not be afraid to examine your motivations. These are the first steps to healing the spirit and uprooting the dwelling places of demons within you because they need fertile ground to remain and grow. The demonic have roots but in order to be effective they need something to attach themselves to. That's where our part comes in; to keep ourselves cleansed and holy because this is exactly what we don't want, sources of attachments for these demons. We must beware of all of the fertilizers that we may be unwittingly using that allow this demonic habitation. Our objective here is to render our "land" uninhabitable to demons by denying these roots an opportunity to take hold within us. We all must learn to look to God and depend on Him as the source of our blessings, and look to Jesus for maintenance and look to the indwelling Holy Spirit for guidance. Blessings have no other source other than God the Father, anything else that *looks* like a blessing is but a counterfeit and in the long run will prove destructive and fallacious.

That is what this book is all about. It's not about making excuses, avoiding embarrassment, or calling something good when it is evil. It's not about hiding the truth or holding something against ourselves or anyone else who may be dealing with problems caused by being in an unenlightened state. This book is about becoming enlightened enough so that we have enough information and courage to face our demons. This book is about shining the light into the darkness of our souls, exposing the hidden forces that work against us. It's about raising our consciousness, facing our demons and kicking them out of our spirit, terminating their lease, uprooting and evicting them forever!

RECOGNITION TIP # 11

Recognize and acknowledge that accepting and owning God as our Father is an important part of our freedom in Christ Jesus. Whether our earthly father was good or bad, remember that spiritually there is no comparison between the two. God is not man.

CHAPTER 12

And when he was demanded of the Pharisees, when the kingdom of God should come, he answered them and said, The kingdom of God cometh not with observation; Neither shall they say, Lo here! Or lo there! For, behold the kingdom of God is within you.—Luke 17:20-21

Demons darken our spiritual walk, confuse our earthly mission and compromise our connection to God while systematically wreaking havoc in our lives. Demons overshadow God's truth and distort reality with lies. Where demons dwell there is darkness. No joy, no peace, no happiness, no love, can find rest in such darkness. If demons dwell in one area of our life, there is darkness and the nature of this darkness is to expand. It ***will not*** stay within the confines of one area for very long. If demons abound in many areas of our lives, the darkness is even darker and even *that* darkness will expand even further. Who among the living wants to live in darkness? We are not nocturnal animals who are meant to live in the night. We need light so that we can see where we are, understand where we came from, know where we're going, or at least we need to be able to read the map to get there!

The spirit, which is directly linked to the emotional and the physical, affects the quality of life that a man is capable of experiencing while on this earth. You cannot experience the fullness of life; happiness, joy, grief, pain, disappointment, revitalization, hope, love, excitement; and all the variables in between that make life worth living, if there is interference with your Christ connection. If a man's spirit is not properly connected to his creator, then that man is vulnerable to connect to anything or anyone else. He is also open for anything and anyone to connect to him, especially that which is not of God. This is not a healthy state; in fact I would venture to say that it is a very dangerous state to be in. Our spirit *must* be acknowledged, our spirit *will* be attended to whether we like it or not. It *cannot* be denied, ignored, retired, or forgotten, without dire consequences, this is the very nature of spirit.

There are terms and diagnoses for the physical and mental just as there are terms and diagnoses for the spiritual. While there are diseases that have no cure and there are mental illnesses that have no cure, ALL spiritual ills have a cure. As far as the spirit is concerned, there is no such thing as the cure, "not being available to man at this time," as may be the case with physical and mental illnesses. Physical and mental illnesses that have no cure and do not respond to treatment are not necessarily demonic; after all, there are cures for various things to be discovered in their own time. Again, just because there is no cure, does not mean that the ailment is demonic! However, the fact that the illness *could* be an indication of demonic activity should not be dismissed either. An authentic mental illness is defined according to *Webster's Encyclopedic Unabridged Dictionary* as follows:

Mental Illness—Any of the various forms of psychosis or severe neurosis. Also called mental disorder, mental disease.

This definition in itself seems a bit generic so I think that it is important for us to look at the definition of psychosis and neurosis.

Psychosis—A mental disorder characterized by symptoms, such as delusions or hallucinations, which indicate impaired contact with reality.

Neurosis—A functional disorder in which feelings of anxiety, obsessive thoughts, compulsive acts, and physical complaints without objective evidence of disease, in various degrees and patterns, dominate the personality.

These definitions are a suspiciously close representation of someone who is being demonized. If you're a victim of Satan's grasp there very well may be delusions and hallucinations that are not of this world but of the spiritual realm. There is anxiety, obsessive thoughts, patterns of behavior that dominate the personality because the personality is being dominated by negative spiritual entities called demons. You may be able to function on some levels because the demons need you to function. They don't know how to pay bills, maintain shelter, and interact with others, even if the interaction is minimal at best. The level of demonic activity within a person can vary depending on how many "doors" have been opened. A person with mental problems may or may not have demonic activity; it depends on the nature of the problems that the person is experiencing.

With demonic activity there are companion activities and symptoms that go along with the mental problems. These activities have nothing to do with one's mental state and cannot be controlled or fabricated by an individual. Examples of such activity include odors, changes in room temperature, very obvious physical changes associated with the face, eyes, and/or body of the possessed. Victims may be capable of abnormal body contortions when demons manifest themselves. There is a presence; victims of possession always feel a presence within them or a presence that surrounds them. Others, who are in the presence of the possessed may also feel this presence, depending on the person witnessing the demons and the level of demonic activity going on. People in the presence of those suppressed by demons will have a sense that there is a darkness or "cloud" that surrounds, precedes and/or follows like a foul residue. When in the presence of demonic activity the air can be charged with negativity and/or discordant vibrations that can easily be mistaken for excitement. These discordant vibrations, while they may be mistaken for excitement, will have a slithery undercurrent like something unholy is making its way through the room. There is an uncomfortable feeling of fear and uncertainty. Satan is making his presence known in situations such as this, and we need to learn to recognize him with all of our senses.

Such variables must be considered before a determination of demonic activity is rendered. For instance, this presence is an important element that divides the mentally ill from the demonically possessed because a sense of a foreboding presence is one of the biggest telltale signs of demons. There is always a presence, whether weak or strong, surrounding the individual. Sometimes the "presence" is not strong enough to be felt outside of the person, but the afflicted individual has a sense that there is someone following, watching, instructing, and empowering them. Again, not only will the person feel this presence; depending on the level of demonic activity and how spiritually sensitive a person is, others can feel it too. There will come a point in a demonized person's life, however, that a person would have to be dead not to feel the presence. As the demons become stronger and gain more control, people are actually repelled by, or drawn to, such people in an extraordinary way. Hitler is a prime example of this phenomenon. Hitler was so possessed by demons that he was able to draw millions of people to him. Hitler had such demonic charisma that his ranting and ravings were hypnotic enough to convince others to not only kill millions of people, but to exterminate these people as if they were inhuman.

Conditions must be factored into the entire picture to get a true determination of demonization or possession. While there is no apparatus to detect demons for sure, the proof is in the cure. We prove a demon's presence by the individual's response to, and results of, spiritual warfare or exorcisms. If the demons flee in the name of Jesus, then we know that there were indeed demons there. This method of detection is sure and foolproof because even if a person wanted to "fake" demonization, this in itself can be characteristic of demonic activity.

Some demons can be dealt with by using continual spiritual warfare to keep them from locking in and developing into strongholds. Once demons attach themselves to us they become strongholds and now the problem becomes a different story. *Now* there must be a tearing away, and many times that "tearing" is violent because this has to be done by force. It's like pulling a tree up by its roots; the longer the tree has had an opportunity to grow, the bigger the tree is and the longer and stronger the roots are. Perhaps when it was smaller it was possible pull it up by hand, break it off and toss it to the side, *this* can be considered *spiritual warfare*; the damage is there but won't present a serious problem as long as there is maintenance. But, the bigger the tree gets, the deeper the roots go, heavy equipment must be brought in to bring it down to a stump. When you have to bring out the heavy equipment to remove the stump and kill the roots: *this is an exorcism.*

As we go along, more and more details will be given about symptoms that may indicate the presence of demons in a person and the need for spiritual warfare or exorcism. Right now let's look at some of the very basic symptoms that we can generally expect when we are in the presence of demons or demonic activity:

The behavior will be very negative, very anti-Jesus, anti-God, becoming progressively disruptive and destructive in the person's life and those of the people around them.

The person may bear fruit, but the "fruit" of their tree will smack of immorality, negativity, deviance, danger and confusion. In other words they can accomplish and have a worldly type of success, but note what they are successful at, and how that success was attained. How many casualties; people or lives destroyed, can be attributed to them?

The inability to have a peaceful night's sleep for weeks at a time may also be an indication of demonic activity. The soul is in a state of unrest.

We can look for and expect moral decay. Moral decay accompanies demonization without fail. The person's behavior and values will deteriorate as the person slips deeper and deeper into darkness. Boundaries disappear and become blurred. Their talk and their behavior may become more lewd and obscene in comparison to previous behavior. Moral integrity cannot be maintained for very long with heavy demonic infestation.

Another indication of demonic activity is physical decay. The person's physical presence may seem to be "melting" as the demons gain ground. The vitality associated with life and the living seems to be draining out of them through their feet. There may even be evidence in their facial features that manifest this "melting" look.

With a demonic activity, there is always confusion. This confusion seems to follow that person relentlessly. There is an inability to make up one's mind, stick to a particular path in life, retain information and/or relate information in a coherent fashion. The person has the ability to leave trails of distress, confusion, and anarchy wherever they may go. Again, there is no peace.

There may be a fascination with opposites. These people enjoy posing arguments just for the sake of arguing. They are fascinated with contradictions and opposites such as; opposites are really the same or the opposite make opposites possible. They enjoy ferreting out contradictions because their mind is being prepped to accept as fact that Jesus is contradictory. The mind of Satan *is* contradictory to the mind of Christ, but demons want to exploit the contradiction to the point of confusion. The object of this mind game is to eventually lead the person to believe that Christ and the devil are somehow melded into one, and that God and the devil really aren't that different. Jesus and Buddha are one and same, so it makes no difference who you look to for salvation. Satan introduces this in to the mind of his victims because he does not want us to realize how powerful the name of Jesus is! If he can't get us to forego the name of Jesus, maybe he will be able to get us to dilute our concept of Jesus.

There is an aversion to hard and fast moral standards and a preoccupation with themselves that leaves little room for anyone else who is not just as interested in *them*, *their* goals, *their* interests, *their* achievements, as they are. There is a distrust and suspicion of anyone or anything that distracts or interferes with their theories, axioms, idioms and beliefs, all of which are beyond the normal range of amusement or speculation.

These people have a tendency to frequently if not totally isolate themselves, living in murky secrecy rather than risk their immoral ideas, codes and values being broken, tampered with, or interrupted. They appear to be the "creepy" loners that people stay away from because something instinctively tells them to stay away from them. They don't want their behaviors being observed too closely by anyone and would prefer most of the time to be alone although to be alone does not necessarily prove to be a tranquil activity for them.

These people will lie *and* charm on a regular basis. It is in no wise a rare thing with them. Many times they lie because they cannot help it because Satan is a liar. It's not that they are compulsive liars; it's just that this is their method and means of getting what they want and keeping people off-guard. They fully realize that later they can use their charm to smooth things over and win their way back into anyone's good graces if they really want to, but as for the moment of the lie, they needed to tell the person what they knew the person wanted to hear so that they could accomplish the necessary task at hand. They are not compelled to tell these lies as a compulsive liar is, these lies are tools used for manipulative purposes. Compulsive liars lie may lie for no reason, demonically compromised individuals always have a reason.

Some are driven, constantly in motion. They attend to foolishness and have an aversion to truth, they cannot hear it. You can talk to these people until you are blue in the face, and unless you notice the vacant look in their eyes, you may actually think that they get it, that they have heard you and are listening to you. However, if you happen to miss the vacant look, their actions will prove to you that you've been spinning your wheels and wasting your breath, for nothing will change—nothing! It is as if the conversation never happened.

Speaking of eyes, note the eyes, they are either vacant or dart furtively about. Do they seem to bore into your soul as they make the most nonsensical remarks or tell tales that are filled with blatant lies that are irreverent in nature. Also, look for a mischievous twinkle that always seems to be there, even when circumstances are not particularly amusing or funny. The expression of the eyes and the gravity of the circumstance don't match up. In some people the eye color may even change.

RECOGNIZING SATAN

There may be a sense that the person is not wielding complete control of himself and/or his actions. They may pick up an object and put it down for no reason, fidget, stand up then sit down; there may be very little, to no impulse control. There may be bursts of emotion that have no apparent reason such as anger, disgust, laughter, crying, or withdrawal.

Spiritual strongholds *can* be dealt with by spiritual warfare but it is a long and exasperating process that may take years. Any stronghold in our lives involves demonic activity that must be eradicated in order for us to live a happy and contented life and the very nature of strongholds is HIGHLY indicative of a need for an exorcism. A spiritual stronghold is something that we've come across in life that is not good for us, but seems to have become a part of who we are physically and mentally. We've come to depend on these things, although they are bad for us and leave us feeling empty and weary. These things become a pattern of behavior that seems impossible to break and impossible to live our lives without these things, however much we may desire to. Some of the most common strongholds that plague our lives are below in bold print. Under them are how these things may manifest themselves in our lives.

ADDICTIONS	**RELATIONSHIPS**	**LIFESTYLE**	**LIES**
Alcohol	Abuse	Homosexuality	deceit
Drugs	Unevenly Yoked	Excessive Partying	kleptomania
Cigarettes	Angry	Immorality	Thievery
Overeating	Violent	Crime	Cheating
Bulimia	Distrust	Uncleanness	Untrustworthy
Anorexia	Unfaithful	Shyness/Arrogance	Denial
Binge Eating	Undependable	Profanity	
Self Mutilation/Cutting		Violence	
(This includes excessive piercing & tattoos)		Promiscuity	
Excessive Behaviors		Undependable	
Gambling		Isolation	
Sex		Scorn	

This list is a list of strongholds and the categories that they fall under. If you have a problem with any one of these things, you have a demon problem that needs to be addressed. There is demonic activity involved with strongholds and we should want nothing about us to be controlled by demons. Strongholds can be prayed about, but a more effective tactic in dealing with the above matters is spiritual warfare; the most effective being exorcism. Strongholds usually respond to treatment but are usually not cured by treatment alone as with many demonic occurrences. But strongholds are more of a problem because it is more difficult and sometimes even impossible to get rid of them unless the person acknowledges that there is a problem. This is why confession of our sins is so important. Usually the problem is acknowledged through treatment or another person whose opinion these people trust and respect. Someone or something has come into their lives to help them see the light of truth, that truth being that there is a problem. With strongholds, even after they are acknowledged which is a very important part in getting rid of them, it does not guarantee that the victims of this malady will respond to treatment because it is very difficult and unless there is a pointed and specific tearing away at these things, many times, they will not leave! This is why we hear about people who've been in treatment for years and have made little or no progress in conquering these monsters. Again spiritual warfare does work in such cases; but it may take years and years to get rid of these demons. One of the drawbacks of such treatment—spiritual warfare, prayer, medical treatment—is that as long as the demons are there and able to operate on any level while this treatment is going on, they will continue to affect the person and those around them; and even worse they may die having *never* conquered them. This is why sometimes we need the quickest and most effective way to get rid of these strongholds, whether they are acknowledged or not, an exorcism. The hold on these people is strong and must be broken by the power of Christ.

RECOGNITION TIP # 12

Recognize and acknowledge that there is a difference in pride and confidence. True confidence is a manifestation of faith and does not hinder our spiritual growth. Pride goeth before a fall and stunts our spiritual growth.

CHAPTER 13

And they bend their tongues like their bow for lies: but they are not valiant for the truth upon the earth; for they proceed from evil to evil, and they know not me, saith the Lord. Take ye heed every one of his neighbour, and trust ye not in any brother: for every brother will utterly supplant, and every neighbour will walk with slanders. And they will deceive every one his neighbour, and will not speak the truth: they have taught their tongue to speak lies, and weary themselves to commit iniquity. Thine habitation is in the midst of deceit; through deceit they refuse to know me, saith the Lord.—Jeremiah 9:3-6

While I can't see how an exorcism could hurt anyone who's not demonized, I would recommend seeing a physician and/or consulting a mental health professional first. If a physician or mental health professional cannot help, then it's time to take the next step; get involved in a spirit filled church. If that doesn't help the next step should be spiritual counseling. The next step after that is spiritual warfare, then exorcism.

One indicator that a person could benefit from spiritual warfare or an exorcism is that a number of people who don't know each other mention the possibility of you or someone you care about being demonized, evil, wicked, scary, strange, or kind of "off." This may come up in conversation or be brought to you as a concern. Before you become offended and go into a rampage of denial, stop and search within yourself to see if this is just an insult or if it may indeed be a fact. Consider the source of this information. Is it coming from a person whose opinion you would generally respect? Have you heard this before or anything similar to it about yourself or the other person at other times in your life? Take the time to pray about it and ask the Holy Spirit for revelation. You don't have to be 100% sure, just reasonably sure that something of a spiritual nature is amiss.

If you are the person who is being called wicked or evil, take a minute to think about it. If you sometimes feel that many of your actions and decisions are done to deliberately hurt somebody, not excluding yourself, but you just can't seem to help it, consider the spiritual. Are you, or have you been aware of a "presence," either recently, since childhood, or for as long as you can remember? Are you prone to unexplainable panic attacks and the victim of frightening visions of monsters, aliens, snakes, or spiders? Do you have a hunch or a feeling that something is not quite right? Do not be afraid to investigate where this "feeling" is coming from. It could save you a lot of sorrows and troubles in your life for it can only benefit us to be aware of how Satan works.

If you suspect someone you know is afflicted or possessed by a devil, pray for them. Don't just sit back and shake your head and avoid all contact with them, send up prayers on their behalf. It is not a time to whisper, gossip, and ridicule a person who is in such a precarious position. We must look for the devil's signature etched within that person's behavior. Sometimes, depending on the demonic forces present, it may be difficult to feel anything at all while you are in the presence of that person, this happens sometimes. It may be that you are only able to sense the evil when you are not in the presence of the person. You may recall something that they said or did; an expression on their face that sends chills through you now that you reflect on the encounter.

I remember being in a grocery store not too far from my home. There was a man there; I would say that he was between the age of twenty-five and thirty. As he walked around he was talking to himself audibly in a desperate whisper. I don't think that he realized that other people could hear him or if he realized that he was speaking out loud. His conversation with himself went something like this; (pardon the inferred language).

"Lord, how in the world did I end up with this b***! Jesus, what's wrong with me, why in hell am I with this *EVIL B***!* What's wrong with me, I need to get away from her, man! I gotta get away from this b***!" He shook his head in confused agony, as he unwittingly beseeched God, in the only way he knew how. He was still muttering to himself as he left the cold cuts and rounded the aisle toward the meat section.

This man more than likely was caught up and held in spiritual bondage via this woman and did not know how to extricate himself from the relationship. He was in a relationship of unholy soul ties. My heart went out to him because I could see by the look on his face and the desperation in his eyes. I could hear it in the passion of his words that he was being tormented as if by demons. I have met people caught in relationships where one person dominates with demonic control and the other gets nothing out of relationship yet they stay. They don't expect the relationship to change, yet they are caught up in the twisted madness. They experience no joy or satisfaction to speak of and are only familiar with the feeling that they are immobilized and trapped. The man knew that this woman was evil, or at the very least not right for him. He also knew that he should leave but didn't know *how* to leave or *why* he had not left. Perhaps he had tried to leave before only to realize that the demonic influence was stronger than he'd bargained for and he had not the spiritual power to reject it. More than likely, there were forces within him that were in agreement with these demonic forces, usually there has to be. Only on rare occasions is this not true and in these cases it is only a matter of time before the offended party leaves.

This is why in circumstances such as this the first line of defense is to check for holes within you. We must take the focus off of the person who has us trapped and look inward to find out what is going on within us spiritually that we find ourselves in this situation. What is going on within our spirit that has allowed such an unholy alliance to form and develop into such a relationship? What is going on within us that will not allow us to leave this person that we know is not right, or this person that we know with everything within us is evil. How can these people have such a hold on us in the first place? Why is it that this evil person is not as disturbed by our goodness as we are disturbed by their evil? What are we doing or not doing that's making this person comfortable enough to stay? What is going on in our spirit or our consciousness that they are not *compelled* to change so that they can remain with us?

There are the spiritually weak and the spiritually strong. It is important that we understand that it does not matter if your spirit is **good** or **bad**; it will still fall somewhere on the scale of being weak or strong. A person can be evil but the strength of their spirit is weak. A person can by nature be sweet and kind, but the strength of their spirit is weak. And so it is with those who are spiritually strong. I'm not talking about those who bully, because bullies in the spiritual world are weak. The spiritually strong are those who act with purpose and intelligence. The spiritually strong, good or evil, have conviction and faith that no human being can hurt them enough, when they are on a mission, where they cannot bounce back. These people are thinkers and risk takers, they are unaffected by your plans and are willing to lose you or anything else that stands in the way of their mission, or what they have come to love or expect out of life. These people, good or bad, are those who have vision and confidence in that vision of themselves and will not allow anyone to interfere with how they see themselves to be. These people, good and bad, are the spiritually strong.

The spiritually strong have no Delilah's outside of themselves. It is no simple task to woo the spiritually strong to the point of handing over their strength to another that they might be destroyed. I use Delilah as an example because Delilah was physically weaker than Samson, but spiritually, she was the stronger because she had more conviction to her evil than he had to his God. We should all strive to be in Christ, for to be in Christ and live for him is to be spiritually strong and the Holy Spirit who is God, dwells within us as our teacher. To be spiritually strong and live only for ourselves is to live for the devil; the spiritually strong who live for Christ can be sure that they are children of God. To be spiritually strong for self-preservation is to give the devil access and give him permission to be our parent and teacher. Christ was not spiritually strong for self-preservation for if he had been he would have never freely given his life for us.

We must understand that Satan launches a campaign for our soul the minute our soul is proposed into being. Have you ever seen baby turtles that are born on the beach during a certain season? The mother turtles' eggs hatch and literally hundreds of turtles break free of their shells and the beach is blanketed with hundreds of turtles instinctively making their way to the water. The reason why the turtles lay so many eggs is because they are slow and the environment that they are born into is very hostile. In order for the species to survive, hundreds of turtles are hatched to make up for the many that will not make it to the water and survive. Jesus died so that our chances of making it into the water, are better than they would have been had he not given His life for us. The hundreds of turtles represent the many chances that he gives us to seek redemption. The turtles that do not make it to the water represent the times that we might falter or fail, but this does not stop the instinctive drive that is within each of us, to reach the safety of the water where there is healing, salvation, forgiveness, hope and mercy.

RECOGNITION TIP # 13

Recognize and acknowledge when you need spiritual help. Do not go into a state of denial, seek it and you will find it. You must go the distance! If you feel that you need and exorcism, you probably do.

CHAPTER 14

And a woman having an issue of blood twelve years, which had spent all her living upon physicians, neither could be healed of any, Came behind him, and touched the border of his garment: and immediately her issue of blood stanched.—Luke 8:43,44

Satan's campaign is more vehement with some than with others. He can work through the mother's mind to the womb, by creating within the woman such a spiritually toxic mindset and atmosphere that it affects the spiritual balance of the child that is growing within her by passing on feelings of negativity to the baby. A mother's spiritual state has the ability to affect the atmosphere of the womb. A mother can unknowingly project feelings of sadness, lack of love, fearfulness, hopelessness, rejection and defeat onto her child. This does not mean, however, that being pregnant and having feelings other than happiness and bliss, will produce a spiritually disturbed child. What it does mean is that if such feelings are sustained, there is a danger of negatively imprinting on the soul of the child. The good news is that the very same phenomena of imprinting can occur if positive expectations and feelings are projected onto the unborn child.

How the imprinting actually affects the child can vary. Sometimes the results of the imprint can be obvious, sometimes not so obvious. A parent may have the feeling that something is not quite right with their child and find that she is studying the child more closely to figure out just what is going on or a parent may go into denial and ignore all symptoms and indications of demonic activity. A parent may see that there is a problem with their child, and ignore it because they are at a loss as to what to do.

Many times a presence presents itself in early childhood. The child may sense something that is friendly or frightening is following him or trying to communicate with him. Someone or something may make the child do things or say things that make the child feel sad, angry or ill at ease. Aberrant behaviors in a child that are not learned or fostered by an outside person should be taken very seriously, especially behaviors that are indicative of an individual well beyond the child's years. Sometimes a demonic presence is drawn to a child because the child is experiencing an extreme in their life such as extreme loneliness, pain, fears or anxieties. Often a parent will have an instinctive feeling that something is not quite right spiritually with their child. If you are a parent and you are having such feelings, get your child to the church and ask the spiritual leaders of the church to pray with you for your child in the name of Jesus. But don't just depend on them to pray, YOU pray in the name of Jesus that your child be protected and delivered from any evil that may have come upon them. In addition to this, go to a mental health professional if you think that this is necessary, but remember take care; by law, mental health professionals are bound by law to report any and all cases of child abuse, and demons are liars and if your child has demons, they WILL lie. A physical examination by a physician may be able to come up with symptoms of abuse or neglect in a child, but the presence of any type of abuse to a child can and does open the doors for demonic infiltration. It is your job as a parent to figure these things out by seeking help on all levels until you find out exactly what the problem may be. *Ask* God to give you wisdom in the matter and *expect* that wisdom in the matter is forthcoming and be prepared to act on what God has shown you.

With young children, I strongly suggest that you seek out a minister who is a spiritual counselor and familiar with the weapons of warfare against the devil. A minister who has a sense of what is demonic and mental illness is best. Don't spend too much time second guessing yourself as to whether you are right or wrong,, however, check it out and move forward. Ask God to show you exactly how you should handle your child. Pray to God the Father in Jesus name, for guidance in dealing with your child and whether or not a mental health professional should be sought. There is a proper way to deal with such issues and there is a fine line between mental and spiritual disturbances. You don't want Satan to "trick" you into handling the child in such a way that you do more harm than good. You don't want to waste time by handling the spiritual without the word of God and neither do you want to waste time when there is a perfectly good physical or mental explanation for what ails your child, which can be handled with counseling and/or medication.

Under no circumstances should any child be mistreated because you "think" that they are demonized, and even if it has been proven beyond a shadow of a doubt that there is demonization, this is no excuse to harm a child. The only acceptable behavior that you should indulge in is to seek help from a reputable person whether that person is spiritual or a secular professional. Remain with your child as much as you possibly can while they are receiving whatever treatment they need. YOU ARE RESPONSIBLE FOR THE WELFARE OF YOUR CHILD. Do not turn your child over to just anyone because they possess an air of authority.

You yourself must be on watch and on guard because Satan is a deceiver. He will try and deceive some parents into thinking that the best thing that they can do for the child is to harm the child in order to help the child. Recognize that this is of an evil mind, and not at all the mind of God. Do not be foolish enough to let just anybody do handle your child either. Keep in mind that whether your child has demons or not, as a parent, you are still responsible for the welfare of your child. You are still the parent, so if a treatment or cure seems to be unnecessary, or makes you uncomfortable, speak up! God gave us all a myriad of helpers, including good old fashion common sense, which should be duly employed. Besides, if your child is so far gone that you feel that an exorcism is warranted, there will be enough evidence to support it and enough scripture in the bible to combat it.

Exorcism is not something that can be accomplished by anything other than the word of God. Amulets, religious symbols, the bible itself are but tools that probably make the users feel more comfortable because Satan has no respect for such. He will defile a cross just as quickly as he would anything else. Nothing is sacred to the devil. The Word of God spoken in the name of Jesus IS the weapon. Otherwise, restraint in order to keep the child from possibly harming himself or others should only be used when absolutely necessary and only then by individuals that have been trained to hold in the most efficient and least harmful way possible. There was a story in the local paper about a child being killed during and exorcism because of the methods that were used to restrain him. Restraining a child is a very delicate thing and should be done carefully! Many times, if the exorcism is done correctly, harsh restraint is not necessary. The presence of one or two trained, spirit filled, able-bodied men to assist when necessary, should suffice.

Adults should definitely be seen by a mental health professional first, then seek spiritual counseling if necessary. This is because by the time we reach adulthood, stress, past traumas, guilt, shame, remorse, and/or bad upbringing may definitely be a factor. If it turns out that it's nothing, fine. If it turns out it's something, you can save yourself a lot of grief and unnecessary suffering. Whatever it turns out to be, our goal should always be to seek and to live a healthy life mentally, physically, and especially spiritually; but we must not suffer in silence because of fear of embarrassment. If demons are trying to take control, you've probably embarrassed yourself a hundred times over being in such a state anyway. If demons have infiltrated your soul, you've blurted out and said stupid and hurtful things to people, and have "ego-tripped" shamelessly to the discomfort of those around you. Satan will convince us that we had good reason to hurt someone's feelings because we know so much more and they just don't get it. He will puff us up to the point whereas we truly feel that we are so blessed that we are untouchable and more spiritually gifted than anyone we know. If we could only see ourselves when we get in such a state, we'd probably go find a corner and hide our face to the wall. That's just how embarrassed we'd be! If we would only see ourselves as we truly are, we'd all be humbled into submission to God. We would appreciate His mercy and wisdom as we see just how He's worked and just how He is working in our lives. We should not allow embarrassment to keep us in bondage, because if anything is embarrassing, it's embarrassing to walk around filled with demons!

For too long now, the suffering spirit has been left unattended to blindly stumble along with no explanations and no expectations of relief or cure. The church continuously exhorts these poor souls to pray and have faith, something that is easier said than done at times like this. Some think that they are exercising faith and patience but in reality what they are doing is nothing more than avoiding dealing with the unpleasant issue of bondage that is before them. Some can manage a prayer, but they are not praying with the expectation that something good will come out of the situation because in their hearts they have made up their minds that they are bound to continue on the same path that they are currently on. Therefore, they pray prayers of futility that haven't the energies to rise as sweet smelling incense to God the Father because in their hearts they are expecting defeat. They have allowed situation to blind them to the mercy of God.

When we do not listen to God's instructions for whatever reason, we put ourselves in harms way and the devil becomes familiar with our rebellious nature and uses it to get us to do his bidding. Whatever reason we may have, whether it's that we consider God's instructions too hard, too much work, too unacceptable, or too uncomfortable, Satan uses these attitudes of rebellion to bring us closer to him. Another thing that he uses is the condition of our hearts. If we have hardness of heart and have no intention of stopping a negative behavior, he uses this to gain entry. An example of this is having an unforgiving heart, a heart of stone, or being cold hearted. Another hindrance to man's freedom from bondage is stubbornness; we have a tendency to think that since *we* would not resolve a situation a certain way, neither would God. Consequently, we put ourselves on a level higher than God and reject God's solution to await a solution that is more to our liking. What many people want is magic and it's not God's nature to be a magician. It's his nature to be God. Satan uses our conception of God that we have created with our human minds, to trap us into believing that God really should think like us, and so should everyone else.

RECOGNITION TIP # 14

Recognize and acknowledge that the choices you make in life are always your own. No one can make choices for us. If we agree to do something, to accept something, to be something, whether it is good or bad, we have made our choice. A circumstance or situation we may not be able to control; however, how we choose to allow it to affect us is our choice.

CHAPTER 15

For the preaching of the cross is to them that perish foolishness; but unto us which are saved it is the power of God.—1 Corinthians 1:18

Many churches have very little concrete or detailed teachings on this malady of the spirit, the methodology of demonic control and infiltration. They speak in general terms rather than specific, as though it's bad luck to talk about such things. Some churches attribute everything to the devil! If the sun wasn't shining brightly enough on the day of the church picnic, the devil was responsible. Sometimes churches may attribute such things to character defects to the devil, using these "character defects" to attack and berate their congregation for not having the decency to "live for God." Character defects and demonization are separate and distinct. We all have character defects, and these defects can help us to recognize our need for the Father and draw us ever closer to Him, however, we are not all demonized because there are defects in our character. Demons want to move us away from God the Father by any means necessary, our character defects draw us closer to the Father unless we allow them to do otherwise. One of the means used by the devil may be character defects if they are not acknowledged and if they're not a part of our prayer life. Demons plague many a lost soul, not character defects which tend to lessen or even disappear with the onset of the Holy Spirit, grace, and age.

People are often left hurting and bound by demonic activity, Christians and non Christians alike. Churchgoers are left spiritually wandering in the wastelands of their minds, coming back time and time again and again to their place of worship hoping for an answer. They hope for an answer to a spiritual problem that they can't seem to define because they have not been educated in the specifics of how Satan launches his attacks against us. Some are not even aware that it is a spiritual problem that they're dealing with, while some give up and turn away from the faith altogether seeking water in dry places.

I once met a man who was so angry with the church that he decided to venture into a philosophy or a religion, I don't know exactly what you would call it, that catered to the individual as God. This, to me was rather self-serving (no pun intended!) Everything was about him; me, me, ME! I went to one of the meetings to investigate the scope of what they were talking about, not to knock them in any way mind you, just to see for myself what they were talking about. There were certain things that they espoused to that I could see. But generally *I* couldn't see it. They wanted to know why it was that I was having a hard time understanding that I am God. I told them that I was too flawed to be God. I needed a God that was greater and more powerful than I. I don't want my God to need contact lenses, have stretch marks, emotional mood fluctuations and not want to be bothered at times. I need a God who is omniscient, omnipresent, having wisdom far above and beyond what I could ever set my consciousness to comprehend. I need a God who has more love for me than I could possibly have for myself or anyone else on my best day.

My spirit can understand that Jesus sacrificed his life on the cross that I should be able to live in such an imperfect state and still know in my heart whether or not I think that I deserve the love of Christ, it is a perfect love, and that I do indeed have it. I understand that because of this crucifixion, the cross is a constant reminder that I don't have to be perfect to be loved, and this gives me peace. It reminds me that, when I am feeling low or overwhelmed by the troubles of this world, if I remember that Satan truly has no power over me because of this supernatural event on the cross. I can pray to the Father and because of His son's resurrection, he will help this imperfect soul that I am. Jesus serves to remind me that I am free, and his Word tells me why I am free; how to go about remaining free; and how to become free again when I am deceived by Satan. I'm glad I'm not God because I know that I would not be very good at it. The pressure would be too much for my frail human body. It is one thing to embody the Holy Spirit within us and another to *be* God. Still I am not here to knock the very few people that were at that meeting; people come to the path of Christ in their own time and in many ways, maybe this is one of them. After all, how should I know, I'm not God!

Some people don't even bother to go any route. Some people get so fed up that they discontinue their search period. They have made up in their minds that what their church offers is all that they can expect from God or anybody else. They suffer in silence because frankly, they're tired of feeling bad about themselves and prefer to live in anger and denial, where they at least feel some semblance of control. If they let others in, they'll know just how bad, ill at ease, and unacceptable they feel, they'd be ridiculed or shamed because of feeling this way. In religious circles, to feel this way is synonymous to being a substandard Christian. If we feel this way we are lacking in our devotional endeavors and that's why we cannot overcome these feelings. We do not want to be labeled as not having enough faith in such a situation because this is tantamount to being stoned to death because of sin. Some of these poor souls go so deep into denial, that their lives are consumed, over-burdened in serving others with little or no time allotted to truly examine their lives. It is a sad fact that they are so caught up that they have little or no time to contemplate the Word or more importantly, wait on the Lord to perform His perfect work in them. These individuals get caught up in the only release system that they have found to work for them. To receive a few seconds of peace, they must constantly prove to themselves or man that they are worthy. This is work and a vicious cycle that is void of the results that *they* are trying to achieve!

I call this type of living collecting distractions, whether it be by helping others, living vicariously through their children, or feeling a need to work fourteen to sixteen hour days. These things are not bad or wrong in and of themselves, but, when they are used to avoid living a full life, it's a method of avoidance or "collecting distractions." The result of living to collect distractions is that these people become so overwhelmed and overworked in trying to avoid facing the inevitable, the turmoil and misery of their own lives that they end up living life without truly knowing Christ. They too seek water in dry places thinking to find relief because they do no have a clue that what they are serving, though they are in church on a regular basis, is not God. Church has become one of the many things on their "to do" list. It has become a social obligation and not a time of worship, an opportunity to learn of Him, and a time for their spirit to be revived.

The church, on the other hand, needs to understand and accept the fact that some people are so demonically afflicted, they *cannot* pray, they *cannot* read the bible, and faith is an unachievable goal with little or no meaning to them. What they have faith in is this; there is no way out except to depend on themselves who they've discovered a long time ago is weak and ineffective. Yet these people continue to hide and berate themselves on a regular basis because they are stuck on a merry-go-round of a no win situation. They do not realize they have been temporarily blinded by the enemy, that there are paths to Christ that are available to them that have become blocked by Satan in some way. No one can fight Satan with purely human resources, because Satan is not human and human beings cannot defeat him in with human powers. Those who are saved and have fallen into bondage to the devil have the foundation to be free; for those that are unsaved, unless they accept Jesus as Lord, this is an impossibility.

The church needs to understand that many afflicted people stop going to church and voluntarily render themselves hostage to the devil. They do this because many times they feel that they have done all that they can do and frankly, they are tired! Attempting to fight Satan on our own makes us tired. It's like trying to fight a serious battle with a wet noodle, why not just give him what he wants and try to live with it. These poor souls have waved the flag of surrender and are that much closer to living their lives far from how God would want them to live. There is a risk that these people will never know true freedom and joy. There is a strong possibility that they may never be fulfilled, and live zombie-like existence; treading water in an ocean of darkness without shores, never knowing the peace of God until possibly—I say possibly; they are on their death bed.

There are those who are of the church and especially those that are *not* of the church, who accept the powers and gifts of the dark side and make a sordid life for themselves, convinced that this is the only way for people like them. They've concluded that the closest to peace that they will ever get, is to acquire power. How and where they get this power is of no care to them. They want power and they want it fast—they want it quick, and they want it strong. God can work this way, but more than likely he won't, so they turn to a power that will; they stop resisting the devil. They have already resigned themselves to the fact that they have lost the fight, not realizing that the reason they fought such a losing battle was because they were using the wrong weapons.

These people live in darkness, filled with demonic thoughts and catering to them in the most sordid and unimaginable ways. They sacrifice the life that God gave them in exchange for what they think is power. They feel that this "power" will bring relief and finally end the constant feelings of fear, confusion, and panic. Of course this doesn't happen; it just gets worse because the nature of the devil is that he is a liar. What does happen is that the feelings do not go away; they learn to ignore the feelings and become numb to their humanity.

What they have unwittingly bought into is being controlled by the dark side where there is no mercy, no forgiveness, ungodly justice, demonic terrors, and death. Serial killers are more than likely a product of this phenomenon.

By shedding light on this subject of demons, we can thwart the powers that we may have innocently or not so innocently allowed into our lives. Doctors have their place in our lives and so do the fine people who are in the mental health industries. But physicians can only refer to the psychologist, the psychologist can refer to the psychiatrist, the psychiatrist can refer an individual to where? Back to the physician, when it should be the church? The church should deal with such problems because it is where such problems must be dealt with. Only the church can educate God's people with a spiritual understanding of such matters and wage a purposeful war against Satan because the gates of hell cannot prevail against it.

When the physician, after examination, pertinent questions, testing of every kind still does not have an answer, he comes to the conclusion that there is nothing physically wrong. There is nothing he can do because it is not his job to cure what does not manifest itself in a physical form. We may, on our own, decide to seek a second, third, or even fourth opinion from other physicians, but if the results are the same, what are we to do? After we've related our story to the fourth doctor, or maybe even before we ever reach the fourth doctor, his response will probably be to refer us to a psychologist to see what is going on in our head. The psychologist will listen to us, maybe test our responses to a battery of tests hoping to find a clue but when he is unable to, may refer us to a psychiatrist. The psychiatrist, doing his job professionally and effectively, tells us that by all indications, you're as normal as anybody else. He may write you a prescription to calm your nerves if he thinks that we're too stressed about our imagined situation. Herein lies the crevice that allows Satan to exist in our lives and to continue to do his evil work. No man can help, therefore we just assume that whatever the malady is, we'll just have to learn to live with it or, maybe it will go away.

Wouldn't it be a wonderful world if the psychiatrists had a list that they automatically referred to, of clergy who were "experts" in the field of spiritual warfare? These experts would be prepared and qualified to help guide us right into the arms of Jesus and out of bondage for relief whether we belonged to their church, or nobody's church for that matter; how long can the unchurched ignore what has helped them so profoundly? Unfortunately, my friend, this is not so. It's a sad fact that it is not common practice for the psychiatric and spiritual communities don't work together, even for experimentation and documentation, when they really should.

When you consider the fact that there are billions of dollars a year being spent on brain disorders, you would think that there would be desperate attempt to clear such a medical impasse. Considering the amount spent for research, there should be no objection to trying conventional and unconventional methods including spiritual repair. Scientists are now convinced that the missing link does not exist and have studied the creation story in the bible and are finding that scientifically, the bible's version of the process of creation does follow a viable scientific pattern that makes sense. If scientists were willing to investigate the Darwinian theory, that has held up over all these years, and Darwin's inconclusive theory has even found it's way into the textbooks of our children, how hesitant should we be about using a technique that has been proven by the spiritual community to work, and to not only work well, but is a permanent cure for many?

Medical professionals, having done limited experiments using the power of prayer in healing. They have found that there is a clear link between the impact of prayer and faith on the healing process and the results are not negligible. Physicians are now coming to understand that the spirit and body are indeed closely related and dependent on each other; and that in fact, one can affect the other in significantly. Many doctors have found that to achieve the optimal effects of treatment and medication, prayers seem to boost the effectiveness of *their* efforts. Indeed, how much damage can result for any health care worker to inquire of a patient about their spiritual beliefs? The doctor should not attempt to influence what someone believes because that is not his job, but it certainly should be recorded in health records if a patient chooses to have it so. Just knowing a person's spiritual belief can give a physician insight into how they look at life. Simple questions, such as:

DO YOU ADHERE TO A PARTICUALAR RELIGION?

DO YOU WANT THIS PHYSICIAN TO HAVE KNOWLEDGE OF THESE RELIGIOUS BELIEFS?

WOULD YOU LIKE A LIST OF SPIRITUAL PROFESSIONALS IN YOUR AREA?

I WOULD PREFER TO KEEP WHAT I BELIEVE OR DO NOT BELIEVE PRIVATE.

This should be a routine practice. Those that choose to divulge their religion, and want a list of professional in their area would be handed a list of religious organizations that are willing to come in and help to facilitate healing on another level. The doctors should continue treatment as he sees treatment is warranted, without interference from the religious organizations, and the religious organizations would do what they do best without judgment from the medical profession. Those who believe in prayer can be helped tremendously; those who don't would just receive their medications and take their prescriptions as directed. No harm no foul just intensive care on all fronts.

Okay, I do admit that I have been accused of being a Pollyanna of sorts, but that's okay. The situation may not go exactly as I described in the previous paragraph, but can't we come as close to it as possible? To continue to leave body and spirit on totally separate fronts is foolish and outdated. We should be well aware by now that the two are in relationship with each other at all times as we go along in life. It's unavoidable.

It seems that the uncharted frontier of mind and spirit is a reluctant collaboration just waiting to be explored by the mental health industry and the church, but imagine the results of such collaboration? Hundreds and thousands of people could be helped immeasurably. If the psychiatric community would acknowledge the benefits of such studies, the money and people would appear. I think the closest that we've come to such an effort is parapsychology, which is not the study of the human mind and spirituality. Parapsychology is more interested in the unusual capabilities of the mind, and paranormal activities attributed to entities in a supernatural realm.

If the proper studies are implemented, the psychiatric community would automatically attribute many maladies that were not a physical, mental or emotional problem to the spirit, where it belongs. Sure the psyche and spirit are intertwined, but they are not one and the same. To treat the psyche without making sure that the individual is in good standing spiritually may be futile and unproductive in the long run, and the circle continues; from the physician to the psychologist, from the psychologist to the psychiatrist, from the psychiatrist to nobody until, something physical or emotional sends them back to the physician.

Unfortunately we live in a world where nobody wants to be the bad guy. The bad guy doesn't even want to be the bad guy; even he has an excuse however implausible! Nobody wants to take on the role of telling someone that there is something unholy going on with them. Theory is okay when it comes to hard science, but when it comes to the spiritual, theory is superstition, not provable, or a by-product of fanaticism and intolerance. Nobody wants to be overzealous or judgmental about others or even worse appear to be some kind of religious fanatic. We want our professionals to remain professional and our clergy to remain humble, cloaked in holiness, and agreeable. In our society we want to keep church and state separate nice and neat so that we don't infringe on the freedom of others because there is a fear that if we do, things will spin out of control and our freedoms will be compromised next.

RECOGNITION TIP # 15

Recognize and acknowledge that Satan has no power over us; only the power he deceives us into giving him.

CHAPTER 16

And always, night and day, he was in the mountains, and in the tombs, crying, and cutting himself with stones. But when he saw Jesus afar off, he ran and worshiped him, And cried with a loud voice, and said, What have I to do with thee, Jesus, thou Son of the most high God? I adjure thee by God, that thou torment me not. For he said to him, Come out of the man, thou unclean spirit. And he asked him, What is thy name? And he answered, saying, My name is Legion: for we are many.—Mark 5:5-9

To accuse someone of having a demon or demons is pretty serious business. One does not feel comfortable doing that sort of thing, does one? Unless of course; a body levitates off of the bed, while the head is spinning in such a way that is physically impossible for any human, a backward language is being spoken, and there is projectile vomiting having the consistency of split pea soup, then, and only then, might it be acceptable to consider that the demonic *might* be involved. Even so, we'd prefer to think that there had to be a reasonable explanation for such activity that has nothing to do with the spiritual, some sort of mental illness.

I'd like to assert here that I strongly suspect that there is a fine line between someone being insane and someone being demonized. I've considered symptoms, research and personal observations here and I attempt to come as close as possible to making the case for recognizing Satan's work without stepping into the shoes of mental health professionals. I'm sure somewhere along the line, mental illness and demonization will cross each other, but theoretically neither should weaken the other's case. The defining factor for mental illness and demonization lies in what method *cures* not *treats* the condition. What method is needed to free these poor tortured souls from bondage?

No one wants to be demonized. No one wants to have a demon. No one wants to be a demonized person's friend, mother, father, lover, child, or associate. No one wants to think that he even *knows* a demonically afflicted person personally. We would prefer that such a state in a man was of movie fantasy or that the person was just plain old crazy. We want for such things not to exist outside of the fantastical. We would prefer that there were concrete labels that could be addressed by some genius psychiatrist that could explain it all away, nice and neatly.

There are diseases that have a name but no cure. There are mental illnesses that have a name, and no cure. Then there are diseases and mental illnesses that have no name, fit into no category of illness, physical or mental, and have no "cure." Many of these maladies have been *forced* into categories by lay people because we don't have an answer. Some things remain hidden like a pit in a peach because it is imperative that some label be given and since there is no name, although we know that the thing exists, it's our way of denying its existence.

People are being given treatments that are designed to alleviate symptoms because the doctors don't know what else to do. They cannot identify the problem, so they treat the symptoms. Although this may provide some relief, it does not solve the problem. There is even the likelihood that the dosage has to be increased or the medication has to be changed altogether because the symptoms no longer respond to a particular medication. Some clergymen have even suggested that medication may actually impede the healing process that is involved with spiritual warfare or exorcisms. While mental situations requiring medical attention such as these do not definitely indicate demonic control or demonic affliction, such situations may bear looking into and would be a good place to investigate to see if a demonic problem is the culprit. After all, there's nothing to lose and everything to gain.

A certifiable mental illness is identified in the psychiatric community through a series of tests, psychological data and information, physiological changes in brain waves and/or chemical imbalances. A mental illness is not assigned to you just because you think you may be suffering from one or want an excuse for bad behavior. Any psychiatrist with an ounce of integrity would never do anything as heinous as this. Spiritually the same is true. A demon cannot be designated as the culprit because you're temporarily exhibiting bad behavior or having a particularly trying day or week, or year. There has to be relevant evidence. In order for a demon to enter our bodies, there must fertile ground for the demonic habitation to occur, and just as with the medical community, the symptoms must add up. Spiritually, conditions must be ripe for demonic infestation and there will be evidence.

So what about the things that ail us that cannot be attributed to an illness of any kind? What about the maladies that cause us to behave in ways that make us feel as if we are a puppet on a string? Knee-jerk reactions that constantly come unbidden and we feel as if someone else has taken hold and spoken the words or committed the offense. What about when there is a feeling that some unknown force has taken control of our being and there is a gut feeling that certain behaviors will in time, ruin our life yet we cannot seem control ourselves or stop the behavior. What of the constant feelings of irrational desperation that seems to grip our very soul forcing us into situations that we do not want to be in and hold us prisoner, refusing to release us no matter how hard we try or how much we pray? Barring a diagnosed mental illness, what would lead us into dangerous and harmful situations that are self-destructive, self-defeating, or even to participate helplessly in perversions that we despise? These behaviors go against the very laws of self-preservation.

What ailment, regardless of its origin, would lead a human being to destroy himself and/or others? Who would glean sheer joy from orchestrating or witnessing the downfall and misfortune of others? What would cause someone to throw himself repeatedly into the fire knowing that it burns his flesh or cause a person's personality to suddenly change from being social and upbeat to being uncharacteristically sullen, negative, irritable and dark, in a fleeting instant?

As I said earlier, barring any detected mental abnormality, why would a human being feel at the mercy of uncontrollable urges to constantly engage in activities and behaviors that prove to be hazardous and life threatening. Not only does the behavior sabotage or destroy the good that he has in his life, it threatens or destroys the good in the lives of those around him. What would make a human being get a sense of release after committing a violent act upon himself or another human being, only to keep these urges temporarily at bay until the next urge overwhelms him again? What is the cause of such private wars that go on within, and how did it come about? Shall we all be lost and suffer the consequences because the behavior does not add up to indicate a concrete illness that fits neatly into a box and cannot diagnosed and treated? Shall the individual be subject to such torture because it is not meet to discuss such things as exorcisms, spiritual warfare, demonization, or demonic affliction? Should we just meanderingly gloss over possibilities and shake our heads, click our tongues, because the medical professionals profess not to know and do not want to become involved any further in our lives beyond a writing a prescription? Or, should we look into other possibilities, like the spiritual? Why should we be afraid or embarrassed to look into the possibility of demonization, especially after all else fails?

When questions like the ones proposed in the above paragraphs cannot be answered medically, there is only one other explanation possible. We must attribute such things to the one who desires to kill our spirit, steal our joy, and destroy our life—the devil! It is the only other valid explanation after all is said and done.

There are many things in life that will remain a mystery. We don't know the answers to all things, and never will. But that's okay. To this day, many of us do not understand the intricacies of radio transmission, but that doesn't stop us from using the radio. All we know is that when we plug it into an outlet and turn it on, it works. When a discovery needs to be made, it is made in its time, what we call; ideas whose time has come. Right now, as I write this, there are souls being born and have been born into the world who have the keys to unlock many of life's great mysteries. Such a person does not have to be some type of genius, but will be a genius in his own right. They may not be born into the upper echelon of society, but may very well be. They will have the perfect parents to facilitate raising them, but by no means does this mean that the parent or parents will be perfect. It is not necessary that he parents be rich or poor; black or white, but however and whenever it has to happen, the circumstance will be perfect and conducive for the type of nurture, or even lack of nurture needed in order for these people to discover the answers to these mysteries.

Jesus was not born into a perfect situation by human standards, but according to the standards that God needed, the conditions were perfect. Mary and Joseph were not equipped to teach Jesus all that he needed to know, but the teaching and the knowledge that he needed were provided. Joseph, son of Jacob in the bible was born into a very dysfunctional family. I mean, come on now; any family that blatantly shows favoritism in this respect *has* to be dysfunctional. Brothers who would sell their own brother as a slave because they were jealous of him, screams dysfunction. Still, God used Joseph to do what he needed him to do despite his circumstances. As Joseph told his brothers, you meant it for evil, but God allowed it for good. This is how our heavenly Father works. He does not work according worldly standards; He works according to His standards. Who among us can judge our creator? Of the wisest among us, who among us has the wisdom of God?

The fact of the matter is there are no perfect people available for God to use. Jesus was without sin because he was God in human form. Unfortunately, we are not. We are fallible but not unusable. God's choices therefore are relegated to the imperfection of our humanity. Our imperfection fortunately, doesn't seem to inhibit God's ability to accomplish what he needs to accomplish through us. He knows our imperfections, each and every one of us, yet that did not stop him from sacrificing his only begotten son that we might be saved. He was sent here to die because of our imperfections. Our lives may fall apart and be in shambles, but God's divine plan goes forth despite our private lives. He uses us as He sees fit. He uses us as we are fit to be used. So when the time comes to reveal a mystery or mysteries, it will be revealed at the perfect time, in the perfect era, by the perfect person to deliver it so that his divine plan can continue to go forth.

This person, man, woman, or child will be given whatever they need in order to be able to accommodate God's plan. Their consciousness will be open and accepting enough so that he can absorb these mysteries and reveal them to the world. The mysteries will be received by the people who were meant to receive it, to others it will fall on deaf ears. Others will hear the mysteries, but will not be able to comprehend it. The people, who are chosen to receive this information, won't reveal this information to the "Herods" of the world, because they will understand that these Herods will try to prevent the mystery from being unlocked or revealed. The receivers of the mysteries will be protected to the extent that they need to be protected so that their vessel spreads the information as God will allow. They, the Herods, would try to destroy it before it's time but it will not happen. Mysteries are protected and evolve according to the receptive nature of the times. When their time comes, when God is ready to reveal them, no one can stop them.

Now, some of you may say, "What in the world does this have to do with exorcism, demonic control or affliction." Well of course it has something to do with this or I would not have included it in this book. Regarding demonic activities, let's just say, suppose the time has come for further investigation into matters such as spiritual warfare and exorcism. Suppose this book is just a drop in a vast sea of what we will come to understand about handling this matter. Suppose, just suppose, someone was freed from demonic bondage because this book or a similar message fell into their hands or the hands of a friend or relative and because of this information they were liberated from Satan's grasp. They were able to access a key to a mystery that had been there all along, but they were not privy to, because the demonic activities kept them in bondage. Suppose the person in bondage to the devil did not realize that they were in bondage, because they we not familiar how the evil one works until they received this vital information.

The less interference that we have in our spirit, the more likely it is that we will hear the still small voice of God. The more we are able to actually hear God, the more likely we are to heed his call. God needs to use people, ordinary as well as extraordinary. People need to be open and free to hear His voice. A person who has gained his freedom through Christ after being demonically controlled is definitely more open for use than one who doesn't have a clue that he is being manipulated by the devil.

Demonization can be something as severe as depicted in the movie *The Exorcist* or *The Silence of the Lambs*, to something as mundane as an unexplained tic or being generally unpleasant and ill-tempered. Most of us in our lifetime will not see anything as severe as *The Exorcist* and will not encounter anyone as demonically controlled as Hannibal Lechter in *The Silence of the Lambs*. It makes sense if you think about it, Satan will employ the least obvious methods to reap the best results because most people would run away from a hideous monster coming their way, but how many more can be drawn into Satan's devious web willingly if the bait were more attractive? Once captured in the devil's lair the affect that such a person would have on those around them would be quite effective in drawing others. The devil has acquired two for one, or three, or four, or five, or maybe even an entire group as with the Jonestown massacre. Those aren't bad odds! Even if he manages to overtake just one individual and like a spider that captures prey in a web, and sucks the very life force out of it leaving just an empty shell of a human where there was once life, I'm sure Satan would have no objections to this.

RECOGNITION TIP # 16

Recognize and acknowledge that our flesh will crave and desire whatever we feed it and what we feed our flesh affects our spirit.

CHAPTER 17

Now we have received, not the spirit of the world, but the spirit which is of God; that we might know the things that are freely given to us of God.—1 Corinthians 2:12

Total and complete demonic possession, the strongest and most severe of Satan's methods is rarely used by Satan these days. As a matter of fact because our spirit belongs to our creator, to be possessed is a misnomer. For the purposes of this book, however, we will continue to us the term, "possession" with the understanding that with God as our creator, no one can be completely possessed because the spirit of God dwells within us all. Only in degrees can Satan take control of our soul. As depicted in *The Exorcist*, to be demonically possessed is to virtually be transformed into a demon. I have heard of such a thing being possible and I have witnessed through the spirit the manifestation of demons on people. When demonic infestation reaches this point, the personality/soul has been so completely subverted or corrupted that the mind and the body are completely and totally under the control of evil, this is as close to possession as we can get, but even this is not total possession. It is not total possession because the spirit of man that belongs to God cannot be possessed by the devil.

We may be so demonically controlled, however, that someone else has to wage spiritual warfare on our behalf because we cannot. Our soul/personality may be so corrupted that we have little or no control over our actions. When this happens we need help because it is very difficult and sometimes impossible for us to help ourselves. We need someone else to intercede on our behalf and stand in the gap until we acquire the strength that we need in order to be in agreement with our desire to overcome whatever stronghold or demon that has us bound. The part of us that is our spirit, desires to live for God, and thirsts for that Christ connection and this is a fact that is true of all humanity. Spiritual warriors who are willing to help us must be capable of reaching that part of us that is subjugated and yet still spiritually open and connected to God. The Catholic Church calls these warriors exorcists.

Exorcists usually train under other exorcists. They do not go about seeking victims of demonization, the victims are usually recommended by friends and family. Out of about 2,000 cases of demonic possession reported to the Catholic Church, only about one or two may be considered authentic enough to warrant an investigation for exorcism. After a recommendation is made for an exorcism, an investigation has to be made to see if there really is a problem of "possession." Before it is accepted that a person is possessed or not, there is thorough examination by medical doctors and psychiatrists. Then there is a reevaluation by not one but many priests of the diocese with the final decision made by a trained exorcist who when presented with the evidence, personally examines the victim again before recommending the exorcism. These things must take place in order to receive an official church sanction for an exorcism to be performed.

Many dioceses in modern times don't practice exorcisms because comparatively, as times go on, there aren't many demonic possessions being reported. This could be because the medical community has been able to diagnose many ailments that were once thought to be cases of demonization, treat symptoms that they are not able to cure on a regular basis with prescription medication, or people are just unaware of the signs and symptoms of demonic activity. According to the Catholic Church there have been thousands of cases of "possession" reported in the past but less as we move forward in time because of the various reasons stated above. At this point, however, I have found no official number of recorded possessions, but it would stand to reason that the majority of humans are not "possessed," or even demonically controlled, Satan is not that powerful. At best there demonic afflictions and strongholds that affect the majority of the population causing us to be unnecessarily bound with troubles that would go away if we were relieved of such things.

There are different levels of demonization. The type of demonization that occurred in *The Exorcist*, on a scale of 1 to 10 would definitely be a 9.999, just a hair away of being totally and completely possessed. When this type of possession occurs, there is an aversion to Christ, spiritual paraphernalia, the church, any material or spiritual thing that represents God and Christ, from bible to crucifix. The goal of a possession such as this is to use the body of the victim to carry out evil deeds as the soul is totally and completely possessed. If death should occur, the demons purpose is to remain lodged within that person through death, its ultimate purpose, to take the soul to hell after the body is deceased along with anyone who comes in its path, especially the soul of anyone who tries to help free the victim of this demonic control. Because it is likely that a person who works within the church would become involved in freeing such an individual who is highly possessed, Satan uses this opportunity to pull out the big guns. The people attempting to save such a soul in the name of Jesus would naturally be spiritual warriors of the highest caliber and directly or indirectly linked with many souls seeking to know Christ as their personal savior. Nothing makes Satan happier than to destroy or possess the souls of any of God's ambassadors! Like the destructive forces of a tornado at the height of its power, those involved in freeing an individual from Satan's grasp, are in the danger zone.

As a matter of fact this would be a good time to mention the fact that although you may not be a priest or a spiritual warrior, ANYONE who desires to see a person free from sin and is actively involved in prayer and believing for the salvation of a sin-sick soul; Satan has a problem with this and he has a problem with you! So if you are a mother praying for your wayward son, or a father praying for your lost daughter, or if you are a wife praying for your husband or a husband praying for your wife; God does hear your prayers, but Satan doesn't like it. You can expect that he will challenge the strength of our faith by interjecting thoughts of anger, disgust, and futility into your mind so that you will tire of praying for them and even tire of dealing with them at all. Satan knows that this is the very time that they need you to send prayers up on their behalf because they cannot and at such times like this, a breakthrough is imminent.

A question may enter your mind to challenge your efforts, such as "How do I know that this is Satan and not God telling me to just let them be?." We know this because while God may tell us to stand still and see the glory of his work, we are to never stop believing and praying for a person no matter what condition that person is in. Jesus helped people that everyone had written off as hopeless to show us that anything is possible with God. If we are in tune with or hear the voice of the Holy Spirit, he may tell us that we need to get away from a person, that we need to let a person go so that *they* can come to Christ for themselves. The Holy Spirit can and will warn us that a person is dangerous or evil and we need to not be in their company, but nowhere in the bible does it ever state in word or parable that we should leave anyone to be consumed by the devices of the devil. However, just because we are tired of dealing with a situation does not mean that the Holy Spirit is telling us not to deal with it. The flesh can also tell us not to deal with a situation because remember, the flesh is all about comfort, it does not like to be uncomfortable. The prompting of the Holy Spirit is not found in anger, weariness, or frustration. We must wait until these emotions subside and then we must listen again to the instructions of voice of the Holy One. We are our brother's keeper, and while some of our brothers need to be kept at more of a distance than others, no where does it say that we are not to pray for sinners. Again, while it may not be wise to be around someone we love, we should still believe and pray for them to one day come to realize Christ as their Lord and Savior and be delivered from a lifestyle whose quotient is misery.

Sometimes we are forced to deal with people from a distance because of the amount of demonic activity that is involved. Make no bones about it, demons who have been allowed to fester and grow to such levels do have strength and they are not to be toyed with by anyone who has not been instructed by the Holy Spirit to deal directly with them and is not strong in the faith. Some demonic activity is so strong that a person must be anointed and spiritually qualified and trained to deal with demons such as these. We must listen to the voice of God because demons constantly look for a home to dwell in and destroy. We do not want to be host to the devil because our ego has told us that you can handle a situation that you are not qualified and/or anointed to handle! Some levels of demonization should be definitely addressed by the spiritually prudent, not some reckless spiritual cowboy who thinks he or she is a tough guy. The biblical account of the seven sons of Sceva shows us what happens to such people.

There are people caught on the cyclonic path of demonic destruction along with the victim. Family members and loved ones suffer right along with the victims of Satan's feeding frenzy. They are the people we love, we may not understand that they are in the grip of Satan; all we know is that something is not right. When our loved ones are under attack, and we are ignorant of Satan's devices, we can easily fall victim because of our association with this individual. When we are unaware of what is going on, we do not access the weapons of spiritual warfare that are available to us. Again, we may know that something is wrong, but in our ignorance, we'll generally try to use human methods to remedy what is constitutionally a spiritual battle.

One of the higher levels of demonization, we'll call it a level eight, these people do not resist the devil's power in any way. At this level the demonic activity in the victim is relatively the same except the demonic energy is controlled, that is to the degree that it can be controlled. These people have willingly turned over their soul and body to be used by Satan. They have given him permission to use them, usually in exchange for something that they feel they either deserve, don't deserve, or God will not provide to them such as money, possessions, power, or fame. These people are children of the devil and do his work on a daily basis. These people can walk into any place of worship and not be affected. They can look at the bible, hold a crucifix, douse themselves with holy water and it will not affect them, because these people are not halt between two opinions, they have made a choice, and they are protected by evil incarnate. They can say the name of Jesus, they may know intellectually that it is claimed that Jesus is the son of God and are able to agree, but they do not believe that Jesus is the son of God or that he is their Lord and Savior or anyone's Lord and Savior for that matter, they don't believe that it affects them one way or the other. They have a mission. That mission is to program and perpetuate evil into whatever person, situation, or profession that they have been assigned to. These people are evil, but they don't feel their "evilness," what they feel is that everything is about them. What they do, they do for self-preservation and do not realize the magnitude of the evil that they do to preserve "self" or even when they do realize the evil of what they do, they are not able to care. This type of evil is why Cain slew Able.

These types of people, who are highly demonized, usually are successful in their worldly endeavors and it may appear that at times they can literally get away with murder, but this is all granted by the devil as an illusion to deceive and draw more people to desire these things. This deception can go a long way when it comes to obtaining and retaining souls. The stronger individuals draw the weaker individuals who crash and burn in their wake. Satan does not play fairly. The highly demonized individual must soon pay the price too, for the higher Satan elevates an individual, the farther and harder they must fall when he drops them. We must pay the price when dealing with the devil, no matter how lofty a position we may find ourselves in.

It is not unusual at all to have such an elevated status or occupy leadership positions in whatever area his workers are involved in. His workers come from all walks of life from the preacher to the usher, from the executive to the laborer, from the principal to the janitor. Once they have agreed to Satan's terms, depending on their usefulness to his kingdom, whatever they take on, they will be good at it and they will be elevated to some position of authority in that area. With all their "success" though uncanny and oftentimes mind-boggling and even awe-inspiring, they will never be able to enjoy their success with peace, an indication of the demonic at work. Joy eludes them and they have to rely on fleshly stimulation or perversions if they are to feel anything at all at this level. Satan leaves us feeling numb or dead to life and perversions help these people to know that they are alive. Unfortunately, the perversions must become more extreme, the more they yield to the devil. If they use profanity, the profanity gets more harsh; if they are into pornography or sexually deviant activity, it must increase; if they are into drugs or alcohol, they go deeper into their addictions; if the stimulation is money, they must acquire more and the more that they acquire, the less they enjoy life, so they must acquire more; if they have a taste for power, they can never have enough to be satisfied. Whatever their particular problem is, it becomes harder and harder to feel alive and they come to depend on it more and more. There is a deadness inside that must be resuscitated on a daily and sometimes even an hourly basis. Life is in Christ, and these people have not accepted Christ, therefore, they have not accepted life and are hooked up to an artificial source that is powered by the acquisition of something. If something is not being done to feed this monster they are the walking dead.

These people many times appear to be quite attractive and personable. I say appear to be because many times it's not the case. They are not as attractive as they seem because to those with a discerning spirit, they can see that thing, and there always is a thing, that makes something about their looks kind of off. They are capable of luring many into their web of iniquity by their appearance, words, emotions, or empty promises that appeal to the ego. Especially vulnerable to the tactics of these evil souls are those who are posted on the fence of indecision and feel that it is possible to serve two, or even more gods, with no consequence or repercussions. People who do not stand for anything are excellent prey for Satan's evil games. Some of these highly possessed people are given assignments of individuals whom they must bring over into the kingdom of darkness. They will wear on this individual, blasting them by various means and wearing them down until they have been convinced that the way of the devil is indeed the only logical way to go.

These highly possessed people do not appear to be miserable. If they appear miserable, then they are not of the genre of the highly possessed. These people have accepted the fact that only what can be acquired in the physical is what is important and anyone who has not acquired worldly possessions is just pretending to get joy out of their meager existence. They are competitive and get a sense of satisfaction out of bending and breaking the rules of society. There is a special satisfaction in "one upping" God's people because they know that what the ordinary person sees, carries more weight than what they don't see. If these highly possessed people can convince the average person that they have a fulfilling, wonderful, powerful life; and are able to display the material evidence necessary to convince a wavering soul that their way of living will be more attractive and therefore more desirable than a "struggling believer," their job is done.

These demoniacs carry out their orders like soldiers. They use the physical body, the mind and the emotions to accomplish victory for their master, who is the devil. They use what they have learned naturally and what Satan reveals to them. They play upon the weaknesses of others in order to manipulate and gain the confidence of those whom they would use to benefit their schemes. In essence, they are con artists of the highest caliber. Like Satan, they believe that everyone has a price, regardless of appearances. These people can detect our weaknesses however minute, a tiny flaw in our character; and they're slithering their way in to acquire another soul for the devil. These people have the instinct of predatory animals.

These demonic executives may have a husband or wife; but the purpose of that husband or wife is to help them accomplish their mission. These people cannot love, they can only possess. They can only figure out what *you* need them to do in order for *you* to feel that you are loved so that they can accomplish their purpose. They are not good people to be around because their range of interaction is limited to imitation and manipulation. They learn to imitate good behavior and to manipulate people and various resources to get want they want. Many times the spouses of these people will stay because they themselves have deep rooted attachments to "gods" that *they* serve, such as money, power, prestige, or anger. The spouses of these demonized souls remain because their needs are being met; in fact their demonized spouses are more than capable of providing a needed reason for such idol worship.

These highly demonized people may have children, but are incapable of love for them just as they cannot truly love their spouse. Children come in handy at times, but for the most part they aren't very important in and of themselves. Only the family as a package may important for appearances sake. These families may seem like the most stable families on earth, but only to those who don't really know them. Those who know them and those who can discern, can see the misery in the individuals that make up this "happy" home. While a spouse may be in denial, generally the children know; even if they can't identify what it is, they know that something is amiss.

If these demonized people are pet owners, the pets will be at a higher ranking order than the children and spouse. There is a strange bond between the owner and the pet. The ties to the pet will be unusually strong and weird, even to the most ardent pet lover.

These high ranking demonic warriors may prey on those who are spiritually weak but influential. They prey on those who do not look beyond the material as evidence of success. Their contacts and associations are with other high ranking demonic warriors. Their line of attack is generally through individuals good or bad, that affects and influences whatever their target might be. These targets can be neighborhoods, schools, institutions, the church, the government as well as the collective conscience of millions of people. They target leaders in society, God's chosen ones, their family members, or closest friends and associates. A person may be spiritually strong, but these demonic souls can spot vulnerability as with an eagle's eye. They understand that attachments such as our family, friendships and associations, can be used to lure a person to unwittingly renounce the ways of Christ and dwell on the dark side of life, thinking all the while that this necessarily must be so.

Highly demonized people are very capable of remaining a husband or a wife because unless the spouse that is not demonized leaves, the demonized spouse is not likely to because there are no genuine emotional feelings to detach from. There are no attachments to that person or anyone else for that matter. As long as the spouse that is not demonized stays in their place, there is no threat to the mission. Like the predators that they are, their sole purpose for positioning themselves in any person's life is to target their weakness so that they can defile these people, open the doors for demonization to occur in them, or at the very least have a cover for their evil operations. This holds true for everyone whose path they may cross, and especially holds true for the spouse. Every person that is a part of their lives must have a purpose that caters to something that they want. There is no friendship just for friendship sake, because they are not capable of a give and take relationship.

Sometimes these demonized people find mates who are also demonized. There are spiritual laws of attraction that do exist that cause this. They recognized something deep within that is evil, and they are attracted to it. What comes from the spirit goes to the spirit. They really are "soul mates" in a sense of the word. Spiritually, we can only attract and attach to ourselves that which we are made of unless we reject what our spirit attempts to communicate to us, this is the only way such a thing can happen. Spiritually sound people should not end up with the devil, and if they find themselves in such a situation because of some lapse in judgment, they do not stay because they *cannot* stay. Spiritually sound people are a peculiar people because they are people of God and evil people can find no rest around them. Nobody can fake a relationship with Christ, their actions and words will expose their true character for even when they make mistakes along the way, as we humans tend to do, you can always count it to their head and not the condition of their heart. So next time you see a couple, and you wonder how a nice guy like that could end up with an evil witch; consider that there is something going on that is compatible in their soul. Consider the fact that this nice guy might be living vicariously through this evil person because he has issues of his own that need to be laid at the feet of the Master. As a person's spirit gets stronger, and their soul begins to heal, the union will have to end because it no longer satisfies a need that is lurking in the soul of the man; it will end that is, IF the demons don't get a chance to overtake or even kill the "nice guy."

This is why it is important to monitor our connection with Christ on a daily basis through prayer, study, meditating on his word and most importantly, our commitment to live for Him. The stronger our connection is to the Christ that is within, the less likely it is that these demonized people will become a part of our lives. The more active our prayer life is the less likely it is that demons will be able to gain a foothold. The stronger our knowledge of God's word, the harder it is for Satan's attempts at deception and confusion to penetrate our spiritual armor. Though they may try, either something in your spirit will reject them, or demons will ultimately reject a relationship with you and simply disappear out of your life. Some demons may hang around a bit longer than others, attempting to defame our character and throw us into a tizzy, but soon, they too realize that we have become aware that Jesus has paid ultimate price for our freedom. Demons recognize when the Christ that is within us is just too big a force to be reckoned with. Many times the bigger demons that understand this will back off and send minor demons in an attempt to tear us down by putting tiny holes in our armor. They will stand back and at every opportunity, anything that might signal weakness, they send in the minor demons to test us to see if we are ripe for the picking. They watch us, trying to figure out how they might overtake us when we are strong. They desire to know the secret of our strength that they may use the very thing that God gave us to protect ourselves and do his work and use it to destroy us. We must put on the whole armor of God that we may have strong resistance on all fronts, consciously and subconsciously, from this devious predator.

The highly demonized individual is, however, not likely to need to partner with someone else who is also highly demonized. It's a waste. Satan is not all seeing and all knowing and he does not have the army of God. He needs as many souls working in as many areas as he can as he tries to make the best of his futile task. He needs them dispersed as much as possible because again, Satan is evil but he is not all powerful like God. Satan's workers may recognize each other and help each other to accomplish their goal when necessary, but there is no love there and they have no problem moving on. Many demons may cluster in a human, but human souls that have been demonically invaded, don't cling to each other in any great number for any extended period of time. There may be a high ranking demonized soul over less ranking demonized souls to serve as their leader, but you will not find high ranking demonized souls hanging out together as loyal friends, they don't need to and frankly one would eventually end up destroying the other. There is no loyalty among these souls. In Satan's kingdom there is much infighting among his elect, unlike the Kingdom of God, there is no peace. If at any time you find such a situation where Satan's elect have assembled together for any period of time, I can only imagine that there is serious trouble a-brewing. There is a network, spoken and unspoken. They don't necessarily need to speak of it because it's more of an attraction than a feeling. They are drawn to each other for various tasks and missions. Their help and support for each other is very generous and forthcoming but without loyalty. Their biggest loyalty is to Satan not those who worship him. A click occurs, and they remain attached for as long as it takes to accomplish a goal, get through a situation, or satisfy Satan's itch. There are no emotional connections, only common goals. They release when it's time to release.

Another indication of a highly demonized person, perhaps a level 7, is that his soul, the way he thinks, feels, his emotions, and how he chooses to spend his life on earth, are pretty much controlled by the devil in the sense that the deeper they are involved with him, the less they tend to hear the voice of God, and when they do hear it, in any form, from anyone, it's considered a great bother and irritant. These people reject Christ altogether and have no problem doing it. They are very angry and hurt people who have allowed anger and pain to overtake them and leave them open to demons. These people have bitterness and hate in their hearts, *demon food*, and are therefore highly infested with demons. They are hateful and hurtful toward others but their circle of influence is not at potent as a level 8. To look at such individuals you would think that they would be in worse shape demonically than a level 8, but the truth is people who are at level 8 has managed to get past the anger that the level 7 feels and is operating with a sense of purpose that is highly influential. Anger and bitterness in the level seven are stumbling blocks that will prevent a level seven from being highly successful at anything for any period of time. A level seven will never be what God has created him to be without somehow sabotaging himself either before reaching his goal or after reaching it. A level seven can feel a call by God for his life but is too wrapped up in his negative experiences to do anything about it; the demons within make sure that these feelings are constantly perpetuated. A level eight cannot feel a call of God on her life at all because she has drifted too far away from her spiritual core. A level 8 is driven to do the work of the devil and will let nothing stand in her way. A level seven has an easier time of coming out of bondage than the level 8 because emotions such anger and bitterness are evidence that our spirit is grieving. Emotions that are attached to nothing higher than oneself is farther away from Christ than having emotions that are attached to a cause other than oneself no matter how despicable the cause. A level seven may seem in a worse state because of the manifestation of such negative emotions which level eight may not exhibit outwardly. A level eight may be more likeable than a level seven which would cause one to think that the level seven is demonized at a higher level.

RECOGNITION TIP # 17

Recognize and acknowledge that God is more important than our religious affiliation.

CHAPTER 18

And even as they did not like to retain God in their knowledge, God gave them over to a reprobate mind, to do those things which are not convenient; Being filled with all unrighteousness, fornication, wickedness, covetousness, maliciousness; full of envy, murder, debate, deceit, malignity; whisperers, Backbiters, haters of God, despiteful, proud, boasters, inventors of evil things, disobedient to parents, without understanding, covenant breakers, without natural affection, implacable, unmerciful: Who knowing the judgment of God that they which commit such things are worthy of death, not only do the same, but have pleasure in them that do them.—Romans 1:28-32

The devil can possess the soul of an individual, but again, the devil cannot possess an individual's spirit. Every aspect of the personality, which is primarily the soul, has been compromised to the point where they are not capable of feeling anything of a positive or loving nature whether it be from within themselves, or from others. Level eight and above may have knowledge that is supernatural and carnal. When a person reaches a level eight and above, their personality and behavior is now to a large degree powered by Satan. We can tell when someone has reached such a stage because at this stage people tend to use Satan's tools of imitation and manipulation. They people shop to see what they can take from whom and revamp what they have taken from someone else's idea, whether it is a style, a look, mannerisms, speech, or how they stand on issues. They use manipulation even when there is no need to because the minds of these people are programmed o operate in such a manner. Level eight and above have only two distinct emotions that are genuine; fear and hate. Many have a zombie-like appearance because their emotions have been so subjugated that their facial expressions oftentimes don't adhere to the wide range of expressions that are inherently human: good, bad, happy or sad. Their faces can have the appearance of being frozen and when they have need to access an expression that is appropriate for an occasion, it almost appears as if their face is cracking under the pressure of trying to bring one forth and it does not look natural.

As I said before, very few people are demonized to this point. Level eight and nine are by no means common. To find a person that is totally possessed, level 10 is to find a demon, not a person with a demon. Level 10 is like Regan *The Exorcist*, and who knows how much of that was theatrics. Now I have heard of people in satanic cults who deliberately invite demons to inhabit their bodies. When this is done, the person literally, it is said, becomes the demon itself. This is done, according to those who are knowledgeable about such things, to acquire more power and achieve a higher hierarchy in Satan's order. Once you achieve a higher position, other demons become subject to your power and they fear you. This is in total contrast to the Kingdom of God where there is no competition. These people, who deliberately open themselves up to demonic possession, want and expect that doing such a thing will yield intense power and erase all fear. They want god-like power! It doesn't matter to them if it comes from the devil. To be in control of one's own destiny and to instill abject fear into people and other demons alike is too attractive an offer to resist.

Again, before I go too far, and instill abject fear in you reader, let me clarify a few things. The average human being does not want this type of power; we fear it because we naturally fear unfamiliar territory be it good or bad. Therefore it is very unlikely that you will run across anyone in your entire lifetime who has knowingly and intentionally invited such profound evil into their body. Secondly to embody such evil is progressive and a person must move through several layers of evil before a soul is open enough to even accommodate such evil. This type of evil is not something that can occur overnight. In order to accommodate such evil a person has to have a reprobate mind, an inability to hear and detect the voice of God, and even if God's permissive will has allowed an individual to develop a reprobate mind, the consequences of what goes along with having a reprobate mind can lead to insanity and death *IF* it does not lead an individual to a change of heart first. If these things do not occur, we are indeed looking at an individual who is possessed, driven, and inhabited by demonic forces. We are looking at a very dangerous and scary individual.

In order for any demon, singular or multiple—strong or weak, to occupy a person, a series of things have to happen. There has to be an OPENING and an OPPORTUNITY. An opening is not necessarily a moment of weakness, or sin. It can be an inherited condition, or a traumatic experience that has opened the door, jarring us into a serious state of panic delivering an overwhelming sense of fear and vulnerability that the evil one uses to constantly remind us of how horribly wicked the world is and how weak and defenseless we are. The devil can keep us so preoccupied with our situation, hurts and fears until we forget that one, two, or fifty unpleasant situations in our lives measured against the amount of time we will spend on this earth in these bodies of clay mean nothing as far as the big picture of our lives and God's destiny for us is concerned. He, the devil, locks us into our moments of despair that have been allowed by God to give us an opportunity to grow, and he uses these same opportunities to stagnate our rightful access to Gods promises.

An opening many times can be an accumulation of moments of weaknesses that have led us to live a life apart from our creator and maker, God. Somehow the mistakes we have made in life consume us and we are so consumed with our mistakes, that we over look the fact that we have made more choices that are healthy and right and good than not. We have chosen good over evil many more times that we have chosen evil over good, but we get caught up on an abortion, an affair, immoral behavior in our past, our disobedience to God about a situation, or guilt over our children, that we allow such circumstances to color our lives forever. Some people even make all their decisions based one unfortunate incident in their lives!

For instance:

I had an affair so I must put up with someone treating me like a subhuman.

I had an affair so I cannot discipline my children because I am such a horrible person to have done such a thing and now I must show my children how much I love them.

I had an affair so I have to be careful not too be friendly to people because I don't know who I might meet through the people I meet and end up having another affair.

I had an affair myself, so what can I tell someone who is having an affair?

I had an affair so I am despicable. How can I expect that things will go well for a person like me? I deserve all the bad things that happen to me.

Insert any circumstance in place of "I had an affair…" This is bondage.

Satan uses such mindsets as an opportunity to keep us in bondage to him. Whether it is in one area or a hundred, these situations and circumstances are openings and opportunities. There are an infinite number of these for Satan to use to bind us and keep us in bondage. There has to be openings first and foremost before Satan can attack us on any level, then there must come from us a sense of acceptance that that we are flawed. There are things that happen by chance and things that are out of our control also. Whether by chance, or by our own conscious decision, these things must be nurtured by us in some way in order for the Satan to be successful. For instance if you are the victim of a traumatic event, the traumatic event can either become a stepping stone to elevate us to a higher level of spirituality, or it can be a cement brick that keeps us burdened and pinned to the ocean floor. When we choose not to allow our circumstances to take us to the level that God has intended for such a circumstance to take us to, the doors are open for demonic habitation.

Satan seizes opportunities as we give in more and more to operating in and because of our fleshly fears and desires. It is important that we take the time to invest in our spiritual nature. We're open when there have been low or no deposits made into the bank of our spirit. Our funds are low and we have little or nothing available to draw upon. When this happens, we are highly susceptible to live a sinful life. We are more likely to refuse to turn to God for help with our inherent weaknesses and find ourselves in a stubborn and rebellious state, hence affording Satan the opportunity of admission into our lives.

To live a life apart from how God would have us to live is called sin. Disobedience to God is called sin. To sin is to miss the mark. Anything that is done with bad intentions is called sin. Any activity that leads us away from realizing the love that God has for us is sin. Anything that goes against the Christ nature is called sin, no matter how good it looks, remember, Lucifer was one of God's most beautiful angels. There are those who do not like this word "sin" and immediately would call this word judgmental. These people would probably prefer terms such as immoral behavior, inconsiderate behavior, bad behavior, unseemly behavior, evil behavior, etc. I prefer the word "sin" because when we talk about sin, we speak of behavior that is not holy. When engaging in behavior that is not pleasing to God, we may operate below or above human standards and society's moral compass. As people who are born into sin, our knowledge about good or bad behavior is determined by many variables that we may or may not have experienced and is hit or miss at best. The word sin goes above and beyond what is legal or illegal, what is moral or immoral according to the sign of the times. It goes beyond what is trendy, acceptable or unacceptable, right for one person and wrong for another. What is pleasing to God is more intricate than what is exciting and what is boring, why we serve versus *that* we serve, our motives versus our actions. What *seems* to be right may not necessarily *be* right according GOD's purpose for a particular situation. What is not sin in one situation may be sin in another if it is not what God would have us do *this particular time*!

The fact of the matter is that what is sin is based on what God says is sin. The bible is our blue print that is indeed subject to interpretation. We can attempt to make a case through the bible to cover any activity that we would like to carry out, all in the name of God. This is why there are so many religions and so many denominations and so many people who are dissatisfied with themselves and others. But God has also given us the Holy Spirit to dwell within that we would not be confused as to what is His "voice" in various situations in our lives. If we have heard the voice of God instructing us in our thought life, there should be confirmation on three levels:

—IT MUST BE BIBLICALLY SOUND
—IT MUST PERPETUATE THE ATTRIBUTES OF CHRIST
—IT MUST BENEFIT OTHERS JUST AS MUCH IF NOT *MORE* THAN THE INDIVIDUAL

If we have confirmation in at least three areas of the three areas mentioned; we can be 99.9% sure that we have heard the voice of God.

Our thought life is very important; what we think, what we think we heard, how we have been conditioned to think and how we have learned to think. It is important because what we think and how we think usually precedes any opening in our spirit and can be an indication of an opening or vulnerability in our spirit. A thought sustained usually insures the action will be taken, if not outright, then to some degree. Sustained unholy thoughts is sin and sustained unholy behavior is sin, other than that, a thought is just a bad thought that flits through our mind, and bad or unholy behavior can be classified as a mistake depending on the intentions of the person perpetrating the behavior. Anyone can have a bad or evil thought in passing or in times of anger, that's a part of human nature and every bad thought that passes through our mind is not necessarily a thought that comes from us. Thoughts can be introduced by demons, or Satan himself. That is why the bible says that we should take every thought captive, so that we may examine where it comes from and accept or reject such a thought in Jesus name, capturing our thoughts give us an opportunity to put them under spiritual examination. Thoughts themselves do not make us bad individuals; however, it is our responsibility to make the thought subject to the word of God.

All of us humans, who have lived any time on this earth, have been involved in behaviors that we are not necessarily proud of, whether they be major or minor misdeeds. We have no doubt in our minds that the behavior is not what God would have had us to be involved in, yet we did it. This does not make the thought right, this does not make the behavior right; but guess what, Jesus died because God knew that we would sin and he knows of Satan's activities. He died so that we wouldn't *have* to live a sinful life subject to the devil's whims and since Jesus' death, we can repent, turn away from sin, ask forgiveness and move on. His shed blood is very powerful and has washed us, but remember, this in itself does not negate the fact that we have to deal with the consequences of our actions. We don't necessarily have to deal with the consequence of a single thought, but we always have to, for better or worse, deal with the consequence of our actions.

Sure, we have free will to accept Christ's death and it's meaning of salvation for all who believe on Him as a statement of fact, but we also have the exact same free will to reject it, in action or by inaction. Whether we believe or not, does not change that fact that we don't *have* to succumb to the activities of the devil and there is a way out—Jesus! That is what ministers mean when they say that Jesus paid the price. A purchase has been made, his death being the ultimate contract eternally binding and irrevocable. Look at your receipt, THE BIBLE. It has all of the itemized details of the authenticity of this purchase.

Satan takes advantage of us at times when we fail to understand and embrace the fact that we have been saved and cleansed by the blood of the Lamb of God. If we have not read the contract or we are not familiar with Jesus, it's difficult to believe God's word and Satan can convince us that there are loopholes, and the contract is meaningless with little or no real substance. The devil can make us question the reality of God and the role of Jesus, and does so every opportunity he gets. He's just doing his job! He's looking for openings and opportunities; seeking those whom he may sift as wheat.

Actually, believe it or not, he does us a service by keeping us on our toes. If we look at what power he truly has in and of himself, which is none; the only power that he has is to use that forked tongue of his to try and convince our free will to accept him over God. He has to convince us to accept Satan's way over God's way; chaos over peace; anger over forgiveness; or fear instead of faith. He keeps us on our toes because if we are to have a quality of life that is worth living, we must be diligent concerning our relationship with Christ. We must protect ourselves from that forked tongue of his by reading God's word and employing His fail-proof weapons of warfare. As with any weapon, the more we use these weapons of warfare the more skilled we become at handling them. The more skilled we become at handling them, the less effective his temptations will be, and the more likely it is that we will be able to avoid Satan's traps and the more capable we are of hearing the voice of God the Father. The war itself won't end, but we become more alert agile in recognizing and dealing with the enemy, winning more and more battles in this ongoing war.

Let's get back to the openings or portals of satanic entry into our lives. We have already stated that there is a thought, and there is a sustained thought. There is a sin, and there is sustained sin; there is trauma and there is inheritance. Many people do not understand that Satin cannot read our thoughts and our heart. Only God can do that. Satan has to watch for physical signs and evidence that you are actually considering taking action on thoughts that he has put into your head. He has to have evidence of anti-God thoughts that are displayed in some physical way. Don't be foolish enough, however, to think that you can hide the thoughts and intentions of your heart so well, Satan is a quick study. He is as cunning as he is evil. It's very important that we don't underestimate the devil and it's just as important that we don't overestimate him. (It seems as the generations have gone by, we have a tendency to do just that, to underestimate or overestimate Satan.) A sustained lustful look at someone other than our spouse, enjoyment when looking at anti-God materials and situations, how and where our anger is directed, how and where our time and money is spent, the words we speak, our actions toward others; all are indicators of openings and weaknesses to Satan. Unlike God, who knows the thoughts and intentions of our hearts, Satan has to have cues and clues that set him in motion. In other words, all we have to do is give him an outward sign that there *might* be an opening and this is how he knows that he can launch an attack against our souls.

After we give him a clue, there has to be an act of consent for him to enter a portal. He cannot take up space in our brains or our body without some kind of express consent given of our own free will. There is verbal consent, and there is nonverbal consent. Sustained anti-God activity and/or thoughts that go unchallenged are part of a spiritual law that permits Satan to have access to our soul, it does not matter if he initiated the thought or if we initiated it. No matter the source of the initial thought, there is always a window of opportunity for rejection or inaction.

Many messages are initiated by the flesh, not Satan. It is the nature of the flesh to yearn for stimulation in all forms; it is the nature of the devil to satisfy that yearning especially when it will work against us. He will satisfy or perpetuate this yearning and use it as a means to an end. Satan will keep coming and coming offering the same thing in different packages until he gets us to consent to his presence or we use the proper weapons of spiritual warfare to resist, fight or stop him. We give him our consent not just by saying "okay" to sinful behavior, but by willfully accepting and consenting to a sinful lifestyle that caters to the flesh. We don't necessarily have to consent verbally; our actions also give him consent. He'll use confusion as to what is acceptable and unacceptable in the eyes of Christ. He uses temptation, guilt, or fear, to acquire our consent, which is aimed specifically at our most vulnerable spot, our ego. The more we cater to our ego, the more likely it is that Satan will be successful. That is why the bible states that the "I" must decrease so that the Christ within can increase. The devil has so many tricks up his sleeve that it would be unrealistic to think that anyone could cover them each specifically in one book or even in one lifetime.

This is how he employs his trade of deception, by changing his appearance like a wolf in sheep's clothing. He'll invade us on the right as we are attentive to what is going on to the left. He'll deceive us with kindness as we set our sights on avoiding obvious evil. He'll "bless" us just to keep us in bondage, and we'll never know that the "blessing" is indeed a curse designed specifically for our personality type. He'll send demons to drain our energy and fog our thoughts. He'll distract us, intimidate us, use us, and turn those that we love against us, if their souls are open to be used in such a way. He'll fling arrows that are harmless at us and we'll expend precious energies, just to avoid getting hit by something that really won't hurt us in the first place; just as we'll spend endless hours fighting paper tigers as he prepares our soul for demonic infestation.

RECOGNITION TIP # 18

Recognize and acknowledge that we should expect to get what we ask for, whether we ask with our mouth or our actions.

CHAPTER 19

...and there came a grievous swarm of flies into the house of Pharaoh, and into his servants' houses, and into, the land of Egypt: the land was corrupted by reason of the swarm of flies.—Exodus 8:24

There are different levels of demonic infestation. Think of it as a home in need of extermination and our bodies, which is the temple of God representing our home.

Scenario I

Perhaps the home is infested, but because it is kept under control by regular extermination and maintenance (bible study, confession, repentance, prayer, etc.), the critters have little chance to accumulate and gain any ground. The home is virtually pest free and the ones that do survive are at death's door or too weak to cause any harm. They may lie dormant and remain harmless or it's just a matter of time before they're gone because they are being deprived of essential living accommodations.

Scenario II

There is the homeowner who feels that by catching a critter here, or killing a critter there, using their own intellectual and amateurish devices will keep the critter problem under control and their home relatively clean. They feel they don't need any outside help if they would just take the time to figure this thing out on their own. No, they don't like the critters, they are a nuisance and a bother, but many days they just let them run unencumbered, because they are just too tired or preoccupied to be on the warpath. These types of homeowners represent those of us who are the every now and then acknowledgers of God the Father and don't understand the power of Christ. They know that God and Christ exist but feel that self-maintenance can be figured out without an instruction book but with common sense and logic. They are preoccupied with "doing" life, and will get back to the critters as time permits; so they fight the good fight, get tired and frustrated. Fight the good fight then ignore them for a while. Fight the good fight, then they just give up until they muster the energy to deal with them again. It's just too hard, after all they're only human and how much can you expect from a human. It's unfortunate for them that they don't acknowledge the power of Christ and futility of their humanity when it comes to things of this nature. It's unfortunate that they don't know that if they were to depend on Jesus, He never gets tired and *He* will give *them* rest.

Scenario III

Then there is a level of infestation where the exterminator may be called, but not on a regular basis and the time that lapses between exterminations is too extended. This allows the critters an opportunity to rebuild their nests and repopulate to a degree that is unhealthy. The offspring of the critters arrive as an unfamiliar breed and are allowed to run free until the person figures out that they too are pests. Their numbers continue to grow until it's like a plague has come upon their home. By the time the exterminator arrives, his job is more difficult and it takes more time because the population of the critters has increased and many have mutated in some respect. Some of the critters respond to his chemicals, but the new ones may need something stronger. The exterminator does his job to the best of his ability and tells them that they'll have to make a follow up appointment so that he can get the rest of the critters, but they don't call because right now it's comfortable enough. In the mean time the call conveniently slips their mind until the problem is once again huge and out of control. This type of homeowner represents those of us who seek Christ only when we're overwhelmed by our growing circumstances.

Scenario IV

There is a level on infestation whereas the homeowner may know that there is a problem, but feel that they do not need to hire an exterminator. These are the people who have incorporated the critters into their livelihood. Live and let live is their motto, and if they were to destroy these critters, *they* are bad because these critters have been an integral part of their life and how they have come to know themselves, regardless of how aggravating and inconvenient the critters my be. They feel that their life will come crashing down all around them because they cannot deal with the guilt that the critters cover up on a daily basis, or live without depending on questionable resources that the critters have come to provide. Surprisingly many people fear that they will have to pay a price if they no longer allow the critters to inhabit their homes such as becoming destitute, weak, or unpopular.

Scenario V

Some people believe that they can live together with these critters in peace, love, and harmony or possibly even train them as one would train a pet or an exotic animal. They don't want to get rid of them and they certainly don't like exterminators.

They don't like exterminators and will be the first to defend, excuse, or allow for, any critters that are running about. They believe in the live and let live philosophy. If the critters are there, they must be there for a reason. There is no need to get rid of them why that would be like asking them to get rid of their personhood, their essence, who they truly are. They cannot understand why it is that they have adopted this happy-go-lucky attitude on the outside and everyone may comment on their upbeat personality, but on the inside they feel like intestinal waste. Or, they may display an attitude of arrogance and confidence as they build a wall to protect their personal critters from harm. In any case, their inner life does not match what they habitually display in their outer life on a daily basis. Their tolerance level for the creatures (yes, I did say creatures because at this point they have been fed and nurtured to such a degree that they have grown stronger, beyond the critter level) has dramatically increased. The average homeowner would not be able to stay if they wanted to but these people do because they have slipped into a protective mode and guard the creatures as they ravage destroy their home.

As the creatures increase, they tend to take up more space than the homeowners thought they would. So the homeowners begin to seek out little pockets and spaces within their own home where they can get a moments rest from these creatures that they have allowed to multiply and dwell in their home, but they soon find that the places of refuge have become smaller and smaller. These types of homeowners represent those being attacked but refuse to get help and refuse to acknowledge that it is the enemy. They may know of God's love and his mercy and his goodness, but are unaware that they should employ any of the weapons of warfare that he speaks of in his word. As the demons multiply, they become confused as to what is of God and what is not, what is clean and what is unclean. As these people sink deeper and deeper into bondage while coddling and protecting the demons, they begin to call good evil, and evil good; they are repressed and oppressed to the extent that they do not think it possible to have peace, love and happiness unencumbered in their lives; pretty soon, they come to expect very little from life and daily, they proceed to eke out some type of life for themselves while attempting to hold on to a semblance of sanity that reeks of anger, dissatisfaction, blame, and incompetence.

Scenario VI

And then there is the homeowner who realizes that the house is plagued, but figures that he does not have to deal with these critters, he'll just move to another house. He discovers some weeks after moving he has unbeknownst to him, brought some of the critters from his old house with him to the new house. The critters were hidden in his belongings and have already begun to repopulate. Ignoring the fact that wherever he goes, the critters seem to appear, this particular homeowner may have to move several times before realizing that the problem is not going to go away because he cannot seem to avoid bringing them with him. This homeowner now realizes that if he moves again, the same thing will more than likely happen. Now he seriously considers using the services of a professional exterminator.

This homeowner represents one of the ones who have tried to control the situation externally, not realizing that the problem is internal. These people play the blame game. It's everybody's fault, they have excuses and reasons that make sense to them; if only everybody else would act right, their lives would be ever so much better! They don't realize the critters are having a field day within their soul; pointing out the faults of others, examining thoroughly and completely any and all dissatisfaction that they may experience; rendering them in a state of denial about their own selfish motivations, and actions; they hide the person's own faults from them behind anger irritation and ego, so that he or she won't examine themselves; and the demons will not allow them to realize the hurt and pain that they cause others. One of the devil's jobs is to keep us in denial!

These homeowners are helped only when they come to realize that their method of moving and looking to change the scenery and the people around them are impotent. They must begin to realize what is truly happening because the critters will return without the help of Jesus no matter how much they run, how much they blame, or how deeply in denial they are. But, even though this type of homeowner may have a realization, it may be a while before he can actually bring himself to do anything about it. There is a realization, and there is denial. They coexist side by side in these people before they finally come to the conclusion that both of them cannot coexist together for any length of time. They must make a choice! Without Jesus, they'll continue to "move."

Scenario VII

Then there is the homeowner that has come to realize that they do need help with these critters. They realize that they don't have the expertise or even the slightest notion of how to rid their homes of these critters but they know they do not want to live under the same roof with the critters, so they call for help. While they may know what an exterminator does in general, they realize that these people have more knowledge than they do. They understand that the exterminator understands the lifestyle, reproduction habits, and feeding patterns of the critters. The exterminators understand what the critters like, what they don't like, why they're there, how they're getting in, what will make them go away, and what will make them stay gone. These people truly believe that the exterminator has the answers to all of these questions and have the know-how to remove these critters from their home. They trust that the exterminator knows his job and are willing to trust him enough to allow him to do their job. They are willing to pay the price and follow the instructions that he gives them; these homeowners are teachable and reachable. Their homes will remain virtually critter-free, and if they do see a critter, they know what to do. These homeowners represent the people who are committed to and stand on the word of God. They are not afraid to use the weapons of warfare that God has provided for us. They are not afraid to delegate to the experts things that they cannot adequately handle.

What scene is being played out in your home. Whatever the level of demon infestation that has occurred in your life, Christ is the terminator of all such activity. His death and resurrection has sealed the deal. The exterminators' role in our lives is to bring our consciousness into remembrance and acceptance of what Christ has already done when the evil one has tricked us into buying into his lie. The exterminators come in to help us when we have believed a lie to such a degree that the very lie itself has taken root in our soul. Christ has freed us from bondage to the devil, his job as our savior is to render the devil powerless and to get rid of the demons in our lives. He has set His church up in such a way that they know how to use His power. With Jesus in the house, the spirit of truth dwells in the house and all these critters that have been fabricated upon the lies of the devil must flee. We have the word of God to instruct us. It is our sword; it is the most vital weapon of warfare that God has provided for his people. There are people who are gifted and trained to eradicate demons, from the simplest form of demonic habitation to the most complicated demons that have become intertwined and hidden in who we think we are. Call them exorcists, deliverance ministers, healers, prayer warriors, demon-caster-outters, exterminators—whatever, with God, these people are capable of getting the job done. These are the people who understand weapons of spiritual warfare, and when they do their work in the name of Jesus, the DEMONS MUST GO.

By the way, if the home that you live in, the one that is made of wood, brick, or stone, is being overrun by critters, rats, roaches, termites, squirrels, ants, spiders, or too many cats or dogs, get it exterminated or cleared out of such things. These animals and pests are just a physical or worldly manifestation to remind us that we should not learn to live with pests or be plagued and overrun by any other life form. God gave us dominion over all creatures; he didn't give them dominion over us. You have dominion over your pets no matter how much you may love them and if it gets to a point where you have so many that they take over your household and finances, you have too many. Our homes should reflect the fact that we will not be invaded or overrun by any thing. Our bodies are symbolic of our personal and individual homes not made by the hands of man; therefore we should also make sure that *it* is free from invasion by demons. We should not allow demonic activities to take up residence in our being no more than we should allow pests and too many animals to take up residence in our man made homes, especially to the point where they push us out, violate our space, and/or tax our resources. We don't have to live with pests in our life or in our spirit.

Make it a priority to get rid of these things. It's alright to love your pet or pets; they can give us comfort, joy, and pleasure. Pets, however, are to be owned by people who live in abodes designed for people who may have pets; not designed for pets who have people catering to them. Pet owners should not be controlled by their pets, this is not biblically sound! Do whatever it takes! Spend the money, take the time, and make the effort to have your home and your pets, decent and in order; this is what God intended for man.

Get rid of the critters that don't belong in your home. Besides the nuisance of the physical presence rodents, pests, and insects, many of these unwelcome house guests carry germs, diseases, and parasites that can make you and your family ill. Get used to owning your physical home and being very protective of what you allow to go on in your home. This easily translates into being aware or our physical body and what we allow in it, what we allow to be done to it, and what we do with it. We should not treat the bodies that God gave us like a piece of trash or waste receptacles. Get used to treasuring your body and acknowledging it as the temple of God that it is. This should become a way of life. We should develop a low tolerance for anything that is ungodly to happen in our home and in our body. We should not allow these types of negative forces to remain in us or exist around us physically or spiritually.

I remember growing up in the public housing projects in Chicago where everybody had roaches. When we moved into the building it was virtually brand spanking new. I believe we were among the first twenty families to live in this building that was designed to hold 160 families and the building was pest free. As time went on, the authorities that be, became lax on the rules and regulations of what was required of you if you were granted permission to live in the building and were not as diligent about maintenance as in the earlier years and we began to see roaches. Well, we'd previously lived in a rat infested two flat so a roach here and there seemed just a matter of squashing them under the heel of your shoe.

As time went on, as the population of the building grew, you could not manage the roaches just by stepping on them and pretty soon the people that ran the building had to hire exterminators. Because each apartment was connected by shared walls, the roaches would just scurry to another unit if the people in other units were not at home to allow the exterminators in. Another problem with the exterminations was that some people, for whatever reason, just did not want the exterminators in their apartment. Therefore of course, the roach problem never disappeared. Everybody had roaches from the filthiest apartments where the children were known to kill them with their bare hand, or brush them off a piece of food and eat it; to the cleanest apartment, who also had them, but housed significantly less. There were no exceptions; everybody had them to some degree because the whole building was infested. On fairly rare occasions we'd spot a roach or two in the classroom of our very clean elementary school. They'd startle us, not because they were unfamiliar to us, but because it was still out of the ordinary, as the nursery rhyme goes about Mary's lamb, *to see a roach at school*. The girls would scream, then a riotous contest by the boys would break out as they competed to stomp the bug as it scurried willy-nilly across the floor. When the bug was finally squished to juicy roach pulp, the teacher would settle us down and we'd go on as usual with our school day.

By the time I went to high school, still having not ventured far from my neighborhood, I thought everybody had roaches unless they were rich or famous. My frame of reference for this was of course, the television. They never showed roaches or even talked about them on my favorite television programs. The blood rushes to my face in embarrassment as I remember the time in high school when a roach was spotted in the girls' locker room. The roach scurried across the floor and girls started screeching and hopping about like they'd seen a scorpion or some such thing. I was about to panic also until I saw that the offending creature was a single, solitary, roach. I walked over to the roach and calmly squished it to smithereens under the sole of my white tennis shoe. As I squished the roach, I remember making some condescending comment to the other girls about them acting as if they'd never seen a roach before. To make matters even worse, I had the pitiful nerve to add, with a bit of arrogance mind you, that everyone had roaches.

Well, needless to say, several of the girls let me know that they did not have roaches in their homes, and they were not used to being around them. I think I blocked their comments out of my mind because it was at that point that I realized that everyone *might* not have roaches, and I'd just given myself away. Everybody didn't have roaches!

This was a day of education for me. After that little fiasco, I had opportunities to visit many of the girls' homes. Not a roach in sight!

RECOGNITION TIP # 19

Recognize and acknowledge that we must resist the devil and that resist is an action word.

CHAPTER 20

Then certain of the vagabond Jews, exorcists, took upon them to call over them which had evil spirits the name of the Lord Jesus, saying, We adjure you by Jesus whom Paul preacheth. And there were seven sons of one Sceva, a Jew, and chief of the priests, which did so. And the evil spirit answered and said, Jesus I know, and Paul I know; but who are ye?—Acts 19:13-15

How many of you readers think that everyone's mind operates in the same way that your demon infested minds works? How many of you think that everyone is selfish because you are selfish? How many of you think that everybody has unbridled no holds barred ambition because you yourself have sold your birthright or would sell your birthright for a piece of bread? How many people are under the assumption that because they have let the devil reek havoc on their soul, allowing him to steal their joy, peace and happiness; that there is no such thing as a person who is truly happy and at peace? And—if you see such a person with such qualities, your first thought is to expose the misery that you know is there because there is no way, they HAVE to be faking contentment. This is an example of the devil at work. He wants you to think that everybody's house has to have roaches, when in reality some people employ the "exterminator," and therefore the roaches may come, but they can't take up residence for very long.

Again, many of us have been living infested for so long and to such a degree that we automatically think that everyone is infested with demons and it's a natural state of being. Well you don't have to embarrass yourself like I embarrassed myself, let me be the one to tell you right now, this is just not true. Sure everyone sins, and everyone has to deal with the antics of the devil at various times in their lives, but everyone is not infested with demons. Everybody's soul is not fertile enough to have the qualities to actually house the demons. Some people are so diligent about their relationship with God, that even though demons may try for a visit, they don't stay because they can't get in and even if they did, there is nothing for the demons to attach themselves to. The demons cannot survive because there is a constant spiritual extermination of some kind going on, and these people are committed to the Lord. This makes living conditions extremely harsh and uninviting for demons, so they cannot stay. God Himself preserves some people, and while they may sin, they will never have demons, it's an unmerited gift from the Father.

We must be careful of what we allow to go on in our homes. We must be careful of what we allow into our temple. Only once in the entire bible does Jesus exhibit significant anger, and that's when the temple of God is defiled. Let's do an analysis of things that were going on in that temple.

First he kicked out all the people who sold and bought in the temple.

We are to freely give of ourselves according to our blessing from God. When people come to the temple, they should not be charged to partake of the Word of God. When people come to us for comfort and godly advice, we should not look to be paid or compensated in any way. If we are blessed with knowledge of God's word, we should bless those who come to us in need of knowledge or encouragement. God's word should not be used as a means to fill pockets or to get money from poor, unfortunate, and suffering souls who are desperately in need of spiritual guidance. Extracting money from those in need of spiritual guidance by the way, is the problem with seeking the advice of fortune tellers.

Then the tables of the money changers were overthrown.

These money changers in the temple were not doing anything that was illegal according to the law of that time. As a matter of fact, that was their profession. The point is; these people were pandering their trade at the wrong time and in the wrong place. While there are some things that may be legal to do according to the law of the land, to do them in the temple of God is strictly out of order. What may be acceptable to society at large, can be totally unacceptable in the House of the Lord.

Some things may be legal according to the government and acceptable to society, but for us to actually allow them to go on in *our* temple, our bodies, is strictly out of order. To do them *in* our temple or *with* our temple is sinful or "illegal" in accordance with how God would have us, his children, to live. He provided our bodies to be a living sacrifice according to His word. Just as with the temple of God, we are not to desecrate it, mutilate it, disrespect it, or defile it. This is important to acknowledge for those who would live their lives for Christ. It is not acceptable for us to do whatever pleases us with our bodies regardless of whether society condones it, or if it is as legal as rain according to society. Our body is the temple of God, and when we desecrate it, defile it, and use it to carry on in unholy ways, forget about opening ourselves up to the devil, Jesus himself hates this and will deal with it by overturning many things in our lives and causing us to experience enough pain and distress in our lives that we cannot bare to continue to desecrate our temple, but as long as we do; the overturning, the pain, and distress in our lives will continue. Do not mistake this as the work of the devil; it is the work of God.

This is probably a good place to talk about addiction. When we become addicted to a substance and continue to put the substance in our bodies on a regular basis this is desecration. We will never have peace because God will not allow there to be peace in desecration because he hates it. Peace cannot be purchased, love cannot be bought, joy cannot be sold. These were the empty promises of the temple merchants and these are the empty promises of drugs, alcohol, and any of the various addictions plaguing mankind in any particular era; be it food, sex, telephones, television, video games, exercise, up to and beyond the mutilation of the body. Addiction promises that whatever it is that we are addicted to will give us a sense of peace, love, and joy; albeit temporarily. The problem is that addiction is progressive and the more that we progress into our addiction the further away we drift from peace, love, joy— the very thing that it promises to deliver. God hates for us to desecrate his temple and Satan uses the choices we make to desecrate our bodies as an opportunity display on the outside the hurt, pain, fear and vulnerability that we feel on the inside; like a calling card to attract demons. Remember that Satan needs a clue because he cannot read your mind, his demons can put thoughts in our minds that we think are our own, but he cannot read our minds. Desecration of our body in any form is a big clue as to where he should aim his fiery darts in order to open the doors for his demons to enter. We should understand that we give the devil a clue for instance because of our addictions and even with our tattoos that say, "Bad to the Bone."

Many of people have begun to use the church as a marketplace to network to help their business grow. There are some who have actually joined a church for this very reason. The church is large and the members fall into a certain income bracket making good contacts for potential clients. While I see no problem with being provoked for whatever reason to attend church, once you get there it should be evident through the teachings as to why one should remain. If we **start** going to church because it makes good business sense or for any other reason for that matter, we should **stay** because we have found that a Christ centered, well rounded life, is better that the one we were living before. If you do not come into the knowledge of Christ while attending this church, big or small, this is not a good church. The word is supposed to show us; how to find peace, how to have joy, how to manage our lives, what love is and what it is not, what success is and what success is not, along with a myriad of other things.

If the main reason we are in church is contrary to worshiping our Lord and Savior, we should play golf, if our main purpose is to be social; we should open a social club; if our main reason is to accumulate business, when should advertise; we should be in show business if our main reason is to be a star; and we should find a hobby, if our primary reason for attending church is that we just want something to do. I'm not saying that people who are in church for these various reasons should stop coming to church; I'm saying that we must realize what our true objective is and pursue it in its proper arena. Church is not a get rich and popular social club and if you think that it is, Satan will use such a mindset to cause you misery and dissatisfaction with the church. Your dissatisfaction will open doors for demonic interference between you, God, and God's people—the church.

Pastors, or those who hold in leadership roles within the church, have an awesome task before them that should not be taken lightly. It is their duty to impress upon us that making boatloads of money will not save us or bring true happiness. It is their responsibility to deliver the word to the saved as well as the unsaved. Not only are the unsaved looking to be helped, but the saved are looking to be fed, replenished and sustained. Many times the unsaved that come to church are at a crossroad in their life, how they are received into the church and their perception of that church, is of vital importance and what they see going on in the church is of vital importance. The purpose or responsibility of the church is not to give the impression that everyone who goes to church and comes to God becomes flawless, that's inherently impossible anyway. The church should give the impression that we are a people who believe the word of God and strive to live in that belief and for that belief; in other words as Christians we strive to incorporate what we know and what we have come to understand about the gospel into our lives so that each day our walk will be more pleasing to God. We may fall from time to time but we have knowledge of whom to go to when we're in need. We get up and help each other up in love, all the while keeping our focus on Christ our savior; this is the most perfect impression we can give anyone who desires is to join the church.

He told those who sold doves not to sell them in the temple.

Doves represent peace. He did not scatter them like he did the large animals. Peace belongs in the temple but is not to be purchased at any price nor should it be sold for a price, yet we constantly attempt to purchase it and/or sell it in some form to those who desire it. As with addictions and abuses mentioned earlier, we try to purchase peace for ourselves through substances and things. We indulge in activities and habits that we feel that we may be able to control, things that we think will bring us peace. The result is, however, that what we have managed to accomplish is a temporary method of altering our state of mind. Abuse of alcohol, drugs, sex, and money represent our way of trying to buy peace within our temples. Peace, which is represented by these doves, cannot be purchased and cannot be brought in the form of something man-made. Even with this temporary escape from our problems, the man made route is only a temporary fix. We must constantly accumulate the means in order to continue to have this type peace because it *is* temporary. As soon as the money, drugs, alcohol or sex dries up, our "peace" is shattered and once again we must be on the prowl again to feel "right." Within us we know that this is not true peace, but day after day, year after year, we're caught up in the lie, engulfed in Satan's deception and we continue to ignore the truth because we are not yet equipped spiritually to resist the devil. The truth that the enemy does not want us to realize is; it is impossible to manufacture peace with human hands.

Our bodies are sacred for our bodies are the temple of Christ; therefore we are to respect it as such. Should alien forces set up camp in our temple, we should experience the righteous indignation that Christ felt in the temple of God when he kick them out. Our bodies are to be filled with love, faith, hope, and truth in Christ, anything contrary to these things, and not a normal and healthy part of human nature, should be forcefully and immediately eradicated. As a matter of fact when we accept Christ into our lives as our Lord and Savior and decide that for Christ we live and for Christ we die, it would not be unusual for us to feel within our "temple" a violent shaking. Thoughts, ideas, energies that once resided in us unencumbered, now have the awesome force of Christ to be reckoned with. In exorcisms this can be seen very clearly as the demons are forced out in the name of Jesus. Jesus cleared the temple of these ungodly inhabitants and Jesus died so that we would not have to live as a habitat for demons.

All sin is not necessarily caused by the devil. We make a choice to sin just like we can choose not to. Whether we are strong enough to make proper choices is a spiritual issue in and of itself. Every bad thought that we have doesn't necessarily come from Satan. I know many "church folk" who think that all of them do, but they don't. Some of them come from emotional garbage. Some of our bad thoughts come from hearing them over and over from the mouths of those who raised us; some of our bad thoughts come from systematic programming by culture, society, or those in authority; some bad thoughts are from Satan, but these thought are usually passing thoughts that have no power, other than the power that we give them. If we let them pass, they will do just that—PASS, with no effect whatsoever. The more power we give to them the easier it is for these thoughts to gain power in our lives and the more power they gain in our lives, the more power they have over us. The more power these thoughts have over us, the easier it is for Satan to open doors for his demons to take up residence in our minds and the more power the demons have in our minds, the more power they have to affect our lives.

Demons may use the resulting action of bad thought to their advantage because we have acted on a thought that should have been allowed to pass because it was a thought, not from our arsenal of experiences, but a thought that was planted by the enemy. Other sources of bad thoughts, as mentioned previously, where we are reacting to past hurt, abuse, or punishment, can be used by the enemy to rationalize and excuse us doing the devil's work. Emotional situations for instance can trigger bad thoughts. If someone hurts us and we are angry, many times what we think about them is far from pleasant. This is a reaction from the flesh that helps us to stay away from what is bad for us. However, anytime the flesh alone is involved in anything, beware! The flesh is one-dimensional and we are not one-dimensional beings, we are not supposed to allow our thoughts to run wild without monitoring them, good and bad alike. We are to bring every thought captive before God to be examined before we capriciously act on them. The bible states that the heart can be a liar, the tongue should not be allowed to fly freely, and the mind needs to be renewed. All of these things must work together and be in agreement before a final action is taken in order for us to be pleasing to God and make us less vulnerable to the devil. At no time should only one part of our anatomy to be in control, and bringing our thought life under subjection to God is how this is accomplished.

Many times we react to things according to the spiritual state of our heart, not because the devil made us do it. Our emotions are a manifestation of our spiritual state. How we react to things is directly relative to our spiritual state. Haven't you noticed that when you are in "good spirits" your reactions are more positive and generally more well thought out, than when you are having a bad day? How some days problems and irritations just seem to roll off of your back like a duck in water?

The overall spiritual state of a man is therefore quite relevant to the choices and decisions that a man makes, regardless of what kind of day he is having. If a man is in good spirits huge problems seem small. If I man is in bad spirits, small problems seem impossible. We can see why it is so important to attend to our spirit. On our spirit can rest important decisions that can be a detour away from our destiny that may take us forty years or better to get back on track *if* we ever do. Or, the state of our spirit will allow us to make decisions that honor God the Father and keep us on the path of glory with all the prescribed ups and downs, as we make our way to our promise land in God's time. The Egyptians wandering in the wilderness is an indication that it is possible to delay or even, forego our destiny. God promised them the promise land, but a whole generation did not make it because of disobedience and bad behavior. The spirit of these people was not steadfast with the Lord, even Moses, their leader, who spoke with God Himself did not make it to the Promised Land although he was allowed to go home to be with God. You see, the devil can stop us from reaching our land of milk and honey, even if he does not succeed in stopping us from going home to be with God before we can see our promise land. If the Christ that is within us is nurtured properly, we will naturally make significantly more good decisions than bad.

We have freedom of choice. Satan can try his hand at convincing us to choose evil, but we're not innately designed to comply with what Satan puts before us. If we are on "empty," however, and have not been building ourselves up through prayer, church, studying God's word and so on; of course it makes it easier for Satan to get us to comply with his wishes and forfeit our Promised Land if he cannot put us in such a position to compromise or sabotage our relationship with Christ so that we will forfeit our souls to hell.

RECOGNITION TIP # 20

Recognize and acknowledge that being in denial about our spiritual state does not mean that we don't have one.

CHAPTER 21

In this the children of God are manifest, and the children of the devil: whosoever doeth not righteousness is not of God, neither he that loveth not his brother. For this is the message that ye heard from the beginning, that we should love one another. Not as Cain, who was of that wicked one, and slew his brother. And wherefore slew he him? Because his own works were evil, and his brother's righteous.—1 John:10-12

I once rode in a cab where the cab driver was neither enamored with nor disenchanted by spiritual matters, particularly the church. He was from Africa and he said that Africans are very religious. He told me that his wife got up everyday at 5:00 a.m. to pray just as his father in law who still lives in Africa continues to do each day. He doesn't have a problem with his wife praying everyday and taking his children to church and teaching his children about God. The problem he has, he said, is that all of these people pray and pray and their lives don't seem to improve at all. In Africa, the poor pray, but they still are poor. In America, the American's pray, but they don't seem to change.

What's the use, he said, "I believe in God, I just don't understand why such poor results!"

This man articulated a rarely acknowledged occurrence within the Christian community. Children have seen their parents serve and there is no change in anything significant in their lives. Parishioners belong to churches where it is not unusual for no one to prosper, yet they still come. Sinners standing on street corners day after day, who will freely acknowledge that they are sinners, see the same people going to church Sunday after Sunday with no improvement in their countenance or their standard of living which is either stagnant, or depleted because they gave up their sinful way of making a living.

It is a fact that many times there is a change on the inside that has occurred some large some small, depending on the grace of God along with their level of understanding. It is also true, however, that there should be a change in all facets of our lives. If we become new creatures in Christ, we should be new, a new form, a new person that is clearly distinguishable from the old, depending on how far we have fallen in sin. Not only should our countenance change, we should be capable of reaching our Promised Land because of what God has promised to us. The bible says that the poor will always be with us, but it also says that there is a Kingdom of Heaven at hand. It also states that there is a place flowing with milk and honey that is there for the children of God who will claim it.

The problem that the cab driver spoke to me of is at least three fold. There is a problem with many Christian not knowing exactly *how* God works, we know *that* God works, but we don't know *how* He works. We know that we love God, but because we come from a human perspective of love that is based many times on emotions and feelings, we cannot comprehend GOD LOVE, which surpasses human love to such an extent, that love in human terms, and LOVE in God's terms should not even be mentioned in the same breath. What the cab driver spoke of without even knowing that he was speaking of it is that Satan blinds the eye of the believer to whatever extent that he can, based many times on the believer's status in life, culture, upbringing, superstitions, and lack of understanding of spiritual things. Satan has Christians in bondage so much so that we cannot enjoy the fruit of many trees that have been planted for us and it is perfectly legal for us to partake of these fruits.

It's the diabolical nature of the devil to mislead us in biblical history, with the story of the forbidden fruit, by using fear and even our reverence of God, to keep us confused with what we should abstain from. Of the many, many trees in the garden, Adam and Eve were to abstain from the fruit of only one; all of the other trees were from God for our enjoyment. Here we recognize diabolical nature of Satan since the beginning of time. By distraction, he keeps us from thinking about how blessed we are, all the things we do have and tempts us to obsess over the what is not meant for us in the first place; this is how he can keep us in bondage. He would have us focus on one thing in our lives, while there are several other ripe and right opportunities that are tailored specifically for us.

When we cannot enjoy what we have in the present because we are preoccupied with something our in our past, this is Satan using the negative to make us afraid to move ahead into our destiny. For instance, if we were mistreated by a person who said that they loved us, the devil will use the results of our pain, which should be caution and discernment, and put a different label on it in our minds. The healthy outcome of this unfortunate situation should be that we develop caution and discernment in future relationships. However, once the devil gets a hold of it in our minds, he has convinced us that the lesson of caution and discernment is not really caution and discernment that we feel, but fear! So instead of taking the lesson as the good Lord intended because he has allowed this to happen, we are convinced that it was not a temporary lapse of judgment or a lesson to take note of, we are convinced that everybody is out to do us wrong and we have no business in a relationship. Now the bad relationship has convinced us that we are unlovable and unworthy of a healthy and Godly relationship. We should not allow the forbidden fruit of one tree convinced us that all of the fruit in the garden should not be eaten.

Satan uses emotions such as **anger, bitterness, loneliness, envy** and **pride** to get to us, but he doesn't necessarily create such conditions in us. Sometimes these emotions, such as the result of a bad relationship for instance, are fostered by pain, grief and sorrow. Such emotions are part of our nature and are not necessarily bad in and of themselves and they do serve a purpose in our lives. These "negative" emotions can act as a barometer of our emotional as well as our spiritual state. Understand that Satan can create nothing because he is not a creator, he can only use what already exists. God is our creator and He knew what he was doing when he created us *and* our colorful emotions, it was not a mistake. Have you ever seen a person who seems devoid of emotions? Scary! Try this. I tried it on my younger sister and it really creeped her out. Smile, but don't let the smile affect your eyes, the window of your soul. *SCARY*! While this is an interesting thing to try on friends and family, it's also a way to recognize demons in people, which will be discussed later, because if there is strong demonic activity going on in a person, demons look a certain way, but it is very difficult for them to show emotions that are genuine and flexible. Demons are imitators of emotions and are first, foremost, and ultimately evil.

Though we all sin, we are not all plagued by demons that've infiltrated our borders and turned us into evil monsters. Some of us have learned to be great warriors in the Lord. David, father of King Solomon, sinned but he was a man after God's heart. Can you imagine that? A sinner, just like me, who was a man, was loved in a special way by God the Father and he wasn't a saint who did everything right. This is good news! It shows that God will love us even though we are sinners, but let's not just stop there, why did God love David in this special way? There were plenty of sinners around, why did he specifically refer to his love of David in such a special way? The reason is so simple and so accomplishable. Why was David loved in this special way despite the fact that he was an undeniable sinner? Because David did not try to deny the fact that he had sinned, an important fact that many of us miss. We spend so much time in denial of our sins that it impossible for us to repent of our sins, you can't repent of something that you're in denial about. David sinned because as humans we are prone to sin and the bible does not state that an evil spirit came upon David that made him to commit these sinful acts. He sinned because his flesh was weak. He sinned because the spirit and the flesh are at odds with each other and the flesh won.

To sin is to go against God and what God would have us do; it is not necessarily to play out what the devil himself has tempted us to do, although to do that *is* to sin. There are sins that we commit in other words, that have nothing to do with Satan and have everything to do with our emotions and us yielding to the flesh. "The spirit is willing but the flesh is weak." It appears that David's sin was that he had a tendency to yield to the flesh. David is an example of a person whose soul is tender and whose spirit is constantly in communication with the Lord. David could still hear the spirit of truth enough to be convicted by truth. David didn't blame his actions on Bathsheba, or the devil; he did not deny his sin or make excuses. He was sorrowful and humble. He was obedient to God and Nathan, God's servant, when his actions were brought before him.

Although David is sometimes momentarily blinded by sin, he never lets his sinful behavior get the best of him. David loves the Lord and he fears or respects the awesome majesty of the Lord. When you fear the Lord you understand that your relationship with Him is more important than life itself. David was truly repentant of his sins, and when we are truly repentant and when we continually seek His face, Satan's opportunistic ways do not have a chance to become a way of life for us. To repent is more than just being sorrowful about our behavior. To repent is being sorrowful enough that we are compelled to stop the errant behavior and if we are too weak to stop, we can never ever again feel comfortable enough in the behavior to continue it without feeling, not *guilty*, but *convicted* in our spirit until God delivers us. When we come to a place in our lives where we are truly repentant, it is impossible for us to continue to have fun in our formally sinful ways. We will sin, but there is no reason to dwell in sin and be in bondage to sin. We are under no obligation because we have sinned to leave the door open for Satan to just walk right in and set up camp. An unrepentant attitude leaves holes and opens doors that present us ripe and ready for Satan to use us for his work. These holes and open doors are portals that usher us as sheep to the slaughter into the demonic world.

The Sadducees and the Pharisees, a powerful and influential political and religious sect during biblical times, were constantly under reproach by Jesus because they were filled with pride and in a constant state of denial about their sinful nature. During those times the people looked up to these people because they were commonly accepted as a very disciplined, very wise and a very learned people. Because their view on anything was so respected, when Jesus came along spouting ideas that seemed in direct contradiction to these people, His teachings were a threat and a great danger to these people. He knew that His personal welfare was at stake because they'd rather kill him than risk their position, or alter their beliefs. Therefore many of the Sadducees and Pharisees chose to remain in denial rather than hear the essence of what Christ was saying. They were so busy looking for the loopholes in Christ's words that they couldn't see the wisdom in them. They were not like David, who when his sins were disclosed, was sorrowful and repentant toward God. He desired restoration and union with the almighty God because now, because of sin, there was a spiritual disconnect within him that needed to be reestablished. His sin, however, did not stop him; his pride did not stop him, his kingship did not stop him from desiring a right relationship with his heavenly father. The Sadducees and the Pharisees were willing to allow their intellect, their pride, and their position, to keep them in a loop that would never lead them to a relationship with God. They were learned men who were respected and revered because of their position, it was not important to them that God be pleased with them as long as their way of life remained comfortable and unchallenged. In light of this contrast between David and the Sadducees and the Pharisees it is no wonder why David, and not the learned and proper Sadducees and the Pharisees, was deemed in the bible as a man after God's heart.

If David's repentant attitude is one of the things that endeared him to God, then we can be endeared to God by having a repentant attitude. This is one of the things that keeps us cleansed of demons. We have to own up to our sins, take responsibility for what we do or what we do not do and be sorrowful enough not to continue the sin. We have to be willing to go to God to ask for forgiveness and faithful enough to know that we are forgiven. It appears that David was not a repeat offender with his sins, being sorrowful long enough to get on God's good side and then engaging in the same sin after a certain amount of time lapsed. David blamed nobody but himself because they were his decisions. They were bad decisions, they were sinful decisions, but they were his decisions. He yielded to his flesh not to the devil. Had he gone the road of denial, the devil would have used his decision to make him a weak puppet of a king, so filled with guilt and anguish that he could not fulfill God's plan for his life.

RECOGNITION TIP # 21

Recognize and acknowledge that each day is an opportunity to get to know God better.

CHAPTER 22

__Now the works of the flesh are manifest, which are these; Adultery, fornication, uncleanness, lasciviousness, Idolatry, witchcraft, hatred, variance, emulations, wrath, strife, seditions, heresies, Envyings, murders, drunkenness, revellings, and such like: of the which I tell you before, as I have also told you in time past, that they which do such things shall not inherit the kingdom of God.—Galatians 5:19-21__

We must be full of care as to what we ascribe to the devil and what a result of us yielding to the flesh is. We cannot use the devil as a scapegoat because we lack discipline over our flesh. Yes, we can and yes we should exercise discipline over our fleshly desires and God has provided us with all the help that we need in order to help us to be more victorious in the battle of the flesh. We have His Word, Jesus, the Holy Spirit, and His mighty angels to help us to gain control of our unruly flesh. Satan generally has his way with people who refuse exercise control of the flesh and believe in living for the moment. Satan doesn't make our personality or our choices but he can and does use both the personality and our choices as a means of accomplishing his plans for us.

Having discipline over the flesh is something we should learn as a child and get better at as an adult because this is one of many portals for demonic intrusion. Other examples of portals or openings are; ways of life or lifestyle choices, ways of thinking, and traumatic experiences that may have opened us up to demonic attack, invasion and infestation. Some of these avenues of intrusion we have control over, some we don't. In the movie *Poltergeist*, the portal was via an actual closet door where the poltergeists entered into the physical world from the spiritual realm. The television set was how the spirits communicated with a child. The portals that demons use to enter us are not that simple, however, the movie does address something very important, symbolically the closet represents things hidden, closed, unattended to, not confessed. The television or media represent things communicated or said to us; things taken in through our eyes and ears that are filtered through our subconscious and find their way into expression on some level in our lives. These too are portals that are commonly used by Satan to gain entrance into us, the "closet"—hidden, closed off and "television"—things seen, heard or communicated.

When Satan has succeeded in entering a portal that we have created or has been created by whatever means and for whatever reason, there are at least seven levels of demonic activity that can occur. At the seventh level of this demonic activity, which is surely demonization, there are other levels akin to opening a trap door; however, all of these levels of possessions can fall under these four categories:

HARASSMENT
AFFLICTION
DEMONIZATION
POSSESSION (soul, not spirit)

HARASSMENT

Harassment is when Satan seeks to determine where you are in your spiritual life. He wants to know where we are strong where we are weakest, and how much time and effort he must put forth in our particular case in order to gain entrance. Do not be flattered to think that you have such an anointed call on your life that he wants you personally; it may be that he's contemplating who he can affect by affecting you and you're being weighed in the balance so to speak. He's been walking to and fro, up and down in the earth seeking souls, and when he chooses you, you will be a victim of his harassment.

When Satan harasses us, he pesters us with little things that distract and annoy us to the point where we spend our time focusing on non-issues. We can never get to the meat of our lives because we are so busy dealing with the mundane, irrational, and the petty issues that demand our focus. The devil will keep throwing the most ridiculous problems at us until before we know it we are overwhelmed by nothing and too tired to focus on anything. We're too irritated to enjoy life and our thoughts are filled with checklists of distractions.

Satan can't read our minds so he has to take us through a series of temptations to see just how or even *if* he can get to us. What will we resist, what weapons will we or won't we employ, are we easy prey or will we be a problem, what are our true feelings about God, do we have faith—if so, how much? We all have been hurt, but the devil needs to know which one of our hurts, if any, can he use to destroy us? Do we in the deepest recesses of our heart blame or resent God, because if we do, that's a plus for him. While God may test us, Satan tempts us, and we must never get the two confused. God tests us to allow *us* realize where our relationship is with him, this helps us to become spiritually mature and we grow in grace when we are successful in passing these tests. God's testing allows us to stretch beyond our complacency with the usual, to higher levels of spiritual understanding. Satan tempts to confuse us and keep us from an elevated understanding of Christ by keeping us in fear and doubt about our relationship with God. He wants to tempt us into a state of confusion by confusing our thoughts so that we think that maybe our misery is God's will when it's not His will at all. Are we passive enough, spiritually uneducated enough, to believe him and not the word of God that says that we should have life, and that more abundantly? How do we deal with our problems; do we deal with them at all or do we internalize them? How's our prayer life—do we even have one or is our prayer life a series of foxhole prayers only when we're desperate or in trouble? Who do we turn to, what's the spiritual condition of our hearts? Satan has to harass us to find out what he can use and how he should go about severing or compromising our relationship with Christ who is our lifeline to God the Father and his eternal threat.

LEVEL 1

Within the category of harassment is level 1. This is the level of weird occurrences and temptations. We may encounter slew of problems. We may lose our job, find out a spouse is cheating, receive a large bill unexpectedly out of the blue, and be diagnosed with a severe illness, all in the same week! We feel like we're boxing an opponent with our arms tied behind our back. When Satan attacks us in this way, we are confounded, confused, bewildered, and off-balance—like we've entered the twilight zone. When something like this happens, we are sufficiently panicked and it is very hard not to resist the temptations and suggestions that Satan may put before us as solutions, especially in the beginning when we're desperate and still reeling from the punches.

If, however, we can get past the initial shock of the onslaught and realize that everything will work out; if we realize that the pain may be uncomfortable but that it is only temporary; and if we realize that this too shall pass and that we will be alright; the devil has nothing coming. However, if we allow the problems to go unresolved for any length of time and do not pray for direction, do not exercise faith, and do not believe that anything good could ever come out of such a situation and the pain becomes more real and intense day by day, the temptations of the devil become more and more appealing. While initially we may have had confidence in ourselves, our resolve will begin to melt under the stress and the pressure as solutions fail to manifest themselves according to our personal time table, we lose hope, drop our guard, and no longer have the will or desire to resist the devil and now he has an opening.

In harassment, the temptations that Satan seduces us with may or may not lead to anti-God activities or sin, if you will, because he is in a "getting to know us" stage. Can he use an inherited condition as a vehicle? Can he use our family members, our fears, and our doubts? Can he exploit our weaknesses, ferret out our deepest and darkest secrets and use them against us? Where are we most vulnerable? At this point he is accessing our "data base" to see what makes us tick. Will we hold on and have faith that God will prevail, or will we drop our guard and allow *him* have his way? How long can we white knuckle it before we finally give up?

After the devil has toyed with our emotions by presenting various temptations and opportunities into our life, some temptations we may have dodged but others we have taken the bait; he can now take inventory of what affects us and what does not. He hasn't begun to truly deal with us, believe it or not, at this point, he is using harassing techniques in order to find out how to deal with us effectively. While we are more concerned with the consequences of the temptation that we have succumbed to, be they good or bad; he is more concerned with our reaction to the consequences of the actions taken. If the outcome to the consequences of his temptations strikes us as positive, he will use our positive feelings about it in order to get us to buy into his scheme again. If the outcome of the consequence of the temptation is negative and we are not pleased, how do we rationalize in our minds as to why it did not turn out so well? Is it that we have done something wrong, and that's the reason for the negative outcome and it's just a matter of us being more careful; or is it that we rationalize that the reason that the outcome is negative is because we should not have done it in the first place, and the likelihood of us doing it again is slim to none.

Many of us don't like negative consequences. We spend a great deal of time lamenting over these consequences until many times we lose sight of the sinful action that led to the consequences in the first place. This is fine with the devil because he realizes the irony that the consequences of our actions many times lead us back to commit the same offense and expect that the results will no longer be negative. Satan knows better than we do that everything will manifest some type of consequence or sequence of events. A watermelon seed is planted, if anything grows at all because of that seed, it will be a watermelon, this is a natural law and a spiritual law that the devil is aware of and uses. If we become fully aware of this law, we wouldn't do half the things that we do that cause us trouble and we would do more of things that ultimately lead to positive outcomes and consequences.

When the inevitable happens and the consequences of our actions are bad, he manipulates our thoughts so that we attribute the negative outcome of our actions as the fault of others, but he would prefer that we blame God. Our resentment and malice toward God and others gives him an opportunity to milk a situation that he did not create, into something that we are no longer in control of. We have opened the doors and he has grabbed the reins. As for the *good* consequences of *bad* actions, he doesn't care who we attribute them to because this makes it easier for us to become more and more comfortable with our bad behavior and the bad behavior leads us away from God and Satan can accomplish his goal.

There are consequences of bad behavior and there are rewards of bad behavior. The consequence of bad behavior is a natural outcome, what an action would naturally render except by the grace of God. The devil, on the other hand, is the only one who rewards bad behavior! Many times people get this confused and call the devil's rewards blessings from God. The purpose of the devil's reward is to keep us off guard, until the time is ripe to disrupt our life, and hopefully disrupt our lives beyond repair. He wants to get us acclimated to living a sinful life, because he knows that one sin is not going to pull you over to his side. This "reward" that the devil has in store for us is designed to draw us away from God and ruin our lives. In order for Satan to get us to serve him rather than God, in the beginning the good consequences of bad behavior *will seem* to outweigh the bad because he has to bait the trap to make it seem as though bad behavior works. Meanwhile, he feeds our minds and grooms our thoughts until we think that his thoughts are our thoughts. He cons us into believing that the way of the world seems to work for us and "our" thoughts and actions are harmless enough. This leads us to develop trust in feelings as we become familiar and comfortable with thoughts and suggestions that are not our own but the devil's. Even so, he has not gained entry, not yet anyway! He is simply harassing our thoughts, standards, and principles.

Once he has gained entrance, the good times and fun will fade into confusion, destruction, disharmony, and tears. Before this can happen, however, we must be entrapped into a way of thinking that flip-flops back and forth up and down, in and out about the proper way to live our lives. Our thinking has to become off-balance before he can proceed further. At level 1, before he actually gains entrance; we may feel all is well and may even feel that these new thoughts and this new way of looking at things is rather freeing.

HARASSMENT LEVEL 2

This level also falls under the category of harassment. At this level we are enjoying to a large extent exciting and unfamiliar territories. We're convinced that what we do, we do because we're just having fun, not necessarily being sinful. After all, we're only human and we are not out of control, we're just having a little fun and adventure. It seems that everybody is engaging in sinful activities, and anyway, how can anybody live a chaste life and have fun? We put away the bibles, and seek other "gods" that satisfy the flesh. We put the Holy Spirit on hold and depend on our worldly knowledge, our worldly friends, and conclusions that we may draw from current events and fads to supplement any lack of knowledge or guidance that we may need. We figure that later on in life, when we're old, or when we accomplish certain goals in life, it will be more fitting for us to be part of the church, read the bible to find out what God says about everything. We figure when we're done accomplishing the things of this world, or when we are old, sin won't be a big problem. After all, how many sins can we possibly need to or would want to commit when we're eighty or have acquired worldly success! Right now, however, for this sweet moment in time, our youth is not spent, and we have things to do, people to see and worlds to conquer. Life is surely meant to be enjoyed, not suppressed!

If we're older, we figure we can live on what we've already learned in life. Our experiences, we believe, have made us wise enough to keep us out of many situations, and clever enough to get us out of practically any dilemma that we may find ourselves in. Besides, who has the time to read the bible regularly, go to church regularly? Prayer may be "doable" in a crunch, but how many prayers have I sent up already? Right now we need a break; we're tired of holding on tenuously to the invisible. Now is the time in our lives when we need to stretch out, have fun, breathe, and stop worrying, because everything is going to work out some kind of way anyway. Maybe we have been a bit too cautious all of our lives and believe that we will have more success if we are willing to give in to our deepest longings. We're at a point where we simply don't give a care how or why things work out; if it's God, fine; if it's the devil, fine; we don't want to think about it. All we know is that we've proven ourselves to be pretty responsible in the past and there's no chance that we'll jump into a cesspool of sin now; we're just sticking our big toe in. Besides, we aren't *really* sinning, we just want to take the chances that we may have missed earlier in life because of too much caution and unnecessary fears. We're like Willie Loman in *The Death of a Salesman*. We've shot our best shot and look back longingly on the "what if I had taken the chance deals."

We're lucky in a sense too because at this point when we act out of the will of God, but within the confines of what society expects or tolerates, it's looked at in a different light *because* of our age; even by people in the church. Society allows certain sins for adults when we're over the age of twenty-one that are acceptable because they are legal. Society also allows for another set of sins when we are a little further along in our lives and has even given these types of sins a label. This label waters down the fact that we are operating in sin so that the behavior seems less serious; it's called a middle aged crisis, or being "grown." Again, this is another way that Satan tricks us when we're older. Instead of running to the throne of grace, confessing and asking the Lord to help us, once again society has given us a label, an excuse, to behave in a sinful manner because we are grown and no longer young and foolish.

Because we accept the devils food, whether we are young, old, or middle aged; our perception begins to change. We are eating from the devil's table and dining with the devils children. Now it seems that everybody that we run into seems to be engage in all sorts of sinful activity with little or no adverse consequences. Again, it only *seems* this way but in reality it's not. It seems this way because it is our perception that has changed, not the world and certainly not God's word; Satan is setting us up. In this world it is logical that we run into good people and bad people at all phases of our lives. We *are* meeting people that are good; it's just that our attention is not drawn toward them to notice their goodness or to even want to be bothered with them. In the places that we go, what draws our attention, what we choose to ignore, and what we chose to give our attention to, has changed and this becomes our "reality" and it is based on our altered perceptions. No, we are not operating in a world filled with devil-may-care sinners; our attention has been diverted from what is good and wholesome to what is foolish and bad.

Any time we're engaged in sinful or negative activities, we run into people who appear to be good and people who appear to be bad. Depending on how we want to feel, we'll seek out the people who don't seem that bad to us. We seek out these "good" bad people so that we can get the thrill without feeling that we're hanging out with a bad crowd or we'll seek out people who are bad but seem powerful and in control of themselves because we want to know that power. These people operate with charm and without conscious and we want to see how it feels to operate this way. We want to be close to the action without having to be totally responsible for the action; kind of like Adam in the Garden of Eden. He's drawn to the disobedience but somehow feels less responsible for the disobedience because it wasn't his idea. How we tend to see the "goodness" or "badness" of a person is relative to our spiritual condition, where we are on our life path, and what we are looking to get out of a given situation, which in turn is related right back to our spiritual condition.

There *are* good people in bad situations just as there are bad people in good situations. There are good people in good situations and bad people in bad situations. Some situations are temporary and a learning experience, some situations are lifestyle choices that will color an individual's life for a very long time, maybe even until it ends. How individuals become a part of our life is in part, based on our perception; our spirit has to be receptive for anyone to becoming a major player in our lives; a major point to remember! This is a spiritual law, and it is because of this spiritual law something or someone that is attractive to us at one stage in our life may hold no value whatsoever at another stage of our life.

As human beings we are constantly changing and evolving within ourselves even our very cells. Every cell in our body regenerates itself, this changes us physically. Who we are at age sixteen, as far as regenerated cells go, is not who we are at age thirty-five. Factor in our personal experiences, and this changes us mentally. Spiritually, we are constantly open to change whether for good or evil. It is this part of our nature that the devil uses to influence our minds and cloud our perception as to what our experiences mean. While God may allow bad, negative and unfortunate situations to strengthen us; Satan's goal is to get us to react in negative and unholy ways that will surely to weaken us. We all have had experiences in which we unfortunately must endure pain, rejection, poverty (whether financial or emotional), loss of a loved one, and our own impending death, are unpleasant experiences that must be endured. Satan hopes to use such common experiences of life to produce long-lasting negative emotions like anger, hate, frustration, dissatisfaction, bitterness and fear. Prolonged negative emotions such as these are a breeding ground for demons so we must be attentive to how our emotions have affected us and how they now affect us.

At level 2, Satan uses demonically controlled people, strategically placed, to entice us into his web of deception and mayhem. In order for these people to be successful, however, we must be receptive to them; our emotional state must be in agreement with them. Satan is a con artist, and a con artist must have some idea of human nature in order for his scheme to work. He knows that we were made in the image of God but we have a sinful nature; therefore he must watch us to learn what it is that he must do to gain a certain individual's confidence.

I had to understand that he was using the love that I have for my spouse to get me to react in a negative fashion to a particular situation that we were going through, which I did. I know that it was not how God would have wanted me to respond to him, regardless of how I felt, but I was tired and frustrated and all of this tumbled out unrestrained. I felt very uncomfortable with my reaction because I felt that this meant that things would get worse and there was not hope and wanted to leave my marriage, not because the situation was so hopeless, but because I felt that I was losing control and I so wanted to feel that God and I had a handle on the situation. Because I blew my top, I thought that maybe I was just fooling myself and God wasn't in this at all. I found myself fantasizing about how much easier it would be for me to live a life free from the emotional challenges that come with marriage, how I could deal with God, pray, and love on God unencumbered by this MAN!. This was good until the Holy Spirit pulled my coattail and I recognized it for what it really was: Satan. The Holy Spirit showed me that everything that was placed in my mind that I should do was negative and against biblical principles, not to mention immature. Not one thing of a positive nature was dropped into my mind, another clue that I had allowed the enemy to take control of the wheel. I also recognized that he was using the part of my nature that I had perfected as a means of protection since childhood, the ability to tune out emotionally if I had to, to entice me into making a bad decision by covering it up with a desire to praise God with no problems.

Many of us have something that we do and have been doing since childhood that brought us relief and comfort and we tend to lapse into whatever it is in order to feel safe. What most of us learned to do, however, was more than likely not the best thing to do, but we worked it as best we could and the older we got, the more comfortable we became with doing it whether it solved a problem or not, it was just comfortable and familiar. The problem with this is that when we depend on these things it is very unhealthy and we come to depend on us and our tactics, and leave God out of the picture, not because of lack of reverence for the almighty but because of habit.

There is a man I know who is notorious for saying, "I've always been this way." He says it often and with pride and dignity. Of course I want to say, "Then you should know better by now because it's not working!" Who needs to have always been some way? Most of us need to change if for no other reason than that a grown man should not behave exactly as he did when he was fourteen years old. Change is inevitable and when we try to stifle it, prevent it, or avoid it—Satan will ultimately use this to keep us stagnated. I've seen churches with this problem, businesses with this problem, and cultures with this problem. Change is necessary for growth and nothing changes without **moving** from one stage to another.

God tells us when to hold on and when to let go. The Holy Spirit moves us to change for the better. If we insist on remaining the same, God cannot work with us or through us, but Satan can. If we are stagnant, more than likely we are sitting on a fence. Unfortunately we are not partial to God or hearing what the Holy Spirit has to say about our lives. We are not getting our rightful blessings and nothing significant can happen in our lives as long as we hold to this position. The devil, however, will send his people right to your fence, not to talk you down but to convince you that you are better off staying right where you are. The devil will convince us to stay with what we know, even if what we know is bad for us or doesn't amount to a hill of beans.

When we're in this state, the enemy is so cunning that we are changing whether we know it or not, we are deteriorating and dying and he wants to make sure that no one comes along to tip us off. Satan will place a particular demonically controlled person in our circle to form friendships with those of us who are on the fence. The whole job of this person is to make sure that you do not get any better. Beware of these people who try to convince you that the fence is comfortable every time you express a desire to make an improvement.

I know a woman who never fails to run into people who convince her that what she has is just fine. People come along and give her exactly what she needs for the moment and she is grateful and thankful, but what I find interesting about the whole situation is that every time she makes a move to better herself in some way, these "blessings" just pop up out of the blue and before she knows it, she has made very little progress in living a life of success and independence. She has come to depend more and more on these "blessings" and less and less on playing a part in her financial and spiritual independence. Her spiritual life exists but it is easily derailed and she often finds herself not engaging at all in spiritual things for long periods of time because when she begins to make progress in developing a relationship with Christ, someone will come along and "give" her advice that challenges the validity of her spiritual walk. Satan has strategically placed people in her life so that she will not change. BUT, in order for this to be successful, something inside of her must buy into it because this cannot happen any other way; this is spiritual law.

We have to be comfortable enough let down our guard before Satan can move us to the next level, level 3.

HARASSMENT LEVEL 3

Level 3 is filled with confusion and disorder as well as various levels of engagement in sinful activities. At level 2, this environment is not yet stabilized enough for demons to inhabit. Here, at level 3, demons may only "visit" because the individual has made no decision to accept his unholy activity as a way of life; they are merely experimenting or dabbling in forbidden territory. Because of the resurrection, and the blood of Jesus, this is not qualifying enough to destroy our lives; it's merely part of our imperfection and freedom to choose.

When we dabble and experiment in sinful activity, however, we must be aware that Satan is in the mix and he is working on recruiting us through the activity or through that we may be involved with. We have given him permission just by virtue of us being involved in sin, to enter as a player in our lives. Now demons have permission to "visit" us during our sinful engagements. No, we won't necessarily physically die, although we could for by engaging in sinful activity we certainly put ourselves at great risk because of the dangers that are inherently involved with the activity. Sin, however, does not have the power in and of itself to destroy us even if we are not aware of the resurrection and have not accepted Jesus Christ as our Lord and Savior. If this were the case, there would be no people left and I would not be writing this book! The bible speaks of the wages of sin and the wages of sin is death. What sin pays at the end of the day is death but we do not die because of sin, we "die" because the wages of sin is death. A lot of people do not want to accept this, but what we all need to realize is that each and every day that we are allowed to experience one moment of joy, no matter how fleeting, it's by the mercy of the Almighty Himself and not because we are without sin.

There are consequences and repercussions for all of our decisions. There are even consequences for honest mistakes that we have made, but Jesus will never reject us if we come to him at any stage in our spiritual development, or lack thereof for that matter. All we have to do is believe that Jesus died for us, confess our sins and repent to receive forgiveness. According to the Word of God, this is all it takes for us to receive forgiveness; ask according to His Word, and we receive according to His Word but we have the hardest time accepting the simplicity of this. At level 2 we are still cognizant and our soul has not been severely compromised; at level 3 we are well on our way to affliction.

AFFLICTION

The demonically afflicted are in a very confused state of mind, regardless of whether they appear highly agitated or as cool as a cucumber on the outside. They cannot think clearly and it feels as if a constant battle is going on in their heads. They cannot understand why they have such a difficult time harnessing their thoughts and headaches are very common with affliction. Eventually, as they progress, the ability to grasp concepts, make proper decisions, exercise self-control and problem solve become more and more difficult which can be very frustrating and very tiring for an individual. Affliction is designed to move us deeper into the devil's territory by pounding down our walls and crashing through barriers that separate good from evil. Satan comes to steal, kill, and destroy and these are the demons afflicting our souls by stealing and confusing our thoughts, killing our hopes, and destroying our dreams. To excel at anything is difficult if not impossible at this point. We are sometimes able to experience glimpses of genius, but nothing of sustained profundity. If there is genius at this point, it's very specific, and anything outside of that genius is chaos. God gives us gifts that the devil cannot take away, but he can convince us not to love the gift, not to embrace the gift, not to nurture the gift, and not to use the gift. Since the devil has no power over what God gives us, he has to exercise his powers in the best way that he can by convincing us that what God has given us is either useless or that it is not a gift at all.

The goal of these demons is to have us not to think at all. Man was made to think; to exist without thinking is to live impulsively without reflection, direction, or consideration. This is contrary to how God would want us to live! How do I know? Because he gave us free will and in order to experience free will one has to be able to think in order to make choices. If the devil can cloud our mind and distort our judgment, he will be successful and the demons will be able to enter into an environment where they can thrive and grow. My oldest brother, who is a preacher, is fond of saying, "We thank you, Lord, for waking us up in our right mind. Someone didn't wake up in their right mind this morning!"

At the point of affliction our souls are at war with the devil. Some souls may be physically afflicted with illness or their bodies do not obey the signals that the brain may be sending it. A person may appear to be out of control and unable to control impulses. Some cannot control their tongue and things fly out of their mouths that would have been better left an unexpressed thought. Sometimes in this condition, a thought doesn't register at all, but the words come out, seemingly out of nowhere. Physical affliction may also come in the form of a disorder or illness. It may be serious but it doesn't have to be. The disorder or illness seems to have no rhyme or reason for its existence, yet it's there as a hindrance in our everyday life.

Demons afflict us to make us doubt our strengths, paralyze our actions, or at least frustrate our attempts to live a holy life. If we are frustrated enough, we will accept these afflictions as a way of life. "I guess I was never meant to have a husband/wife." "Maybe I was never meant to be successful and I'm beating a dead horse." "I can't do anything right!" "I'm so accident prone!"

"Nobody likes me, but I don't care." "I'm always sick with something, and the doctors can never find anything wrong with me!" These are only some of the hundreds of thoughts that provoke the mind of the afflicted.

Those of us who are afflicted are doomed to live very shallow and unproductive lives. We will find ourselves unhappy and unfulfilled in our lives regardless of what blessings we have because we fail to see the significance of it all. The few blessings that we manage to see are easily attributed to something that *we* did or because of something that *we refused* to do and not at all to the sovereign power of God our Father. To be afflicted is to be caught in a vicious circle of thoughts and visions that may make their way through the haze and yield nothing. It's difficult if not impossible to plant seeds because it's hard to recognize the seeds and if they are recognized, we may look at them and think they are worthless. The demonically afflicted have a difficult time with success in life whether personal, financial, or emotional.

Souls who are demonically afflicted are very easily hurt or angered because Satan's demons have their souls off balance and have managed to focus their attention on the darkness instead of the light. Every human being can be hurt, because we are designed with emotions; this is part of our fleshly nature, but when we get to the point of sorrow and hurt as an everyday occurrence, demonization should be considered as the cause. Some experience righteous indignation on a daily basis because of this type of affliction and there is nothing holy or righteous about it because this is anger along with negative emotions that have been nursed or left to fester. This negative energy is truly *energy* and energy is active; it has force. The force of this energy will push its way out into the atmosphere being expelled from the body yet hover around the body. Negative energy has negative effects when expelled and somebody is going to get hurt, whether it is the afflicted person or an innocent bystander. The problem with negativity in life is that it begins in generalities but eventually takes on a life of its own in specifics. The hate list of the afflicted grows to include short people, tall people, men, women, teens, kids, people with brown eyes, people with blue eyes, people who wear red, people who wear hats.... This presents a problem because as this list grows constitutionally, there is an unwillingness to fully engage in the life that God has given them because they are so preoccupied with hate. Of course such people have problems feeling positive and vital. They cannot have genuine affection toward anyone, including themselves! Why would they?

The afflicted cannot stand to be accused because of all of the accusations that they are experiencing within. To have the accusing voice of the demons along with the accusing voice of someone standing before them is too much to bear and it's not uncommon for these people to "snap" or throw a tantrum when confronted about something that seems to tarnish their character or question their self-worth, especially if it's true! In those who are not afflicted, such confrontation and accusation may cause sadness, a desire to correct or explain ourselves, and even anger, but our reactions are in response to what is said to us by someone on the outside, not a response to a chorus of torments and accusations that we are experiencing on the inside.

Genuine affection toward others decreases proportionally to our demonic affliction and intolerance for others begins to spread like a cancer. The afflicted soul is at war with himself and everyone around him. The list of people that have done them wrong increases and many times they may find a person or group of people to be extra nice to, just so that they feel justified. If they can be nice to some people and they like them, they can't be all that bad. The demonically afflicted must find a person that sees them in a way that is above average.

It's hard for the afflicted to be satisfied with life itself. In the eyes of the afflicted there are very few people who deserve the life that they have if it is good, and if it is bad, they feel that the people deserve it and have a hard time feeling compassion for them. In the eyes of theses afflicted souls, everybody else has a problem, not them. Everyone is against them at some point and/or trying to control them in other instances. They feel this way at first about one, then maybe two or three people. Then the feeling of intolerance and paranoia cannot help but spread and their social circle of friends and associates get smaller and smaller right along with their views on life.

AFFLICTION LEVEL 2

When we creep into the second stage of affliction, the cancer begins to spread beyond people who are familiar to us to other areas of our life and on to groups of peoples, cultures, and nations. We start to feel disdain for perfect strangers based on any obscure reason that we can come up with. This cancer at some point will eventually evolve into a pessimistic attitude fueled by the voices of the demons. The demons are whispering in our ears and we believe it is the voice of reason within, leading us and guiding us to do what is right. At this stage we may resist the voice to some extent because we have not developed the courage to act on these unfamiliar thoughts and feelings.

The devil is using negative thoughts, feelings and emotions to gain a more secure foothold. There are mixed feelings about many things and we may try different tactics to see what type of reaction we will get. In this stage of affliction we will target a loved one or someone close to us to release our anger against to test the powers that our new thought process promises will bring us relief. This allows us to be safe enough to see if it can work as we to try it on for size because it is perpetrated against someone that we know without a doubt, loves us. The demons use our volatile emotions as trip wires to release thoughts that are evil and/or combative in nature. These thoughts are filled with hate and rage that do not come from us, but from the demons as they try to remove any support system that we may have in jeopardizing their mission to deceive us. What they are attempting to do is to remove the first line of defense that we have against attack, our loved ones, by making them feel helpless or disgusted as we unload our garbage all over them or by driving us angered and embittered away from our support system by bombarding us with thoughts that are false but powerful.

A little further along on this scale is a person who needs to make all of the decisions regarding a situation and is uncomfortable or disturbed with anyone else who would dare come up with a suggestion or opinion. They can be prone to an excessive amount of energy needing little sleep or rest, yet, they'll refuse to expend the energy that it would take in to get past the roadblock of this affliction because it is too overwhelming and exhausting a task to undertake. They feel this excess energy in their bodies and know that it must be expelled so they exhaust their energy on either meaningless tasks and busyness or taking over other peoples' lives. They are distracted with the mundane and the negative in life and if asked to do something worthwhile and positive, like attending to spiritual things, they are not necessarily disagreeable, but the likelihood that they actually will actually follow through is slim to none. I guess it can be summed up that these people are operating in the darkness and lack the fortitude to turn on the light. They'd rather spend the time and energy trying to light a candle with a wet book of matches than doing what it takes to turn on a light. They are busy accomplishing nothing.

AFFLICTION 3

We can be sure we are demonically afflicted when we have an unforgiving spirit. Satan would not like us to let go of anger and resentment, but to hold onto it forever if possible. This is the third state of affliction which may not look as bad as the first two stages, but in reality it is the most dangerous because we have shut doors and made up our minds. Once we have made up our minds to let evil reign by being unforgiving, angry, bitter, resentful and mean-spirited, Satan has permission to do what he does best—use our body and soul for his evil deeds. He'll use this as fuel along with our anger, resentment, and our fears to create strongholds in our lives while he uses our minds to concoct various notions and ideas that foster hatred, disconnection, depression, revenge or even an emotional paralysis. As long as he can keep us in an unforgiving state about anything in our lives, he knows that it has a trickle-down effect. The less we forgive the harder it is for us *to* forgive, and the more likely it is that we will develop an unforgiving spirit and THAT he can work with! If we harbor an unforgiving spirit we can never embrace and understand the awesome forgiving nature of God the Father through His son Jesus Christ; this allows for spiritual disconnection and an obvious portal for demonic activity.

Satan uses affliction to wage a soul war to wear us down and discourage us in key areas of our lives, but believe it or not, there is an upside to such an attack. The very area of our affliction and attack probably holds the key to unlocking our life's mission and purpose. You see, Satan afflicts us to make sure that we ignore the things within our personality that are key to our destiny. If key areas are undeveloped or underdeveloped, Satan wants to make sure, through affliction, that these areas remain so. He knows that, in terms of yielding high dividends in the spirit realm, should we be successful in overcoming him and developing these areas of our personality, there is the threat that we will become the person that God has put us here to become, which of course he does not want us to become. If we can only remember that the areas in which or lives are plagued with afflictions *are* indications of the very areas wherein much of our strength lies, we can use how the devil afflicts us to actually achieve success in life.

For example, considering Satan's job description and his very nature, why would he waste what little time he has badgering us about something that will never amount to anything anyway? He doesn't want us to amount to anything, and if we're on the path to destruction anyway, why bother going through the motions to destroy something that we ourselves are proving quite capable of destroying on our own? He needs to afflict us in areas that are significant to us as individuals created by God to do His work. He attempts to separate us from the love of Christ or at least bow down before him and serve him as we are meant to serve the only true and living God. Satan knows that we cannot serve two gods, for we will either love the one and hate the other or go crazy! A house divided surely falls. God the Father and Satan have two separate agendas for our lives. One is toward love, peace, atonement, and an abundant life in Christ; the other fosters divisiveness, confusion, destruction and death.

Why would Satan use his minions to tamper with the thought process of an individual who is not naturally equipped to be a deep thinker? Why would he afflict someone who has no interest in athletics and who is not athletically inclined to doubt his athletic abilities to hinder their performance level? Why would he orchestrate writer's block for those who are not writers, or try to squash the artistic talents of someone who is not artistically inclined?

If you're being afflicted, you may find it almost impossible to get it together in a specific area in your life, more so than other areas. While we may have problems in many areas of our life, a specific area is more problematic, ongoing and a constant struggle. This specific area feels like we are trying to scale a brick wall of impossible heights, like we have been given a task that is impossible, but guess what? Our destiny is more than likely behind that wall or those barriers! Our personal promised land can never be attained if we cannot get beyond that wall and yet another lie that the devil perpetuates! We are *designed* to get past the wall and the only reason this wall is allowed to exist in the first place is to develop our muscles and increase our knowledge and understanding about what it takes to live in our respective promised lands. It is there to remind us that in order to get over obstacles and break down barriers, we must defer to the Father in the name of Jesus and allow Him to instruct us on what tools we need to use to become conquerors, and over comers in Jesus' name. We must be willing participants in tearing down theses walls in order for God to accomplish His work through us because even as we walk with God in overcoming the walls in our lives, Satan is busy looking for reason and opportunity to rebuild the walls to weary us. It is up to us to not allow our thoughts and our actions to give the devil a reason or an opportunity by being diligent with our walk.

Wherever you are afflicted, you will be sure to find that the area does not remain isolated and confined. The one area of affliction *will* by its nature affect other areas of your life. Affliction is designed to keep us diffused and confused for a vast portion of our lives; at least long enough so that we never accomplish our goals or have a wholesome relationship with Christ. The devil knows the importance of our relationship with Christ as we battle the many arrows that the devil flings our way. It's his way of keeping us confined to a way of thinking and a way of being that will not allow us to be able to receive what God has placed before us. It is a way to blind us to the obvious by keeping us distracted with the petty and insignificant. The devil constantly attacks our self-esteem because it is so vulnerable. If our esteem is high, the thoughts that he places in our minds may move us from egotistic to megalomania. Where our self-esteem may be low, the devil may move us from shy and withdrawn to becoming victimized and suicidal.

If we come to understand that where people are moved to compliment us, consult with us, or admire us, we will come to understand that these are the very tools which God has gifted us with in order for us to fulfill our destiny in Him. Obviously, if this is the case, these very things will be points of attack that Satan will use to place fear, doubt, insecurity, and adversity within us. When Jesus is attacked in the bible, in every case, it is initiated because there is a threat of breaking barriers that the enemy has constructed to conceal the truth or to hinder his progress toward his destiny as savior of the world. These biblical instances of Jesus being harassed, attacked, and ridiculed, illustrate that it is in this way that Satan attacks us to hinder our progress. Satan loves to kill our desire for our true destiny in Christ. He wants us to reject God's plan for us and anything else that he has to offer that would lead us toward salvation. When we find ourselves rejecting our gifts, rebelling against our finer points, not utilizing what is good and at hand, the enemy is at work in us. Satan does not want us to discover the keys within us that would allow us to discover our destiny specifically because he has nothing to gain and not only does he lose a soul, he loses all of the souls that we are destined to draw to Christ through our obedience so that their destinies are fulfilled also.

If we are at the point where we think that there is no point in living, and feel that our occupation of this earthly plane is without merit, this is an attack and should be considered as such. We should not be ashamed to seek help! There are sincere spiritual leaders who can help. We must be determined and ask God to lead us to those who can help us. There's no sense in wasting time by allowing Satan to have his way and bombard us with shameless detours and distractions in and effort to steal our birthright.

AFFLICTION LEVEL 4

There is a war going on for your soul. At this level we have moved to dalliances and experimentation. Now, not only has the portal been opened, but we have no desire to confess, repent, or ask forgiveness for anything that we are engaged in. We have given our consent by willingly and readily engaging in anti-God activities. We have accepted the negative and it just doesn't seem that bad from where we stand. We do not realize that have immersed ourselves *in* the lifestyle, we're no longer just seeing what it's like. To us we're doing nothing wrong, or it's just not that serious. If someone has something negative to say about our behavior, we look at them as a nuisance, boring or out of the loop because there's nothing to worry about. We count those concerned with our well-being as unknowledgeable and controlling. After all we're engaged in certain activities and so far, lightning and thunderbolts haven't come crashing down; we haven't experienced the wrath of God and our lives have not fallen apart; as a matter of fact it's relaxing not having so many hang-ups.

Somewhere along the line in this stage, we've learned to ignore any conviction we feel in our heart. Our anti-God activities have become so routine that we no longer feel conviction, and if we do, we've learned to label it as something else or even worse, we've become experts at squashing the feeling as we would an irritating gnat as soon as it tries to surface. We'll pick up a phone, turn on the television, throw in a movie, and turn on the stereo, anything to squash that feeling until we can feel it no more. Eventually the power of conviction that we feel gradually diminishes and we no longer play a part in exercising control of our thoughts and actions. As we learn to ignore the Holy Spirit, we become involved in physically and mentally destructive behaviors that take us deeper into the abyss of Satan's lair. At this level we are engaging in two activities: squashing and ignoring. We must do either one or the other to deal with the cacophony of thoughts that surge through our brains. This is a very dangerous state and definitely fertile ground for demons to sink their claws in and prepare for long-term dwelling.

AFFLICTION LEVEL 5

If we reach this level, we may have already encountered a harassing spirit or two, if not at level 4 of affliction at level 5 we surely will. These spirits may have no dwelling place within a body but they come around like vultures to rotting flesh. Just like scavenging birds, they circle those who are spiritually dying hoping that they do not find their way to safety hoping that help does not find it's way and they can commence to devour their prey.

These demons now harass their victims in different ways. Voices incite a rebellious attitude; they instill fear, discouragement, and hopelessness. Spirits may even manifest themselves and follow or hang around us, impersonating guardian angels or helpers. The demons may even take on the form of ghostly apparitions or doppelgangers that we just miss out of the corner of our eye. These harassing spirits may hop in and out of people at levels three and higher to talk to us, convince us to do things or think a certain way in order to seal the deal. At this point, we may see people, total strangers, who look familiar to us, we don't know them in a personal way, and yet we are familiar with something about them that we have seen over and over again. They have the same expressions as other total strangers and we may wonder what it's all about. At times, when looking in the mirror, we may see in our own reflection someone else who has that very same look or expression, looking back at us; if only for a fleeting moment. We may see dead people walking around, "ghosts," or be victims of "poltergeist" activity.

At this stage, some of us we may even experience powers to the amazement of ourselves or others. Unlike earlier levels, our ability to do and perform everyday or specific activities may be enhanced, we may actually feel more capable, more spiritual, and may be given knowledge of the spiritual-supernatural sort. These powers and special gifts are to encourage our confidence by feeding our ego so that we have no desire to seek help.(This is a very important distinction because God does not feed our ego, he touches our spirit.) Our ability to spot threats to our survival, spiritually and physically may be uncanny. It's unbelievable how much we know and at times and we delight in the fact that people who mean us harm, may be frightened off because they feel such a powerful presence surrounding us. The presence of course, is the presence of evil! We feel like we're on top of the world and nothing is impossible. We don't really need people, they need us! At this point it is easy for us to believe that the sky's the limit!

There's one thing about these weird occurrences however; there is a feeling that someone is watching us, following us, or listening to our conversation at times. We have a sense of restlessness and a fear that death is breathing its foul breath down our back. We have a sense that evil is all round us, watching and waiting and that we must be on guard against something that is intangible. There are the strange mood swings; one day social, the next day everybody and everything grates our nerves to the very core. One day we're bold and antagonistic, the next frightened uncertain and meek. We do not want to be alone because the feelings that we experience when we are alone are almost too much to bear. Our ability to relax and enjoy life is almost non existent although most people who know us would never believe it to be so. If we are able to get a few hours sleep, that's as much relaxation as we get—except for the nightmares. Oh yes, silence is definitely not golden because we never know what is lurking within that silence and to be totally alone is torture. We keep the television or radio on if we are not around people to distract us from our very own thoughts, or to drown out the "noise" in our brain. One of the methods that we use to combat these eerie and uncomfortable feelings is to have our ear constantly pressed to the phone in constant conversation or in surrounding ourselves with bodies, trying to feel safe from *something*.

There is a dichotomy going on in and around us; we feel both powerful and vulnerable. We are desperate to control the people and situations around us because only in this control can we feel some type of leverage however misguided. Like a wayward child, we must have our way or the violators will pay! People must give us what we want or we obsess until we figure out how to manipulate the situation in our favor. If this does not work, we will gain control of the situation even if we have to use force or destroy the good name and reputation of others to do it. It's all about us and what we want. As a matter of fact it's not unthinkable that we are willing not only to hurt others to get what we want, we are just as willing to hurt ourselves to get what we want! We'll do what we have to do to feel in control because only at times like this, do we feel *any* control in our *out* of control lives.

At this stage of affliction, there is a price that people who love, admire, or feel close to us to must pay. That price is that they will most likely be the recipient of our bad behavior, and the target of much of our evil. Those who venture into our orbit will be hurt mentally, emotionally, spiritually, and even physically sometimes. Our loved ones are on the front lines in our personal war as we relinquish control to the enemy. As we desperately and grandiosely unleash our pain, hurt, dissatisfaction, and evil thoughts along with our violent and destructive behavior, those who truly care about us will not be spared. A total stranger will fare better at this stage of the devil's activity, in fact; the closer you are to us the harder you will be hit!

What is interesting about this phenomenon is that unless you are spiritual, you will not be aware that you are in the midst of a spiritual battle. If you are not in tune and educated on spiritual things, you'll take it personally and do exactly what the devil will have you do—not be bothered. Nobody wants to be disrespected and abused, so many give the devil what he wants without even thinking about what they are doing. If you love someone, however, you should not give up on them in the midst of this warfare. Even if you do not consider yourself a Christian, try to learn the right thing to do and do your best to do it, but don't give up. Not giving up is not putting up with negative and harmful activity and behavior; not giving up is to constantly believe the best for the person, even if you come to the conclusion that you can no longer be around the person. Keeping the person in your thoughts and in your prayers is a form of not giving up on a person. Believing more for that person than they can believe for themselves is also a form of not giving up. Having a forgiving attitude and a space in your heart for the person, is not giving up on the person that you love, even if it has to be done at a distance.

AFFLICTION LEVEL 6
DEMONIZATION

At this level, if this thing is not nipped in the bud, you'll experience level 6 of affliction which is also the first stage of demonization. At this level, temptation has become harassment, harassment has become sin, and sin has become a way of life. When sin becomes a way of life, then a lifestyle choice has been made. An acceptance has been made and we have decided to embrace the lifestyle. We have consented and decided that the lifestyle that Satan has manipulated us into having because of our anti-God attitude and bad choices is acceptable to us. We are no longer back and forth in our thinking of what is right and what is wrong. We may not have decided to what extent we actually want to take the sinful behavior, but we are definitely in agreement with it because our lives have finally changed. We have justified and rationalized our behavior and accomplishments. Some of us get fame, fortune, the guy or girl we want, a strong career, knowledge and power. It's refreshing not to feel so weak and powerless anymore. Finally, we have something that sets us apart, that makes us special and we are no longer average or below average. We can let down our guard and be whatever we want, have whatever we want, and not feel the aggravation of guilt and shame. We are no longer back and forth, up and down. We have "power" and we feel fearless—at least most of the time we feel fearless.

Remember, Satan's abilities are only effective because of the choices *we* make. God gives us this freedom to make such choices so that we may worship and honor him of our own free will. We do have a choice, and one of them is to reject God if we wish to do so, and this is the choice that the enemy wants us to make. If we make the choice to reject what God is offering us, the enemy wants to use that choice to move us into his camp where all choices are designed by him to shackle and destroy. His desire is to possess your will and leave you with the feeling that you have little or no choices in life, however, regardless of what the devil may say, we do have a choice and the choice is as simple and as uncomplicated as: Whom will you serve, God or the devil? Once we have made the choice in any particular area or areas in our life, be it good and wholesome or unwise and ungodly, *we* have opened ourselves up to the consequences of *our* choice. When we make a choice, we make a choice to be, do, act, live, and think in such a way that is conducive to our choice and by the time we reach level 6, we have made a choice not to serve God. Satan is playing a major role in our lives. Now, we're wide open for demonization.

The choice has been made to accept a sinful life, regardless of what led us to accept this sinful life. At this point the soil is ripe for demonic infestation with the possibility of possession of the soul. At this level the demons have rightful access. Which demons will actually have the staying power to reside within us for long periods of time is the only question that remains. We are, because of our lifestyle of sin and our refusal to accept Jesus Christ as our Lord and Savior, opened up sufficiently to be infested with demons. As I said earlier, in the beginning it feels like we're being blessed because the "powers" and "gifts" that we have work well, but we are still at the 6th level or affliction and the first level of true demonization, but we are inexperienced. We're learning what works and what does not work and how to use this new form of energy. At times it's great but then there's the slow and steady decline into depravity and our very humanity is at stake.

Whatever is gained via this evil and wicked behavior is touted as a blessing to anyone who will listen. The question that begs to be asked is why God would bless sinful behavior. That in itself goes against Him and again, a house divided cannot stand. Yet someone is "blessing" these people and according to God's spiritual laws, there is no way it's Him. There is the matter of God's permissive will, but His permissive will is His permissive will and not a blessing. Granted, God may allow the wicked to lay up treasures for the just, but it does not seem that He is necessarily the one who provides the treasures that they lay up; these are ill-gotten goods He has allowed this through His permissive will. These are not gifts or blessings from God.

Regardless of the treasures that we may or may not have at this level, in some area of our lives we are living in a morally depraved condition. We put a lot of effort into hiding this part of ourselves. We can rationalize these new behaviors in the weirdest ways; we either give up caring about what others may think or we fancy ourselves smarter or having a keener insight than the average person. We could teach a lot of people at lot of things *if* they were as spiritually astute as were are. There are many secrets in the lives of these people, a clear indicator that something is amiss. Sure, there is a certain a privacy of life that we all should enjoy, and then there are secrets that help perpetuate and seal our bondage to Satan.

Of course, at this level there is still room for repentance; some people will—some people won't. Again, this stage of demon infestation is very attractive because of the sense of freedom and power it brings with it. Some may be frightened by it all and realize that they are sinking fast and these people will run to some type of program, institution, organization, or church for help. At this point, anything other than Jesus will only keep the demons at bay for periods of time for it has moved beyond being a social problem and has now become a spiritual problem. As long as the demons haven't infested, nonspiritual help may work to strengthen our resolve to be a good person and make better choices; good choices versus evil choices. It is the consistency of these evil choices that lead to demonic infestation. However, even if we try to consistently make better choices, this will prove to be a huge exercise in just how flawed our humanity really is. You see, we are human and our judgment is not perfect. We may be able to make better decisions and stop the behavior for a time, but these things will not save us from Satan because he is always on the lookout for opportunity. There will be a substitutes to replace errant behavior which in due time yields Satan the very same opportunities to continue his quest for our destruction. If we are not diligent in our spiritual warfare, Satan will continue to gain ground via our very ignorance. As we become immersed in his world of sin, there is no renewing of the mind, confession, and acceptance of Christ as savior because sin has a way of blinding us to the truth of what is right and what is wrong. We can get so caught up that whatever it is that we are involved in feels normal; how scary is that?

Nothing on this earth can **defeat** Satan except the blood of Jesus; any other method does not work. If for a time it seems that we've escaped him by using another method, let me assure you that what has happened is that we've been merely placed on hold until he figures out what method he can use to gain control and hold us hostage. When we are at a point where we embrace a lifestyle of sin, direct or implied, demons have our consent to take up residence within us.

DEMONIZATION LEVEL 2

At this level, we are experiencing demonization. We have given our consent because of our lifestyle and choices we have made. We have opened the door and the demons are now using our mind as a dwelling place. We are free-falling into diverse anti-God activities, thought patterns, and belief systems. There are secrets and perversions in our lives that have control over us and if we desire control over our own lives it is not forthcoming; the control that we might gain yields nothing or negativity for our struggles. All of our religious or spiritual activities are monitored down to a science by the demons so that we do not accept Jesus Christ as the son of God and our savior where it counts, in our minds and in our hearts. Sure, we can participate in such activities as being a bench member, singing in the choir, or playing instruments for the church but there is always an invisible barrier, a wall, that is very real. We can see through the wall, but we cannot overcome the adversary who stands guard at the wall because our defenses are weak and have been compromised voluntarily by us. The devil has a tenuous position and will not be easily shaken; he will do whatever it takes so that this barrier remains. He will destroy families, reputations, careers, finances, and ultimately our very souls in order to keep us on the other side of that wall.

At this level we might go to church, or we might not go to church. Regardless, it's not for the right reasons that we do go. At this level we may go because we hold a particular position of authority that the devil is using for his purpose. We may go church to defame the preacher, spread gossip, get a woman or man, or to put up a front so that it takes people longer to catch on to our demonized condition. Sometimes it is torturous for us to go in this demonized condition, and if we could get away with not going to church, we wouldn't go, but because it may give others a clue that something is amiss, we continue to go. We can espouse any reason as to why we continue to go to church, but if we were to be honest, which many times we can't, it **won't** be for the pure sweet worship of Christ.

The name Satan means adversary. He is portrayed in the bible as the chief antagonist of God and man. He is also known as the devil and Apollyon which is the Hebrew form of Abaddon, meaning destruction or destroyer. He's known as Beelzebub, lord of the exalted abode or lord of the manure pile and Lucifer—more so during the earlier years before his eviction from heaven—which means being or angel of light. Belial is another of Satan's names and that means worthlessness. Other names which he is known by are pretty self-explanatory: the evil one, the father of lies, god of this world, prince of the power of the air, prince of the world, the tempter, the serpent and so on. All of these names represent his nature.

If the devil is in control, you will undoubtedly be deceived and begin to take on various aspects of his nature as his aforementioned names suggest. Satan wants you to think that you have *his* nature and have no choice in several matters in your life because *it's a part of your nature*. When we feel worthless, this is Satan's nature. God did not design us as worthless human beings. To feel worthless even on our worst day is not of God. To feel sad is one thing, to feel discouraged is another thing. To feel defeated is not the same thing as feeling worthless. When we feel that we have no worth, we are not only convinced that we lack viable choices but that we are incapable of making proper choices, and the more Satan can convince us of this, the less control we have as it becomes more and more difficult to exercise our free will. Eventually we succumb to the nature of the devil if something is not done to put the brakes on this downhill slide. When this happens, Satan gains the ground he needs to ruin a life.

It is now that the devil has gained direct access to our soul, and now that Satan has gained entry; there is much turmoil within. There is power, but our free will is compromised. There is no peace because demons tend to be very vociferous and demanding. There is a feeling of isolation and loneliness even in the biggest crowds because the spirit of joy and peace has been compromised and many times all but extinguished. There may be a type of paralysis that occurs where we stop striving and growing or there may be constant activity that looks like fun, happiness, and success; but true to the nature of Satan, it is counterfeit, there is no true joy when he enters the picture. Demons may have us believing that material things are what will protect us from the bad things that happen in life. He will have us think that immoral behavior is the key to not getting hurt because sin requires no self-control and the heart is not involved. We're convinced that many people would want to live this way because it is the nature of man to fantasize about living without boundaries and a nagging conscience. When we're in this state, we're close to living out this lurid fantasy and if only people were as courageous and as willing as we are to step into his world of nefarious and apathetic behavior, they'd feel this power that we feel growing inside us.

At this level there is isolation because the demons are actually residing inside our heads and acting as our navigator through life; the less interference from outside forces, the better. There has to be a divide between us and the people that love us in order for the devil to be successful. We are no longer the captain of our ship. The demons tell us how to act, how not to act; how to feel, how not to feel; what to wear; what to say; what to eat or not eat; who to trust, who not to trust; etc. The demons may even reveal to us the demons or sins of others and be quite accurate...depending on their motive! Never forget that Satan is a deceiver and while he can be accurate, it is not his nature to be truthful.

Satan desires to sift us as wheat, to have us as his puppet at the end of a string. He would be just as satisfied to have us in bondage if he cannot totally possess our soul. God did not mean for us to be like puppets or a victim of bondage to the devil. We are free, according to His Word, to accept Jesus Christ as our Lord and Savior, or to not accept him as our Lord and Savior. By the way, this is where the difference in good and evil can be plainly seen in any situation. Satan wants to control and keep us in bondage. God wants us to *make choices* of our own free will that will allow us to experience true freedom along with love in the fullness of Christ. Making choices that lead us toward freedom in Christ is how God would have us be. The enemy wants us to make bad and thoughtless choices that will ultimately destroy us because he does not have the heart of Christ and it is his desire to render us powerless to sin and negative behavior. Therefore any person, situation, or idea that will render us powerless to sin by not allowing us to freely love, freely forgive, freely give, freely make good choices, or freely hold to unadulterated truths is from the devil.

The realm in which Satan dwells is forever in opposition to God; this will not change. He knows what is destined to happen to him because Satan knows scripture, Satan knows God, but thus far, this hasn't stopped him from getting himself into the position that he's in now! Satan with all of his cunning ways will not take no for an answer no matter what the cost. The enemy is tenacious and unyielding and despite the odds being against him, he will not yield as long as he has his hand in our lives even if it is only to the "nth" degree. When we think that we're better, different, smarter, and more spiritual than other people, our guard and defenses are down because we are buoyed by pride and not Christ. The bible tells us to watch and pray always lest we succumb to the wiles of the devil. When we are foolhardy, we will immerse ourselves in sin but we do not expect the results to be the same as it was with "Tom." It's an illogical way to think when the bible constantly warns against his antics. We understand that Satan plunges himself with abandon into his work of keeping us from truth. It is he who would have us believe that the price we must pay for sin will not be exacted on us, knowing full well the bitter truth that the wages of sin is death. He knows his time is limited and is fully aware of his ultimate demise, but he also knows that when we continue to sin we give him the permission he needs to orchestrate our demise.

Lucifer was an angel; he therefore has angelic powers and abilities. I don't recall reading where God took away his powers when he cast him from heaven. Angels have the ability to talk to us, bestow certain powers upon us, guide us, and intercede in times of trouble. They appear in various forms and in and to various individuals. They perform miracles, deliver messages, kill, protect or destroy. Newsflash! Satan can do all of these things, except he doesn't have the pure heart of one of God's holy angels who follow the instructions of God, their creator. His whole nature is that of rebellion against God and if you are constantly in rebellion against God, your nature is that of the devil. Lucifer wanted to change the way heaven was! He wanted to run things his way and not accept the instructions of his creator. We shouldn't be like Lucifer and reject God's word in our heart! We should strive for obedience to the Holy Spirit. When we harbor rebelliousness toward God, recognize that this is the nature of the devil and must resist this feeling with all our might. We should cry out to the Lord, read the bible, pray, sing, praise the Lord, listen to spiritual music, listen to a sermon, or remember to say over and over again, if we have to: JESUS IS LORD! JESUS IS LORD! until that suffocating, oppressiveness that comes from the enemy is lifted.

These things are important to remember, but let me get back to level two of demonization, because at this level, the last thing we feel like doing or are likely to do at this stage is pray, call on the Lord and so forth. It can happen; anything is possible, but it is highly unlikely. When we are at this stage, the level of demonic activity within us is proportional to the level of suppression of our will, the level of spiritual warfare being waged on our behalf, and our original belief system and spiritual state because the suppression of the will is directly related to the original state of the person's will in the first place. A willful person who is stubborn and prone to resist authority will more than likely be the type of person who would probably resist the will of God in favor of doing things their way. Their nature is rebellious so Satan can work through this because Satan is also against being under authority; it's his nature. He will use the opening of rebellion to turn us against all things in authority, good and bad. He doesn't care; he wants us off-balanced in as many ways as possible because he and his demons relish the chaos.

For example, the ego is not a bad thing in and of itself, but of course an ego out of control is a great weapon for him to use. The ego, as in all aspects of man's psyche, is designed to assist us in the realization of God. It is designed that we might desire and expect the best of ourselves and the people around us. It helps us to be concerned to some extent about what people think of us and what we think of ourselves. The ego furnishes us with the desire for accomplishment so that we feel good about ourselves during our time on this earth. It can help us to keep things in perspective regarding our emotional and spiritual growth. It is designed to protect us from mental harm and anguish, a buffer of sorts that helps us pull ourselves up by our "bootstraps" and continue the path of success despite how prevalent negative outside forces may be. The ego fuels our desire for personal excellence, but an ego out of control or used in the negative sense is selfish, unforgiving, brash, haughty, untouchable, unreachable, unteachable, and dangerous—just the thing that can open us up for demonic attack.

We are naturally spiritually vulnerable because we are spiritual beings and God has designed us in such a way intending that our spirit is open for relationship with Him, for God is Spirit. He knows that we need Him in order that we might live in a healthy spiritual state which is the very essence of our core design. Satan, on the other hand, uses our natural desire to deceive us into believing that *anything* will do to placate this longing. Though to be spiritual is the core of who we are, we are very ineffective when it comes to dealing with spiritual matters versus worldly matters on our own; therefore we need God. God knew that we needed Jesus to pay the price of our sinful ways so that Satan would once and for all have no power to destroy us. He left His word for us to study that we might be prepared with the tools we need to achieve such a healthy spiritual state. We *must* use spiritual warfare because there is danger for us if we do not. Lack of spiritual warfare being waged in the heavens on our behalf by us or the people who love and care for us perpetuates Satan's plan by making his job easier—the less resistance, the better.

There is the original spiritual state of a man that understands that there is a superior course other than what he himself can manage on his own. If we are between two opinions, we can wind up stranded anywhere and serving anything that a spiritually uneducated mind can grasp or comprehend. Again, I caution that there are no substitutions for having Jesus in your life, only diversions and counterfeits! Therefore, according to the word of God, if a man has not found Christ to be his Lord and Savior, anything and/or anyone else he comes to depend on is either a counterfeit or diversion and Satan operates as both.

We may participate in church activities and attend church regularly and that's great. We may be on a spiritual quest with honorable intentions of finding the truth. We may be into meditation, prayer, and religious books of whatever denomination, or spiritual activities that do not ascribe to any specific denomination. Unfortunately, whatever we do aside and apart from God the Father, God the Son, and God the Holy Spirit, we put ourselves at risk. For if we go to a church for the wrong reasons and we are abused by the people in leadership positions or its members, Satan will use such things to discourage us from seeking the truth. If we go to a church where the Word is not going forth, Satan can use that preacher to deceive us, just as he uses evil people and bogus spiritual encounters by placing them in key positions along our journey in life.

We need to have foundation in the Word. A strong foundation can prove very helpful in times of trouble. A strong foundation can hold us even when we don't quite understand the storms that confront us in life. If all we have come to understand is that Jesus is help in times of trouble, it's better than looking to our weary, frustrated selves trying to figure out how to pull strength where we have exhausted all strength. Conversely, if we have no foundation in the Word, we can find ourselves cavorting about and agreeing with anyone or anything that appeals to our mood or fancy at the moment. When we have no foundation, we are more likely to find ourselves sitting at the feet of people who are not what they portray, such as false prophets and con artists.

We may find ourselves worshiping a person whose presence may be very charismatic and awesome, but they are not at all of God's Kingdom; they are of the kingdom of Satan. It does not matter what we *thought*. As the saying goes, "The road to hell is paved with good intentions," and there are spiritual laws that will go forth whether we like it or not. We have the written word of God at hand, and it is our responsibility to study it and use it so that we are not fooled by wolves in sheep's clothing. His Word familiarizes our spirit with His voice and we come to understand that God's Word does not contradict itself while Satan's work is filled with confusion, strife, and contradictions. Even if we don't have the bible around, there is His spirit that he has placed in each and every one of us: good, bad, or indifferent—that lets us know in the most general way, right from wrong.

Some of us, for various reasons, chose to have no spiritual preferences at all. We don't have a spiritual foundation and we don't want a spiritual foundation. We just want to figure this thing called life out, have good manners, be a relatively decent human being and achieve success. We don't understand that by doing this, we put ourselves in grave danger. Satan quickly seizes the opportunity to frolic in this lukewarm and indecisive state, and unlike God the Father, he'll gladly make the choice for us because we are not grounded in anything in particular and the doors are wide open for attack. The devil will allow you to have material success because it is a consequence of your hard work, but he won't allow you to have happiness and your unhappiness will lead you to do things, *anything* that looks like it might provide a moment of happiness. When we do not choose, this means that there is lack of choice. When there is a lack of choice, this means that we have *not* chosen Christ as our Lord and Savior; how can it be any other way? Jesus is not something that is gotten by default. WE must choose HIM as our Lord and Savior; he has already chosen us. There can be no relationship in the natural where one person chooses to be in a relationship and the other chooses not to be. This is no less in the spiritual realm. God has chosen to be in a relationship with us, but if we do not choose to be in relationship with him, there is no relating.

As for those of us who do choose, we are covered in our sins because Christ has offered us the way out. He is our Savior and we understand that making a choice is not about making a choice to go to church, serve in a certain ministry, volunteer our time and money to the church, though all of these things are very admirable if our motivations are pure, but choosing to do these things is not choosing and accepting Jesus Christ as our Lord and Savior. If we choose to sing in the choir—this is not choosing Christ. If we choose to be a deacon—this is not choosing Christ. If we choose to be obedient to the call of our ministry—this is not choosing Christ, this is choosing to do a job. There are people in the church today who have not accepted or chosen Jesus, people in the church who have not chosen to have a relationship with God, one of the most important things that a person can do for spiritual safety. Although we may confess and believe that Christ died for our sins, this does not take the place of having a day-to-day, ongoing relationship with the Father. We have not come to expect, as anyone in a healthy relationship should, that there are certain things that we expect in any relationship, and there are certain things that are expected of us in any relationship.

As Christians, we are to understand that we are carried by the love of Christ during our times of weakness and trials and tribulations. This is why it is possible for Christians to have demons. It is possible for us to have demons because if we serve in the church without understanding, doors are open for demonization. If we serve in the church without relationship, doors are open for demonization. If we serve in the church without using weapons of spiritual warfare, we are open; we cannot fight what is spiritual with what we have learned from the world. I have seen many a Christian stagnant and bound by Satan because if he cannot get us totally, he will get us in part. If we confess that Jesus Christ is Lord with our mouth, it is all but impossible for the soul of a Christian to be totally possessed and taken to hell, but we surely place limits on what God can do for us while we are on earth as the enemy preps our minds to block our reception of the blessings of God.

Even as backsliders, it is impossible to be fully demonically controlled because of our confession of having accepted Jesus as our Lord and Savior because once we make our confession, we are protected from hell, but not from a life of misery. When Christians backslide, just as with anyone else, our sin is a doorway for Satan's operations, giving him legal access to our soul. His demons have a right to inhabit you wherever there is an existing and *consistent* opening that has not been dealt with by prayer or confession and repentance, according to spiritual law. As we become immersed in sin, it's only a matter of time before there is a rejection of the Christ life and an open invitation to the devil. The deeper we go into sin, the harder it is for us hear the voice of the Father.

The amount of demons that one individual can have in them is undetermined. The demonized man among the tombs of Gadarenes had about 2,000 so it stands to reason that we can have as few as one and as many as 2,000. That's a lot of demons! One demon is one too many! Actually, "Legion," the name of the possessed man in the book of Mark, in the Greek means a large and unspecified amount. Satan took a third of the angels with him when he was kicked out of heaven and they operate in the demonic and nobody knows the exact number of angels that he took with him, and although we do know that the majority of them, two-thirds, stayed with our heavenly Father, unfortunately the third are here on earth under the wing of the devil.

POSSESSION

Some people call being at this level of demonization being perfectly possessed. There is too much contradictory evidence that supports the fact that our spirit belongs to God. To ascribe to the fact that someone's spirit can be possessed is a questionable stance to take and to believe that someone can be perfectly possessed is probably just a misnomer for what is really happening because in order for someone to be perfectly possessed they *are* a demon and not a human being. God made every human being; Satan lacks such a divine ability to do this because he cannot create. The only thing that he can do is imitate, manipulate, and complicate. He has to work with what we give him and what God allows him to work with according to his permissive will. He cannot use God's creations to create a genre of people that represent him. To be perfectly possessed is to be possessed of soul, body, and spirit. The question of whether a soul can be perfectly possessed is another matter, but the spirit, that is God's divine umbilical cord connecting us to him as our creator, can never be possessed. God can only be disregarded by us on various levels and in varying degrees but He is the only one that has the power to sever this connection, not Satan.

People at this level of demonization, who are called perfectly possessed, I prefer to call highly demonized. People who are highly demonized will not cringe at the sight of religious symbols and paraphernalia such as crucifixes, bibles, and holy water. They will not necessarily be put off by general discussions of God and even his son Jesus. These people are generally very cold, unemotional, and efficient, or veer toward the other extreme of being active and very likable on the surface. They will never let you in below the surface as they rarely if ever come to know anyone intimately. As is their nature, they are excellent liars as well as eager bearers of hardcore truth, especially if that truth saddens, offends, or discourages us. Whether these people are standoffish or amicable, there is usually something extraordinarily strange about them; something out of place that does not quite fit the personality. These people, although they are not what they seem, can rarely deceive a person who truly knows the Father and may even become agitated in their presence. This agitation that they feel toward these God-fearing souls may be mistakenly interpreted by the unenlightened as anger, disdain, arrogance, impatience, or a strong and unreasonable dislike of a person. The highly demonized will let you know where you stand spiritually if you're in their presence for any amount of time. If they don't want to be bothered with you, you're probably spiritually in good standing. They won't want to be around you and yet they may spend many hours studying you, trying to figure if there is an inlet. They'll ask about you, talk about you, and sometimes even obsess about you, always through others; they don't want to be your friend because they don't want you to discern their spirit.

If by chance these highly demonized people are caught when they are not on their guard, you will be witness to a look that is unmistakably evil. Their facial expressions will take on a totally unfamiliar and sometimes even bizarre expression. If you happen to catch a glimpse of a smile at such times, you will see that such a smile is hideous, illustrious of evil itself. These people seek to pervert the ways and teachings of Jesus, making them to seem infantile, unnecessary and even laughable. They challenge virtue and innocence, love and anything else that is indicative of a beautiful and loving soul and spirit.

These souls can occupy blue collar jobs and are generally quite satisfied with their position and have no ambition to elevate their status beyond a mediocre existence because they have been stationed there by the devil. They are constantly at odds with management and coworkers, their goal is to spread misery and mayhem in whatever way they can. They are generally jealous, vindictive, petty, and prejudiced above and beyond what would be considered normal for such human defects. Do not be fooled, however, if the person is not loud or boisterous, they can also be quiet and sneaky, giving you a sense that they are always watching. Many times we may overlook those whose methods are less aggressive and covert, but they are just as dangerous and sometimes even more dangerous because we never see them coming.

Earlier I discussed people who experience demonization and are high-ranking souls who do Satan's work; though the people at this level are highly demonized, they are not necessarily high-ranking souls in Satan's kingdom. Those who experience high-ranking demonization are still at a high level and stronger than someone at an average level of infiltration but there are levels in the demonic realm that range from the weakest demonic activity to the strongest, from privates to generals. The highest ranking demonized souls operate in the higher echelons of society as discussed earlier. These people represent the genre of souls who worship Satan and have renounced Christ as the Savior of the world. These people have literally sold their soul to the devil and are capable of manifesting demonic powers at will because their loyalty to the cause of evil is so strong. These people have become voluntarily "possessed" of the devil, having surrendered their souls and bodies to be inhabited by demons.

RECOGNITION TIP # 22

Recognize and acknowledge that when God became Jesus, he gave us access to His power through the Holy Spirit.

CHAPTER 23

Or ever the silver cord be loosed, or the golden bowl be broken, or the pitcher be broken at the fountain, or the wheel broken at he cistern. Then shall the dust return to the earth as it was: and the spirit shall return unto God who gave it—Ecclesiastes 12:6, 7

SPIRITUALITY

Any method of spirituality will not work. So if you're sitting around contemplating thoughts such as, "I like to cleanse the air of negative energies with my crystals or incense" or "All one needs to do is think more positive" or "They're just weak-minded, I can handle whatever the devil wants to dish out," you're ripe for attack by the enemy. There are some who have become involved in the occult and would not give it up for the world because it makes them feel more powerful. They feel that by learning and performing certain rituals they have tangible control over not only their mind, but their situations, circumstances, environment and the minds of others. They pity us because we are not strong enough to exist in this life independent of some invisible force, such as God, as a crutch. Many of these people who have become involved with the occult claim to have seen the devil himself; how many of God's people can claim that they have seen God Himself?

Then there are those who do not understand why the rest of us cannot use the power of our mind to extricate ourselves from any situation based on our intellect and wit. If you buy into that then you'd better be prepared to pay the exorbitantly high spiritual price of such thinking. When dealing with demons, buyers beware. Demons will not release you because the scent of chamomile is floating through the air. They will not obey what you say because you have more degrees than your wall can hold. They will not relent because you believe in mind over matter and they will not neglect you because you're the nicest person you'd ever want to meet. They will not flee in the name of Buddha, Paul, or Mary and even your meditations may yield demonic visions that Satan masquerades as deep and profound truths of God while Satan turn your chants into satanic verse. Whatever your spirituality is, there is only one way to be released from the clutches of the devil: the name of Jesus.

Any form of spirituality or religion that does not acknowledge Christ as the son of God and denies power in the blood of Jesus is invalid in spiritual warfare. I'm not saying this to hurt your feelings or to judge your religion, but no other religion teaches of spiritual warfare and the message of salvation and the immediate availability of this salvation through anyone, and if a religion is absent of these things, it leaves us susceptible to spiritual domination by opposing enemy forces. It is simply impossible for us to be good enough to discourage the enemy. If we have not accepted Christ as our Lord and Savior, we are against the true and living God and the bible makes it very clear that we must choose sides. We cannot be for whom we are against. There is no middle ground; there is no such thing as being lukewarm in Christ. Lukewarm means that we have not chosen God and yet we have not denounced or denied Satan. As a matter of fact, it is the lukewarm Christian that is highly vulnerable to Satan more so than the ones that have no preference at all because Satan is not concerned with those who have no preference; he can do with them as he pleases and even ignore them without losing a step. The lukewarm Christians are the ones that are trying to have their cake and eat it too and that's more attractive to Satan because they know *about* God but just aren't quite interested in living *for* God. They walk the line playing around the perimeter of a soft-served or negligible allegiance to God. Tentative souls as these are quite the prize for Satan as it is easy to lead them away from something that they are not firm about in the first place. Satan has always been an adversary to God; nothing gives him more pleasure than to rip a soul who *might* choose Christ. These people have their own agenda in mind and Satan knows that in reality their agenda is self-serving and full of holes. When we choose this path that lacks commitment, it makes us highly susceptible to Satan because this condition leaves us "holey," not holy.

Spirit is our divine connection to our creator. The mind, emotions, and will make up the soul. The soul is what Satan is after because he knows that our spirit belongs to God and God makes the final decision on whether a soul goes to heaven or hell based on our relationship with Him. Satan is not a creator of anything! But he does understand that if he succeeds in capturing the mind and the emotions, the will is subject to follow. Once we give him our consent, in whatever form, our spiritual connection to our creator can be obscured even to the point where it appears to us to be nonexistent.

The will is the glue that connects the spirit to the soul. Once the mind, emotions, and will have been captured, our ability to hear God's will lessens in proportion to the level of sin that we now embrace. The more we sin without repentance, the harder it is for us to adhere to the prompting of the Holy Spirit and the farther we are from our Christ connection. We become more apt to habitually ignore the spirit in deference to the flesh. Remember, God created us all with free will and we can choose to serve Him or not to serve Him; we can choose to develop a relationship with Him or not to develop a relationship with Him; we can choose to love Him or not to. Technically, however, we all belong to God. It's like owning a dependable car and never choosing to drive it. It's in the garage among the tools and boxes of storage items but we've forgotten about it in favor of perhaps a sportier albeit less dependable ride. It makes no sense that we would not choose the dependable car; it makes no sense that we put our money, time and energy into a vehicle that is substandard, especially when we have a more reliable vehicle available but we do this when we refuse to choose God.

God knows our heart. What a man truly believes lies in his heart. There is a difference in searching haphazardly for answers, experimenting with certain lifestyles, studying different methods of expressing ourselves spiritually, and actually embracing these things as a way of life. If, on our journey, our techniques lead us in a roundabout way to God the Father and His son Jesus, then all is well and what we would have lost is time, provided we don't die in the process. If on the other hand our journey or path leads us away from God the Father or a denial of Christ, this is a very unfortunate problem. As I said, God knows our heart, and He does not fault us for the natural desire to make a spiritual connection because God is spirit and He made us to seek Him who is spirit. However, that does not mean that as with any action we undertake, we won't have to suffer the consequences of that search, experimentation, or study.

God's ways are mysterious to us, but all of His ways are wise and righteous. We as human beings can never attain God's level of goodness and wisdom, which is why we must guard our heart with all diligence, especially when we are exploring the spiritual realm. There are good and evil forces in the spirit realm and the nature of the evil forces can be, without a doubt, very deceptive to us humans. The flesh, which is an essential part of the soul, yearns for stimulation and what may seem right to the most moral and well-intentioned person is not necessarily what is acceptable to God. There are many things that sound good in theory, but in practice they lose all substance and in God's eyes they are blatant sin against Him. In other words, with our best thinking we still miss the mark. This soulish part of us all can be used by Satan to draw us away from beliefs that we once held near and dear in our hearts and lead us astray. We must allow God to be God and in order for Him to do His work, He must be allowed by us to work with us and through us. *His* will must be acknowledged and allowed by us to manifest itself in our lives.

We venture into dangerous territory when we try to control or manipulate the spirit realm. We are open and vulnerable to whatever is lurking there as we become susceptible to forces that are beyond human control as our mind and psyche can be thrown into a dangerous bevy of confusion. Beliefs that we once held to be good and true suddenly become cloudy and very much open to compromise, confusion or even rejection. We should not monkey around with the spirit realm in any way without being purposeful and well-informed about what we are getting into. If we are determined to go this route, it is imperative that we understand spiritual laws and respect them. We cannot change them and we cannot manipulate them to our own personal taste and style. God alone has the power to override spiritual law if He so chooses. We as humans have no other choice but to honor them or pay the high price of admission: our soul!

Satan has to gain entrance into us and to do this he to attacks the soul—more precisely, the mind/emotion/flesh which is directly linked with the spirit though it is not the spirit. Satan challenged Jesus in the desert by challenging things pertaining to the soul such as his flesh. He challenged him to make the stones to bread to satisfy the hunger that his body was experiencing. He challenged Christ's emotions by telling him that God's angels would take care of him regardless of what he did. He challenged his mind or ego by offering him the world.

Jesus answered him in three ways:

1. Don't do anything for a piece of bread.
2. Don't put yourself in obvious danger.
3. Don't serve the ego; everything we attain in life should have God as its source.

Remember, we fight not against flesh and blood; flesh and blood can only fight flesh and blood. Flesh and blood, except for the blood of Jesus, cannot fight what is not of flesh and blood. Satan knows that the mind/emotion is only a tool and he must get us to accept his will in order for him to be successful in his quest for our soul. When the mind/emotion part of the soul is captured, he knows that it's only a matter of time, unless there is a successful intervention, before the will follows. Once we relinquish our will to him, we are under demonic forces in whatever particular area or areas we have accepted Satan's will to be our own, but even then, beware because there are trapdoors to that!

We have now allowed the demons to infiltrate and therefore they have direct access to various areas of our lives like the pests mentioned earlier. He is now able to gain more ground because we have given him the openings that he needs. Now that he has gained entrance, temptation becomes almost impossible to resist. With Satan's invasions, the flesh gains more control as it pushes our spirit to the background as it grows and grows. Our anti-God actions, lack of faith, belief system and behavior give him the cue that his plan to sift us like wheat can now be executed because we are now more apt to allow the flesh to overrule our spirit and what feels good becomes more important that what IS good. The flesh is in control, and the flesh will force us to feed it so that it can continue to grow and gain control. The more the flesh controls, the more out of control we feel.

Now Satan proceeds to turn the lemonade in our life to lemons. He skews and interrupts our thought processes to make us discontented with the good and familiar and more open to the vile and unfamiliar. He violates anything within us that is innocent, decent, and pure; probing and testing the recesses of our minds with the smooth agility of a slithering snake. Our ability to focus on what is good, right and beautiful is violently hampered and joy and contentment seem unattainable. Our ability to live in the present is obscured as visions of a tainted past dominate our minds and the future is only a fuzzy cloud barely visible in the distance. Confusion sets in as we enter into a futile battle, using the wrong weapons, against Satan's bevy of demons as they slowly and deliberately overtake our soul.

Once the door is open even to the smallest degree, his task is to get us to voluntarily open it wider and wider. He'll use frustration, a feeling of hopelessness, impotence, anger, as his tools of force create a false scenario in our mind as a system to force the door wider and wider; when it comes to

Satan he has no particular preference, just his ageless goal of destruction. The wider we open up to him, the more his demons can fill us up leaving our spiritual connection in a state of being pressed down, or depressed. Satan propositioned Jesus, a man with no sin, therefore he'll proposition anyone, so don't be foolish enough to think that we can be good enough to keep Satan off our back. We should not be offended when the enemy comes, just be prepared. You see, sin doesn't necessarily make us attractive to Satan although it yields a very powerful leverage. We do not have to sin for an attack of the enemy to occur, although man is prone to sin. Jesus, who is God in the flesh and surely without sin and Job who was a man considered perfect and upright in the eyes of God, were both targets of Satan, proving that being sinless (which is and impossibility with man) does not mean that Satan will leave us alone. The bible makes it very clear that Satan left Jesus for a "season," indicating that even Jesus would encounter him again.

A good indication that Satan is attempting to gain entrance and doors are open is depression and/or confusion. He confronted Jesus when he was physically hungry and weak; symbolically he confronts us when we do not feed our spirit or when our spirit is on a junk food diet. Jesus' spirit never flinched and he answered Satan with appropriate scripture. What does this show us? This shows us that in matters of satisfying the flesh, talking just to show Satan how powerful and unafraid we are does not work and only God's words should be used when dealing with the devil. This is the importance of knowing scripture; not only does it acquaint us with the trinity, scripture comforts, corrects, and protects in any and all areas of our life. It lets us know that the enemy will not win, so for all of you tough guys out there, Satan does not respond to anger and threats. In fact he will likely use your anger and threats to get you to do exactly what he would have you do. Use scripture if you want results; don't think to employ powers of intimidation against the devil because he's not afraid of you.

GAINING ENTRANCE

The methods that Satan uses so that his demons gain entrance are both simple and complex. Satan is not necessarily the cause of our sins as many of us would like to think; he uses them only because they are unresolved issues that we have not taken to the cross. He knows that he cannot use sins and issues that we have truly repented of because of our relationship with Christ. In fact Satan realizes more than we do that Jesus saves! Now if the devil, being Jesus' adversary, has a full and working knowledge of Jesus and his powers, shouldn't we be just as knowledgeable, and even more so, of just how powerful our Savior is? Shouldn't we be aware of Satan's devices and the tools that he uses to gain entrance into our lives and be at the ready to repent and take all our problems to Christ? Shouldn't we be intimately familiar with scripture so that when we are in a desert place in our lives we will be able to use it against the devil?

Denial is one method that allows Satan to gain entrance. To be in denial about anything is to open doors and grant entrance to the enemy. If we deny that we are ignorant of God's law, if we deny who we are or where we come from, if we deny that we have problems, that we feel sad, that we feel scared or uncertain—we set ourselves up. Denial is a powerful tool of the devil. If we deny our sins, the more likely it is that Satan will use such denial as an opportunity to justify his role in our lives. When we are in denial of our sins, we deny that there is anything wrong with the way we live, think, or with the things we choose to do. If, therefore, we feel that nothing is amiss in our lives, what cause do we have to pray about an issue? In denial, we are closed to help from friends, relatives and loved ones and, because of our God-given free will, even Jesus. When we are in denial, we recognize what we are doing and maybe even feel the pain that it causes, but we think that the cause of our pain is not because of our actions or behavior but because of our methods. We figure that it wouldn't be so bad if we could keep the bad behavior and have it under control. So consequently, many times we blame our technique and outcome, not the behavior. We blame ourselves for our inability to control a behavior, and fault lack of discipline instead of placing the bad behavior in the category of a sin where it belongs. If we categorize the behavior as sin, this would force us to look at it as such. If we look at sin and accept sin for what it is, it would not be difficult for us to understand that sin cannot be permanently controlled; this is documented throughout the entire bible. We sin, we will sin, but if we lock onto one sin and continue to do this thing over and over again hating the sin, either our will is somehow fueling the sin or it is a stronghold that the enemy has us believing that we are locked into it.

Unfortunately the deeper we go into denial about our behavior and/or a belief system that does not adhere to the Word, the more bizarre we become.

In order to remain in sinful behaviors, our thought process must be in alignment with our belief system or else we are divided within ourselves and open to insanity. We cannot remain on both sides of the fence for very long if we want to keep our sanity—we must choose. The longer we take to choose, the closer we come to insanity. We *must* go through the necessary changes and make the necessary choices to accommodate our way of living and our way of thinking if we are to keep a grip on our reality. We find a way to include people and events in our scenario even if we must go outside of our present environment because as humans, and the devil knows this, we need to be validated. In order to validate our sinful lifestyles we blame some and avoid others in our journey find those who are like us. Like radar, we seek out others whose souls are in agreement with ours as we methodically target our fury and discontent upon those who voice any discrepancies.

As we journey through, if we find ourselves on the fence, there is an urgency to make up our minds one way or another because we realize that it is impossible to remain on the fence for any length of time. We shift and re-shift, restless, trying to find a comfortable position when there is no comfortable position. When we are lodged on a fence, there is no comfort, only the threat of falling down or apart, as we find ourselves in denial about many aberrant behaviors whether it is ours or someone else's. When we are in denial, our ability to discern is compromised because our sanity depends on us not breaking up, falling apart, or compromising our belief system no matter how inconvenient it is or how little sense it makes. Satan gains entrance into our lives through sustained sinful behavior and his demons sit poised at the fences that we sit on in our lives. They know that soon a decision will have to be made or the "sitting duck" is theirs by default. Again, sinning once does not give Satan the right to own our soul; anyone can make a mistake and we all are sinners. In order for demons to have permission to occupy, there must be immersion and acceptance.

Spiritual paraphernalia or objects that are believed to possess certain powers open us up to the spiritual realm, another point of demonic entrance because by using them we are voluntarily allowing our spirit to be vulnerable to the realm of spirits; we never know if what we are opening ourselves up to is from God or the devil. Evil spirits may appear to be good and good spirits may appear to be malevolent if we are in such a state of rebellion and confusion that we cannot comprehend the benevolence of the good spirit or the malevolence of the bad. Here on earth there are earthlings; in the spirit realm there are spiritual beings. As on earth, where people can be either good or bad, the same holds true in the spirit realm. The two-thirds of the angels that Satan took with him from heaven while rebelling against God operate in the unseen. Since angels are spirit beings and angels do not die, where would we expect that they should dwell? This spirit realm is dangerous. It is dangerous because it is very hard to control by those who are experienced and even harder to control by those who are inexperienced. Those who dare venture into it for unholy purposes—be they good, bad, novice, or experienced—place themselves at the highest risk for demonic control. People who venture into it for holy purposes are highly susceptible for the same reason and are at risk if they are not diligent in employing the weapons of warfare.

Spiritual paraphernalia—the Ouija board, tarot cards, crystal balls and charms—open us up to be a voluntary victim in the realm of spirit. By using such things we open ourselves up, not to God, but to other forces that use the objects as a vehicle to manifest themselves. These things cannot be of God who wants us to seek *Him* for all the issues of life. He left his word in bible form and made His word flesh in the form of Jesus and gave us access to the Holy Spirit. Some say that God can communicate with us in various ways. Why wouldn't the Ouija board, tarot cards and such be viable and acceptable forms of God's methods of communication? Well, God did not list these objects as weapons of spiritual warfare nor does it say in His word that "thou should seek me in thy crystal ball!" Seriously, however, my answer to this is that we should be wary of anything that claims to open the door to the mysteries of the spirit world because we never know what door we are walking through. More importantly, are we prepared to handle what comes through that door?

Let me relate to you one of the many things that has happened to me during my naivete. As I relate this, please understand that I am not going to inject apologies and excuses for why I did what I did because it will interrupt the flow of the story. While I now understand how dangerous and foolish it is to fool around with such things, during that time in my life, I was unafraid and just plain curious. Being a person who shuns anything that may present an unnecessary threat to my physical person, I was pretty fearless when it came to experiencing an "adventure" in the spirit and boy, was I excited about the "adventure" I was about to experience.

I, like many of you out there, had not read anywhere in the bible "thou shalt not use Ouija boards." I was not a teenager but a grown woman, married with two children, the first time I used the Ouija board with a friend of mine. I'll call her Sue. She was also married with children. I'd heard of the Ouija board but had never used it before so when she said that she had one, I jumped at the opportunity to experience it with her. She seemed like a relatively level-headed and sensible woman at the time, so I figured if she had used it before, she would know what to do and be able to guide me through it, and I figured that she wouldn't cheat or resort to trickery; after all she was a grown woman with children for God's sake—like me!

I was tense with excitement the first time Sue and I used the board, excited to finally see for myself if the stories I had heard were true or if it was all about college students and children pretending to be scared just to have a little fun. Up to this point in my life, I'd never encountered a real Ouija board and had only seen them on television and in movies and based on what little I'd seen and heard about them, they were scary enough that I wouldn't consider buying one as a toy for my children, and yet interesting enough to arouse my curiosity.

Palms sweaty, I rubbed them back and forth on the lap of my jeans to get rid of the moisture. I was finally going to experience this Ouija board thing! There was a part of me that felt the whole thing was imagination and nothing at all would happen, but there was also a part of me that wanted it to work and wanted desperately for it to be true and not be a hoax so that I would be able to experience this phenomena first-hand. I love adventure that doesn't require me to leave the ground surrounded by five thousand tons of metal, or that doesn't pose a threat of breaking bones or dying. Sure, I never would have bought a Ouija board for myself because of what I'd heard and seen in horror films but because I wasn't exactly opposed to them, when the opportunity presented itself, the conditions were just right for me.

Before we used the Ouija board, thank God Sue had the good sense to put the children out of the room where we were using it and shut the door. As a matter of fact, we went down into the basement of the house to use it while our children played under the supervision of our husbands upstairs. I don't really know how much good that did, but in retrospect, I'm thankful that we did. My sweaty palms, along with my no-questions-asked attitude about all the precautionary measures taken, revealed that I did have a sense of danger and inappropriateness of what we were about to do, but that didn't stop me; if anything the adrenaline rush added to the fact that I *would* do it and nothing would stop me. I had to see for myself because I could not understand how a manmade board, purchased from a toy store, could have the power to do anything other than manipulate someone's imagination like children trying to frighten each other with tales of seeing the boogey man. Well, by golly, I was no longer a child! I figured that I had enough wits about me not to depend on my imagination or someone's sleight of hand, and as I said before, Sue didn't seem like the kind of person that would engage in such childish folly anyway if there was no validity to it.

Once we were secure in the basement, Sue instructed me as to how I should position my fingers on the planchette. She told me that I wouldn't have to do anything special except not allow the heaviness of my fingers to weigh the planchette down. She did all the talking, asking the questions out loud with the crisp precise English of a well-educated woman. We did not have to close our eyes or recite some spooky incantation; fingers in place, Sue simply asked into the air if a spirit by the name of Tom was there. She only had to beckon him a few times before the planchette started to move on its own! I could feel my heart pounding in my throat by now. As she talked with this Tom spirit, soul, or ghost, whatever he was, conversing with him like he was an old friend, I watched in amazement as the planchette floated across the board under our fingertips spelling out his answers to her questions.

Sue told me that she had talked to him on numerous occasions and he was really a nice spirit. She introduced me to him by name and told him that I was her good friend. I sat in disbelief and said nothing as the planchette moved around in response to her innocuous inquiries with fluidity. I watched her, I watched our fingers, I watched the board; I can attest to the fact that my fingertips were oh-so-light on this widget, until there was no possibility that I moved that thing of my own power. In fact if either one of us made the mistake of leaning too heavily upon the planchette, it wouldn't move at all.

She talked with Tom asking about his death and where his body was buried. He gladly related all of this information with no hesitation. After a while, I got up the nerve to ask Sue to ask Tom questions; simple questions that she didn't know the answers to but I did, such as what was the color of the jacket I wore to the zoo the previous weekend. Tom was right on target with all his answers. Then Sue asked Tom if it would be alright if I spoke with him and asked him the questions directly and he said it was okay. As you can probably gather by now, I became a bit more at ease and my curiosity had to be satisfied. I asked him where he was; was he in heaven, hell, or a type of limbo? His response was that if anything, the closest description of where he was would be that he was in limbo. I asked him how he got there and why he didn't go to a place of rest. I know that he responded but I do not recall what he said; what I do remember is that he did not answer my question and the planchette began to move slower and heavier.

Sue, in response to the change in energy, informed me that the spirit that was in control of the board was no longer Tom. She knew Tom's energy and said that she didn't really talk to spirits that she didn't know because some of the beings, wherever they were, were not so friendly. She said "goodbye" and signed off. She said that we would have to try again later to reach Tom.

I was fascinated! Never before had I experienced anything remotely like that before. I could hardly wait. I had questions; lots of them; and the possibility that I was going to get them answered was almost too much to bear. I cursed that heavy force for its untimely intervention. I couldn't wait to play again, which we did about twenty minutes later.

This time Tom came through as he usually did with her, but she sensed that something was wrong.

"What's wrong. Tom? You don't seem yourself," Sue said, "This is Tom, isn't it?"

It was. Tom told Sue that he was afraid.

"Afraid of what, Tom?" Sue wanted to know.

He told her that he was afraid that she wouldn't come anymore and that they wouldn't be friends like they were now.

"Tom, I'll always be your friend," Sue said, comforting him. "Why would you say something like that?"

Tom then proceeded to spell out the reason he felt that she would no longer be his friend; it was because of "A-U-D-R-E-Y."

My heart skipped a beat and I was a bit frightened and concerned for reasons that I didn't understand. I didn't say anything; I took my hands off of the planchette and looked at Sue who was already working to remedy the situation. She was soothing Tom's hurt feelings by telling him that there was no need to be jealous or afraid because I wanted to be his friend too. Tom disagreed and I don't remember him coming back for another one of our sessions.

We got together for this Ouija board experience a couple of times after that. Once we encountered a spirit who had been murdered and according to her,

her murder, which was bloody and gruesome, took place in the very house where Sue lived. We encountered a spirit who told us to check on our children upstairs because some vile spirit wanted them, for what I don't know. I do know that we left the basement immediately to check on our children upstairs and discontinued our use that day. Then there was the very eerie time when my husband joined in and the planchette was very heavy but just couldn't seem to get enough power behind it to even move. To this day he doesn't know if Ouija boards really do what people claim they do based on his experience. On another day when we used the board, just asking general questions, like what color sweater was I wearing, what had we done on that day, etc., the board was always accurate in its reply to any question asked about ourselves or Sue's husband, but was confused, disoriented, and plain wrong about anything that we asked about my husband Brian. At that time Brian had been called to the ministry. I should have gotten a clue then.

I ended up telling my friend Catherine about my experiences with the board and she was just as excited and curious as I was about it; she asked me to ask Sue if we could borrow it. I was hesitant because I didn't know if it was appropriate to borrow someone else's Ouija board. I wasn't familiar with Ouija board etiquette. While I contemplated this, Catherine said that we should buy one for us to use. I told her in no uncertain terms that I didn't want one and there was no way that I would buy one or even bring one into my house.

"Okay, I'll buy it then," Catherine eagerly volunteered, "and we can play it at my house."

I told her that would be fine and I'd go to the store with her to purchase *her* Ouija board. Meanwhile I called my older sister whom I'd told about my experiences with the board and told her that Catherine was about to buy one. I invited her to participate. She too was thrilled and I told her that I would pick her up from her apartment.

When we got to Catherine's apartment we eagerly unpacked the board and prepared to use it. It was my older sister who suggested that we pray before we used it so that no malevolent spirits would be able to find their way through. We held hands and prayed the Lord's Prayer and asked Him to watch over us. Before we played my sister needed to go to the washroom and Catherine, who was too excited to wait, said we'd get started and she could just join in.

I wasn't as nervous about using the board as I'd been before but was anxious to show them what I'd experienced. We both put our fingers on the planchette and began by asking simple questions that were quite obvious to anyone who could observe what was going on in the room. The board did not respond at all. Catherine was beginning to become disappointed because it didn't seem that she would be able to witness what I'd so enthusiastically told her about. We persisted and continued to ask simple mundane questions. A few times the planchette seemed to try and move but nothing notable happened. Then I thought about the prayer that we'd done just before we'd started and wondered if that might have anything to do with the board not responding. I guess I'd thought of this because Sue and I had not prayed before we'd used the board.

"Wait a minute, Catherine," I said, "Let's try this."

I instructed her to put her fingers back on the planchette, and then I posed my question to the board, "Is this Ouija board evil?"

The planchette moved slow and very heavy, but still there was no definite response. I asked Catherine to make sure her fingers were not leaning on the planchette too heavily because that could be the problem. She double checked to make sure that her touch was delicate and light upon the planchette. I asked the question again.

"Is this Ouija board evil?"

Again we received the same heavy response with no answer.

I raised my voice and in a more demanding tone and asked, "Is this an evil Ouija board?!"

Slowly the board answered, "Yes."

Catherine and I looked at each other, eyes wide with fear. Instinctively we withdrew our hands from the planchette. Neither one of us said anything; we didn't know what to say. Then I had another bright idea. We placed our hands back on it and I asked, "Are all Ouija boards evil?"

Before I could get the "vil" all the way out of my mouth, the planchette shot, it seemed, at supernatural speed to "yes."

I can't speak for Catherine, but at that moment, abject fear went through me. It was as if something vile had pushed and broken its way through into the atmosphere. The blood drained from Catherine's face, and this left no doubt in my mind that she'd felt it too. Without saying a word, we started packing the board back into its original container as fast as we could move.

As we were packing the board my sister came out from the washroom and with a puzzled look on her face she asked us what we were doing. We related what had happened while she wasn't present. You would have to know my sister in order for me to describe the look that she had on her face—not shock, not fear, but a kind of matter-of-fact look as she slowly shook her head as if thinking to herself, *I figured something like this could happen.*

"I can't believe I brought this evil thing into my home." Catherine was shaky and quite upset.

"We've got to get rid of it," I said. "How can we get rid of it? I heard that you aren't supposed to just throw these things away!" I was panicking now because there was no doubt in my mind that *that* thing was evil, and as long as we had it around us there was evil around us. It had told us, succinctly and specifically, leaving no room for doubt! What did we have to do? My mind was gripped by fear, and I couldn't think.

"Well," my sister began in her matter-of-fact way. "I know this lady from work who said she had an experience with one of these. She's very religious and she could probably tell us what to do."

By this time it was rather late in the evening, about eleven or twelve o'clock at night. She was reluctant to call the woman at such an hour. I understood her position; it was an older woman and my sister figured that she'd be asleep by ten o'clock, but I didn't know what else to do and frankly I must say, I didn't care about interrupting her sleep or anything else! We needed someone who knew what to do; this was serious!

We tossed a few ideas back and forth when I unequivocally realized we were going to have to call this woman, wake her up out of her sleep or, if necessary, drive to her house and pull her out of her bed!

"This is an emergency!" I blurted out unable to control my desperation. "You have to call! Tell her you're sorry to wake her, but you have to call. We've got to dispose of this thing and we have to dispose of it the right way!"

She agreed and picked up the phone to call, but couldn't remember the woman's number.

"C'mon now, you've got to remember that number." I was almost hysterical. "THINK!"

She couldn't think of it. It seemed that Catherine was in some state of shock because she just looked from me to my sister and from my sister to me, ringing her hands.

"I can't *believe* I brought that *evil* thing into my house! Lord Jesus, I can't *believe* I brought that *evil* thing into my house." She would murmur this intermittently as she watched the antics of me and my sister.

"Maybe it's in your telephone book!" Words were shooting out of my mouth fast and furious like bullets. "Do you know anybody else you can call to get her number?"

"Well, let me see," my sister said, thinking, a little too calmly and a little too slowly for my taste, but all I could do was wait. The clock was ticking, time was a-wasting. If this woman was a deep sleeper, suppose she didn't even answer the phone!

Finally she phoned another friend and got the number of the woman from her. I was so anxious; I wanted to rip the phone from her hands to dial the number myself because it seemed that she was taking an eternity to dial seven digits. There I was in the room with evil, and I wanted to be anywhere but in that kitchen with that godforsaken Ouija board! She dialed the number and Catherine and I stood in the background clutching each other's hands and praying, "God, please let her answer the phone, please let her answer the phone!"

Hallelujah! The woman answered the phone, and yes, she did have such an experience, and yes, she did know the correct way to get rid of a Ouija board, and yes, it was a good idea not to just throw it in the trash.

She gave us several specific passages to read from the bible. I couldn't tell you which ones they were to this day, but we read every single one of those passages out loud with much fervor. According to the woman, we had to cleanse ourselves and our environment of any lingering evil spirits and these verses would help us to do just that. She also told us that we needed to take the Ouija board to the lake and toss it into the water. We had church in Catherine's kitchen that night as we prepared to take the object of evil to the cold, dark waters of Lake Michigan.

We all donned our hats, gloves, and coats and got in my car for the trip to the lake, which was less than fifteen minutes away. Nobody wanted to carry the board or even sit next to the board in the car. I reminded Catherine that it was *her* board and if she wanted it out of *her* house she would have to get it from her house to the car. Sure, this wasn't the best of situations to force someone to do something that you were afraid to do, but I'm pretty sure she would have gladly put me in that very same position had I been the one who'd bought the Ouija board and wanted it out of my home. Catherine, who ironically donned a long black hooded maxi coat, hands clad in black leather gloves, grabbed the box off the table and said dramatically, "Let's get this thing out of my house!"

RECOGNIZING SATAN

I drove to the lake with my sister, who had refused to sit next to the Ouija board, in the front seat, and Catherine and the Ouija board in the back seat. By now it was about twelve-thirty in the morning and by now we were all getting a second wind from all the excitement. As we drove, we praised the Lord, thanked Him for His mercy and kindness, and hallelujahed our way all the way to the lake.

It was pitch black at the lake with the exception of one or two streetlights that gave some light. The night seemed to swallow us as we got out of the car. Our boots crunched through the hard snow as we made our way as close to the water's edge as we possibly could without falling off the break rocks. As we got as closer, another problem presented itself that we had not anticipated. It seemed to me that there was an effort by someone or something to thwart our mission. First there were the barrier rocks which would allow us to get only so close and then there was an even bigger problem—the lake was frozen from the shores up to about a half a mile into the lake. How in heaven were we going to throw the board into the lake water beyond this expanse of ice?

"Well, maybe we could just throw it on the ice," I suggested. I figured that the ice would melt and the Ouija board would just fall in sometime around the spring.

"No," my sister said. "She said that the Ouija board must be thrown into the lake, into the water."

"Nobody can throw that far, it's impossible. So what do we do now, we can't wait for spring?"

"I don't know," my sister said. "We may have to."

I'd been holding the box because I wanted the honors of throwing the Ouija board into the water to its "death," when suddenly Catherine ripped the box from my hands with such force I almost lost my balance on the icy snow.

"Gimme this thing," she said with a look of sheer determination on her face. "*I'll* get it to the water."

Now Catherine is more physically inclined than either me or my sister, but I doubted that she was going to be able throw that box far enough to hit water. The fear that she wouldn't be able to do it and the idea that the Ouija board would be on the ice and not *in* the lake was enough to make me feel faint. As she walked closer to the water along the rocks I called out to her, "Catherine, be careful, it's slippery, you could fall!"

Catherine didn't acknowledge whether she heard me or not. I just remember seeing the lone figure of a woman in a long black hooded coat moving along the rocks of Lake Michigan with a Ouija board under her arm. Suddenly frightening thought occurred to me as I watched Catherine on those rocks. Suppose the evil spirits caused her to lose her balance and fall to her death? This would be my last memory of one of my oldest and dearest friends and I wouldn't be able to help her because I couldn't swim and my sister couldn't swim very well either. As these thoughts crossed my mind, I called to Catherine but she didn't acknowledge. My sister and I clung to each other as the wintry winds viciously whipped around us.

Catherine stood on the rocks; she'd gone much farther than I ever would have. The evil spirits would have had to eat me for lunch before I would have gone half as far as she did. I started a silent prayer: *Lord, keep her safe, and don't let anything happen to her.*

She only had one shot to get the board into the water. It wasn't like we could walk out there to get it and try again if she didn't make it. If she didn't make it then we would not have fulfilled the requirements that the woman had told us. What would happen then? Would we be haunted forever by evil spirits as a result of our failed attempt to dispose of the board properly? Was there some other evil price that we would have to pay as a result of our failed mission? Was there something else that we could do if the board landed on the ice? Catherine was our only hope. If that board didn't hit the water…

My sister and I looked on as Catherine twisted her body like one of those discus throwers in the Olympics, and with all of her strength, a force of sound erupted from her throat as she threw the Ouija board toward the lake. We watched in awed silence as the box twirled through the blackness of the starless sky. It flew like it had wings, like a rectangular Frisbee, whipping the night air. Whipping further and further into the darkness, getting smaller and smaller, past the thick frozen ice, even reaching toward the heart of the lake until we could no longer see it. Finally, we heard the splash that signaled victory.

You couldn't imagine the whooping and jumping and hugging that followed that splash. Yes, three grown women at almost two o'clock in the morning, one in a long black hooded coat, shrouded in the darkness of Lake Michigan, isolated from the rest of the city, laughing and jumping up and down like school children at recess, celebrating that splash. Hearing that splash meant that we had done it. We had accomplished all the tasks put before us, and by the law of evil spirits we should be free of all forces associated with the Ouija board.

We headed back to the car delighted at our accomplishments, when suddenly my sister stopped dead in her tracks, shushing us to be quiet.

RECOGNIZING SATAN

"Listen!" she whispered. "Do you hear that? Did you hear that?"
"Hear what?" I asked anxiously. "I didn't hear anything!"
"Me either, hear what?" asked Catherine.
"The screaming," she said. "Like many voices, screaming in the distance far away."

Catherine and I didn't hear any voices and we didn't stop to verify if my sister heard voices; we just headed for the car, crunching as fast as we could across the icy snow, hoping that my sister was right behind us.

Needless to say that little adventure taught me a lot. There are spiritual forces to be reckoned with and these forces exist to do evil to all who dare to tap into their world. Whether we open the doors willingly or unwittingly, there are dangers and if we are not prepared to defend ourselves with the knowledge of how Jesus figures into the picture, we are at risk. We must come to an understanding about how the Holy Spirit works, what we should and should not do and what we should and should not accept. In essence, being prepared means that we should familiarize ourselves with the word of God, even on a daily basis. His Word is so complex that we can never in many lifetimes be done with its study, yet it is so simple that revelation from His Word on a daily basis is as ordinary as the rising of the sun. Thanks be to God that we don't have to become experts in order to experience Him, that's what God's grace and mercy are all about. That's also why He sent the Holy Spirit, because not everyone can read, and not everyone can read with an understanding, but anybody with the most general knowledge of Jesus can accept Him as their Lord and Savior.

RECOGNITION TIP # 23

Recognize and acknowledge that God does not act independently of people. God can provide all our needs, and sometimes he provides them in the form of others coming to our aid.

CHAPTER 24

Why do ye not understand my speech? even because ye cannot hear my word. Ye are of your father the devil, and the lusts of the father ye will do. He was a murderer from the beginning, and abode not in the truth, because there is no truth in him. When he speaketh a lie, he speaketh of his own: for he is a liar, and the father of it—John 8:43, 44

I don't know how information gets to a "Tom" floating around out there in limbo. I don't know how it got to the young girl in the bible that kept following Paul. Where the energy comes from that moves the planchette with this type of divination paraphernalia, I don't know, but wherever it comes from, whether it was from my conscious or subconscious, whether it was from some entity entombed in the world of spirits or whether it was from the devil I'm not here to determine. I'm just bearing witness to my experience with this thing. Here is something that I do know. I know that I have consciously recognized within myself and I am now persuaded that the Ouija board is evil! Even on a subconscious level, when I had a feeling that something was not good and not right with this thing, I should have respected that because the Holy Spirit has a way of working at the subconscious level before it reaches the conscious level. I thank God for the Holy Spirit which should always be respected, and I thank God for the subconscious through which the Holy Spirit can access us regardless of the level of denial we may currently be experiencing.

If some disembodied entity from another dimension felt compelled to inform me that the board was evil, that's okay too because my subconscious would have agreed with the disembodied entity before I would have fully understood why. As far as where the information came from, should that be a really big concern of ours? We don't *have* to use the Ouija board to exist on this earth. So those of you out there who would insist that there is nothing wrong with such things, and who consider yourselves spiritual, if you truly are spiritual you don't really *need* a Ouija board, do you? If you insist that your information is coming from God, God does not need the help of such things. The devil uses such things to draw in those that feel weak and powerless because Satan does not have at his disposal "All Power" the way God does. God made a donkey talk because He needed the donkey to relay a message but that does not mean that we should all go out and buy a donkey so that we can receive a word from the Lord. When God needs to give us information it comes in more credible ways.

This is why it is important to study His word because not only are we at risk for falling victim to the Ouija board and getting caught up in depending on psychics and prophets to tell us our every move, we can be deceived and find ourselves caught up in cults and worshiping some demon-infested human being. When we study, we come to understand that Satan is a deceiver and a counterfeit. For everything good he has a counterfeit designed specifically to deceive us in various areas of our life. The following is a list of counterfeits that Satan uses in his attempts to confuse us and to get us to defy our Lord and Savior, Jesus Christ; keep these things in mind. It's another tool to help you to recognize the works of the devil.

TRUTH	**CONTERFEIT**
LOVE	LUST
KINDNESS	MANIPULATION
STRENGTH	CRUELTY
GOOD STEWARDSHIP	PARSIMONY
FAITH	ARROGANCE
CHARITY	CONTROL
PATIENCE	FEAR
SPIRITUAL AWARENESS	EMOTIONAL RELEASE
PEACE	APATHY
JOY	LACK OF DISCRETION
POWER	LACK OF COMPASSION
HOPE	AVARICE
LONG SUFFERING	INDOLENCE
PRAYER	BARGAINING

Notice that the words on the left are very positive character traits and very Christ-like spiritual qualities; we all should have them. Yet on the right, we see how Satan masks negative qualities passing them off as positive ones for his purpose. The devil has a counterfeit for everything that is good and holy; these are just a few key examples. We accept that we are operating on God's behalf many times in our minds even when we are not; it's all a part of our psyche trying not to be a house divided against itself by accepting the counterfeit deceptions of the enemy.

For instance, I've heard people use the statement that they are being patient and waiting on the Lord but what is really happening is that they may be (check the list) operating in fear and indolence. If so, they're actually **refusing** to do their part because they choose to be lazy and the devil has instilled fear in them. Our mouths can say anything that sounds good, but the devil knows what is really happening because he's been studying your sinful ways trying to find inroads. He doesn't care that you *call* your *fear* patience or your *indolence* long-suffering; it doesn't matter to the devil. Despite our ignorance and denial, he knows when we have fallen for his handiwork.

Take another look at this list and you will notice something else; everything on the right is intrinsically adversarial to the qualities on the left:

Love has nothing to do with lust. According to *The American Heritage dictionary*,

—Love is having a deep affection and warm feeling for another.

—Lust is having an intense, excessive or unrestrained sexual desire.

While we can lust for the one that we love, we don't necessarily have to love the ones we lust after.

Satan uses such subtleties to confound our senses and make a mockery of Christ-like attributes. He will take something that is pure and genuine and sully it with evil. What is of the flesh, Satan will disguise it to make it appear of the spirit. Even within the definition of lust, the paradox is confirmed; the devil would have us be unrestrained, excessive and intense in our flesh.

Moving down the list, just to hit upon a few things, when Satan is in the driver's seat we see:

—Kindness being used as a form of manipulation.

—Participation in spiritual things being used for an emotional release.

—Peace being an illusion for what is really apathy.

—Faith exercised as a form of arrogance, to pump up our ego for material gain.

—Joy being confused with lack of discretion.

—Prayer being used as a bargaining tool to obtain the most ungodly things in life. I've even heard of prayer being used to get another woman's husband. Madonna, the pop singer, says a prayer before she gets on stage and does the most lewd and lascivious acts that she can think of.

It is very important that we have the ability to label and recognize Satan's tactics of deception because to make the error of taking a person who is operating on Satan's behalf for face value is dangerous. To rationalize bad behavior and label its counterfeit as good is a mistake that is made out of ignorance of how the devil and his demons operate. We must guard our heart with diligence, and part of guarding our heart is being informed enough to recognize the devil's actions and not mistake them for the work of God. The bible says that His sheep know His voice, but Satan is a deceiver, counterfeiting all that he can to get us to turn away from God and turn to him. Yes, Satan can counterfeit the voice of God! One of his favorite prey has to be the unlearned and immature in matters of Christ. Since spirit is directly linked with the emotions and the emotions are directly linked with the heart, it stands to reason that the heart must be guarded with all diligence. A heart can be hardened by unfortunate circumstances. If we fail to examine a matter closely, we may fail to see God's hand on a circumstance or event and attribute the misfortune to the work of the devil when it really is the hand of God strengthening and preparing us, as only He can, for his work. We must guard our heart to insure that we don't become bitter, embracing a spirit of rejection instead of realizing God's spirit of adoption. In no way should we want to give Satan the opportunity to employ us by default to do his evil work.

RECOGNITION TIP # 24

Recognize that when we choose sin and folly, we are not choosing God and we open ourselves to the wiles of the devil.

CHAPTER 25

Salvation is far from the wicked: for they seek not thy statutes.—Psalm 119:155

The devil will take us for an unbelievable ride if we allow him to. I remember going on a ride a Disneyland. I must have been about fourteen or fifteen years old. I think the name of the ride was "Mr. Toad's Adventure" or "Mr. Toad's Wild Ride." Well, I went on this ride because it looked innocent enough because Mr. Toad was a character of children's stories. How harmful could this be? I would never go on a roller coaster or anything that went faster than ten miles per hour. I do not go on anything that leaves the ground or spins too rapidly around in circles so Mr. Toad seemed the perfect choice for me. So while my younger brother and sister rode the roller coasters and all the other daring rides, I went on "Mr. Toad's Adventure." I don't remember everything about the ride, but I'll tell you this. I remember that it caused me to have nightmares for weeks after that. There were doors opening unexpectedly, creatures popping up out of nowhere, eerie music—the operatic kind that you hear played in medieval movies when they want to give you a sense of urgency, and loud spooky sounds that erupted out of the darkness. The car twirled and spun in the darkened rooms as one door after another flew open for you to find yourself face to face with various goblins and creatures. I tell you, I felt as if I would go mad and the ride seemed to go on forever! When the ride was finally over, I stumbled out of that car close to tears and shaking like a leaf.

The devil is like this. Things that we become voluntarily involved in may appear to be innocuous enough and yet we find ourselves spinning out of control, coming face to face with demons that we never thought would be there and being forced through doors to places that we never expected to go. Our innocence and good intentions may not prepare us for what our choices may bring, but being informed and enlightened can help us to be prepared for any battle that presents itself. We don't have to come out of it shaking and traumatized; we can come out of the "wild ride" with renewed strength and experiences under our belt that give us power and help us to be better disciples for Christ. When we deal with fears, the unexpected, trials, tribulations, and emotional devastation and we find that we have successfully learned to depend on the Almighty and survived with our soul uncompromised, the enemy has once again been defeated.

We may have experienced an emotional roller coaster, but our emotions have remained intact and we are ready for the next wild ride, and there is to be one. We all have emotions and all of these emotions serve a purpose and the purpose of these emotions is not to destroy us. The purpose of our emotions is actually to deter us from becoming caught up in strongholds. This may sound weird because most strongholds appear to be emotional attachments. Strongholds appear to be emotional because the emotion that shows up is really a counterfeit that blocks what is true and what is of God. We take the feeling of lust, for example, to be the emotion of love and strongholds are born out of such a counterfeit. It is not the real thing that we are holding on to and cannot let go, it is a feeling emanating from the flesh, a counterfeit. Emotions can appear to be positive or emotions can appear to be negative to an observer, but ultimately all emotions are positive. What makes an emotion appear negative is the way that an emotion is acted upon. Emotions that are considered negative, such as anger, sorrow and jealousy, are positive emotions that are used by the devil in negative ways because the very nature of these emotions make them susceptible to be used in a negative manner.

The following examples are three intrinsically negative emotions and what they really mean in the lives man.

ANGER

This emotion keeps us grounded. It lets us know whether something is pleasing or displeasing to us. It can make us hunger for justice or revenge. It can lead us to examine our own values and the values of the people who make us angry. Anger makes us look at the general condition of our lives and decide if our circumstances need to change. When we're angry, we go automatically through a litany of thoughts rational and irrational to deal with the situation or person that has made us angry in an effort to find relief from the uncomfortable feelings that it produces. It can prompt us to release tears, confront the uncomfortable, attend to our closest relationships, and realize our need for Christ in our life.

If handled properly, anger can be used to produce positive results that bring us closer to our creator. If not handled properly, kept bottled up for instance, it is like a keg of dynamite and it doesn't take very much to ignite an explosion. Explosions can release other negative emotions that go off like firecrackers damaging innocent bystanders in their wake. Contrary to what most people may think, however, the bible does not discourage anger, and this makes sense, for to discourage this very human emotion is foolish and impossible to achieve without the negative result mentioned; what the bible discourages is responding to anger in a sinful or negative way. Anger is there for a reason and if used properly the results can yield a very healthy individual.

To deny anger is to deny our humanity, to deny our fallibility, to deny our need for God. Those who refuse to experience their anger experience something that's even worse—lack of joy and lack of connection to the human race. The more anger is denied, the more likely it is that you feel no joy in your spirit. It is impossible to be human and not experience anger at least a few hundred times in your life. Anger must be acknowledged or the "rocks will cry out." In other words, it will manifest itself in almost any area in your life—your body, your relationships, your job, your make up, the way you dress, the way you eat, your organs, your love life, sickness, disease, tattoos, self-mutilation and various other ways. Anger is an emotion that when not handled properly, presses the spirit down causing what is commonly known as depression.

There are many people who suffer from this malady of depression who do not understand that misinterpretation of emotions and unexpressed anger gives way to demons whose job it is to enter us and *steal* the very joy of life from us. We must be conscientiously involved in monitoring and interpreting our emotions because of this. We cannot deny, cover, ignore, or downplay them because our emotions are typical portals for demons to enter into us if they are left unchecked for any period of time.

SORROW/GRIEF

This "negative" emotion can help us to be more appreciative if allowed to run its course, and like anger, is used properly. Sorrow can help us be more productive as a result of our loss or grief. The results of sorrow and grief can be a more intense love of what is meaningful and yet so fragile in our lives. It leads us to examine what is worth our attention and what is just a diversion and unimportant. Sorrow can lead us to understand and appreciate just how precious our lives really are.

As with anger, this emotion can also foster a closer relationship to God. We can go to Him in our weakness and He will hear our groaning. Our faith is strengthened as we endure the pain of sorrow as we wait with knowing anticipation that what lies behind that illusive veil of pain, that thing that we once thought was beyond endurance, we endure because we have no choice. We then grasp the meaning of it all, however painful it is and however reluctant we may be to learn the lesson, we learn. The sorrow and grief allow us to let go and give us permission to lean on God after we realize that there is nothing else or no one else that can fill the hole. It is in such times that we can become totally dependent upon God if we allow the grief and sorrow to take us to Him. We finally come to terms with the fact that we have no power to reconfigure things to our own personal satisfaction and our personal wants must take a back seat to a higher power that has the greater authority and wisdom. We find that we must either bow down in desperation to God or allow our response to that pain to plunge us into the deep pits of despair.

Should we choose to react negatively to sorrow and grief, we open ourselves up to Satan. He will use our sorrow to point out to us just how unfair, apathetic, and unjust God is. Satan feeds into such negativity and exacerbates the pain with taunts and harassments of his own" "If God cares, then why…" This is to convince us that what we are facing is not only negative circumstances, but long-term negative circumstances and if we don't do something to help ourselves out of such abject misery, nothing will ever change and we will die, filled with sorrow. He tries to convince us that the feelings will go from bad to worse and nobody can possibly understand how *you* feel and therefore there is no relief in sight for you. He interjects a sense of hopelessness within us that seems impossible to overcome.

Sorrow in its purest form, however, can show us just how much we can endure under pressure. It can heighten our sense of awareness to others who may have gone through something similar. It can make us empathize with the pain of others and soften our hearts to those less fortunate than ourselves. Sorrow can keep us humble, realizing that we are vulnerable and because the experience is not a pleasant one, we do not want to be the catalyst for someone else's grief. It can also soften our heart as it teaches us to step back and allow God to refine us for His use. Grief and sorrow are beneficial in that they can teach us to have hope in our darkest hours because like a physical pain, the intensity of it diminishes with time and it does not last forever.

JEALOUSY

God is a jealous God. He would have us have no god before him. Jealousy is an emotion that may seem to some to be unfortunate for those who must deal with the green-eyed monster, but what can be so bad about an emotion that even God had? Well God is God and man is not, but it does have its purpose.

Jealousy, in its proper place, prompts us to do better because we see through someone else that it *can* be done better. We can be jealous for someone's talents, skills, family life, spiritual gifts, kindness, wisdom, or faith; this is good. Jealousy is meant for such things so that we can aspire to be better in our hearts, making it more perfect toward God. Jealousy prompts us to want to be better and not settle for mediocrity when it comes to the good things in life.

Unfortunately many of us spend this emotion frivolously on things that are transitory, such as material possessions, money, fame and beauty. These things of this world mean nothing to God. God's jealousy for us is not something we can see with our eyes or touch with our fingers. God owns our spirit; His jealousy is for our will to be in alignment with His will. His jealously is that we love Him with our free will as much as we as humans possibly can. God is jealous for us, not jealous of us and *we* should be jealous for all the attributes of God. To be jealous for any other reason, we waste our time and energy. Jealousy *of* something should be quickly categorized as admiration or a desire for that experience.

It is quite easy for Satan to use this emotion to do his will because many do not take the time to figure out what the jealousy indicates for them. Jealousy can indicate lack and unless we examine the emotion, we won't have a clue as to what that lack indicates about our lives. Are we jealous of a beautiful woman because we're harboring feelings of rejection, fears of incompetence, and feelings of inadequacy? Does our relationship need work and we don't want to admit it, or have we been negligent about maintaining our own physical body? Is it the fact that we should have more confidence in whom and how God has made us and this beautiful woman exudes that confidence? Is there something on the inside of that person that shines through, like joy and peace in Christ that makes you jealous to be that woman?

Men, could the reason why you cannot get a grip on your jealousy toward your wife or mate be because your love is not pure and you do not love her as Christ loves the church? Does jealousy over her abilities or competency lead to anger that translates into disrespect and sometimes even violence? Being jealous of her being with other people, men and women, could mean that you are not doing what you are supposed to do and you don't want her to see what a healthy relationship looks like so that you can continue your evil ways. Are you afraid that someone may enlighten her about something that you purposely try to keep her in the dark about? This is not love and it surely is not of God.

If we examine our emotions very carefully, we wouldn't be so quick to push them aside. In fact pushing our emotions aside can cause a huge amount of damage and leave us open to the devil. When we use them as God intended for them to be used, we do not give place to the devil by being in denial. We must learn to recognize the works of Satan when we see them. We must be willing and open to receive help spiritually on all levels including, if necessary, an all-out exorcism.

Our spiritual leaders must be taught and made aware of how to use spiritual warfare when necessary; they must teach their congregation of spiritual warfare; they must engage in spiritual warfare if they are led to do so by the Holy Spirit and not run from it. They should not be ignorant of this. Our leaders must also learn how to use and when to employ a violent wrenching or exorcism, when necessary. This, spiritual warfare and exorcism could save millions of people from spiritual death and misery, whether it's their personal death and misery or the death and misery that these demonized souls inflict upon others.

YOU CAN'T BE FRIENDS WITH THE DEVIL
—DAWN